Phil Spencer is one of the best-known faces on British television, co-presenting the hit Channel 4 series *Location, Location, Location* and *Relocation, Relocation*. Phil trained as a general practice surveyor and, in 1996, was one of the first people to set up a property buying agency. He has written columns for, among others, *The Sunday Times*, *GQ* and *Country Life* and appears regularly on radio to discuss property issues. He also hosts a successful Classic FM radio show.

www.philspencer.tv

Adding Value to Your Home

Phil Spencer

The Property Expert

Vermilion
LONDON

1 3 5 7 9 10 8 6 4 2

Published in 2010 by Vermilion, an imprint of Ebury Publishing

Ebury Publishing is a Random House Group company

The Random House Group Limited Reg. No. 954009

Addresses for companies within the Random House Group can be found at www.rbooks.co.uk

A CIP catalogue record for this book is available from the British Library

The Random House Group Limited supports The Forest Stewardship Council (FSC), the leading international forest certification organisation. All our titles that are printed on Greenpeace approved FSC certified paper carry the FSC logo. Our paper procurement policy can be found at www.rbooks.co.uk/environment

Printed and bound in Great Britain by
Clays Ltd, St Ives Plc

ISBN 9780091935368

Copies are available at special rates for bulk orders. Contact the sales development team on 020 7840 8487 for more information.

To buy books by your favourite authors and register for offers, visit www.rbooks.co.uk

The information in this book is general in nature and not intended to constitute nor be relied on for specific financial or any other professional advice. The author and publishers disclaim, as far as the law allows, any liability arising directly or indirectly from the use or misuse of the information contained in this book.

This book is a work of non-fiction. The names of people in the case studies have been changed solely to protect the privacy of others.

To my inspiring, amazing and supportive family.
I love you all.

Contents

ACKNOWLEDGEMENTS

My friend and writing colleague Cheryl Markosky deserves the biggest thanks in the world. She managed to nurture and develop my ideas, and I'm hugely grateful for her involvement.

Big thanks also to everyone at Vermilion for believing in me and publishing this book. Particularly to my editor, Julia Kellaway, for her support, encouragement and wise counsel throughout.

To Channel 4 for continuing to broadcast my TV series; to the crews and production teams at IWC for their massive efforts over the last 10 years; to Arlington Enterprises who make it all possible; and to Jonathan Conway for his professionalism and dedication to this book.

Thanks also to my special friend Kirstie, who was no help at all with this book, but without whom life would never be quite as much fun!

And finally, I'd like to thank and thank and thank my wife Fiona for always encouraging and supporting me, and my two boys Jake and Ben for making me so proud to be their dad.

Introduction

Adding *Value to Your Home* is about making your property a better place for you to live, and enhancing the value of your principal asset should you decide to sell. It combines our twin loves of building our own castle – it is an Englishman's home, after all – and reaping its rewards when the time comes to part with it.

As well as presenting *Location, Location, Location*; *Relocation, Relocation, Relocation,* and other property specials for Channel 4 television, I have accrued useful experience in other parts of the property world too. As a search agent representing buyers, I find homes for private clients and advise large property funds on what they should buy and what is likely to retain its worth. Through developing properties for sale and helping purchase them as part of a portfolio for buy-to-let investors, I have seen nearly every facet of the residential property world, which I can share with you.

I have always had an interest in property in one form or another. Brought up on a Kent farm, I naturally fell into agricultural sales, qualifying as a surveyor and picking up a degree in estate management from London's South Bank University. Early on, it dawned on me how incredibly biased British estate agency can be, which isn't true in the agricultural commercial property market, or even in other parts of the world. It seemed peculiar to me that you spend the greatest amount of money on the biggest deal of your life with the odds stacked against you. Remember that in Britain, the agent almost always represents the seller – never the buyer. When you walk into the agent's office as a purchaser, you are not the customer.

A six-month stint I did as an estate agent during the property recession in 1991 was demanding, but highly instructive. I was only 22 and business was tough. Agents were so desperate for sales they were carrying out all sorts of underhand deals. Young, keen and principled, I'm afraid I wouldn't do what I was asked to do. I think when I left they were pretty glad to see the back of me. For me, though, this was the turning point. This brush with how certain parts of the property world can operate led me to become one of Britain's first house finders. To help redress the imbalance in the world of estate agency, I decided to work solely for the buyer, and I continue to do so to this day.

Now, with nearly 20 years' experience, I think I am well equipped with my combined knowledge as a surveyor, agent, house finder and television property expert to advise and guide people. I have always seen it as a privilege helping someone find what he regards as his dream home – and in some instances, even help change his life.

I would like to think the advice I have given people on and off the screen has never been about making money as such, but about finding a home. The problem is, people expect to make money from their homes in this country. This is fine on one level, but traditionally you go out to work to make money, and a house is a place where you shelter your family. My constant advice has been to buy for the long term, to buy something that can be adapted to suit your needs as they evolve, or to buy something to improve and add value.

This was my attitude four years ago when I bought our family home in south-west London, where I live with my wife and two small sons. I wanted to create a home that the family could grow into. I bought it for the location. I identified the street I wanted, then the best section of the street and the right side of the street. I wasn't fussy about the house; I knew I could adapt that. I am finding it a pleasure watching the house change as my family's needs change and I try to add value as I go. Right now, I am concentrating on sorting out a playroom for the boys, a space that is likely to evolve into something else as they grow older.

Adding value is about enhancing your property so it is a place to take pleasure from; it is not about simply turning a fast buck when you sell it. Of course, everyone hopes to get his or her money back, along with some profit on top. With this in mind, I hope to give you the information you need to achieve this two-fold goal of increasing the worth of your home both while you are in residence and when you decide it is time to move on.

CHAPTER ONE

What Adding Value Really Means

In a competitive property market it is important to understand what adding value is all about. Investing in your home means it can become the most attractive house on the block, so if you do decide to move, yours will get the most attention from buyers and usually sell quicker and for more cash. And in a leaner market when more people might choose to stay put in their homes, adding value makes great sense. Why not create a comfortable and friendly space for you, your family and friends to enjoy?

There are many ways to add value to your home. It can mean anything from simple DIY projects or insulating the loft, to coming up with a well-planned and well-executed extension. Some projects, however, offer a more clear-cut return than others. While many home improvements add to the saleability of a property, the cost of the project does not necessarily always add an equal amount to the asking price.

New central heating, for example, almost always pays for itself, and is nearly always guaranteed to leave the homeowner with a profit when they sell. The cost to install central heating ranges from £1,000 to £3,000 depending on the system you choose, but the value added can be as much as £5,000.

Many homeowners waste valuable time and money on gimmicks, such as installing expensive gadgets, when they could be better off concentrating on the infrastructure. Is it really a good idea to install that expensive cappuccino maker, for instance, when you haven't fitted a good working boiler or decent flooring? What about the value added by sprucing up the bathroom and losing that avocado suite with gold taps? And will it be worth spending a fortune on expensive fittings, or will B&Q do the job? In the complicated world of home improvements, when planning where to focus your energy and how best to spend your budget it is every bit as important to know what *not* to do. Not everything adds value in cash terms, but some ideas could make your house easier to sell.

This book is here to help you understand what could work best for you, and what will make the overall feel of a house more valuable in the eyes of its owner – and, one day, in the eyes of a potential buyer.

Which Improvements Add the Most Value?

Research shows that the average renovation project costs £17,402, but that it will add £21,207 worth of value on to a home.

Before embarking on any kind of work, it pays to know what will add the most value to your property. Although surveys are worth noting, you need to take some of them with a pinch of salt. Frequently commissioned by researchers at companies selling certain products, their judgement might be coloured. The most useful surveys are likely to come from independent researchers, or those who are acting as independently as possible within the bounds of their jobs. Before trusting a survey, first find out who commissioned it, or for whose benefit it was carried out. For instance, a company selling boiler systems might well declare that installing a new boiler adds significant value to your property. Just keep the origins of the research in mind – it might not be as impartial as you think.

Popular projects

. . . and the estimated value they can add to your property.

Personally, I am not wedded to the idea of apportioning actual figures to home improvements, because it can be hard quantifying the value of everything you do. However, it can be reassuring to know that all the time and labour spent on certain projects should attract some profit when you decide to sell your home. Remember, though, that there is also a value of love – you will enjoy your property more by making it a better place to live, although this doesn't always translate itself into profit. According to the mortgage lender GE Money, which interviewed 110 estate agents, here are some key projects and the values they attach to the work:

- **Loft conversion** Converting a loft to create an extra bedroom, bathroom or office space is said to be the favourite renovation project, typically adding 12.5 per cent to the selling price.
- **An extension** This is the second most popular project. An extension could add on a family room or an extra bedroom or extend an existing living room. Estate agents believe this adds an average of 11 per cent to the value of a home.
- **A conservatory** can add 6.7 per cent.
- **A new kitchen** can add 4.6 per cent.
- **Installing central heating** can add 3.4 per cent.
- **A new bathroom** can add 2.88 per cent.
- **Redecorating bedrooms and the living room** can add 2.6 per cent.
- **A new driveway** can add 2.2 per cent.
- **Installing decking or a patio** can add 2 per cent.
- **Digging out a new basement** to create a whole extra floor is deemed to be a good idea, although there is some debate whether it adds to a property's value. I think it can, but it depends on where you live and how much the work costs.

Going green

Eco home improvements will boost your green credentials and cut down on your energy bills at the same time, but according to a survey from mortgage lender GE Money this could add less than 1 per cent to your home's value. However, I would argue that green additions might prove to be more valuable than some people currently realise. As the cost of energy increases and people are more conscious of resource-saving devices, incorporating some in your home could pay off on several levels one day. I think you need to weigh up the short-term versus long-term gain in this instance.

Outside a boom market, when people are trying to make as many savings as possible, money-saving green devices could be a serious consideration, especially if your home will be marketed to those watching their pennies – say, cash-strapped retirees or first-time buyers.

Your Home is Your Castle

I find it frustrating when people see value only in terms of money. I want you to enjoy living in your home while you are there, not just view adding value as a last-ditch attempt to get as much money as you can when you put up that 'For Sale' sign. There is nothing wrong with trying to make your home as attractive as possible when you sell it in order to get the highest possible price. But adding value is about far more than counting up how much you can earn when you move.

The main point of adding value should be making where you live a better place. There is no point in doing this just before you sell – unless, of course, you are not in a position to do so earlier. If you are planning to spend a certain sum on improving your property, you might as well do it straight away and get the benefit – and the pleasure – out of it yourself.

With more people remaining longer in their homes, whether a first flat, a small starter maisonette or a family house, now is the ideal time to concentrate on improving what you already have. The mantra 'improve, don't move' has never been more apposite. Look upon the current climate as an opportunity to get your home up to scratch.

Shift into Gear: Instant Added Value

I compare giving instant extra value to a home with buying a second-hand car in need of a bit of attention. In most cases, the new owner would book the car in for a service, replace the squeaking brakes and maybe splash out on a new radio or a set of floor mats. This gives you peace of mind and makes travelling about a more pleasurable experience.

Similar thinking should apply to your home. For your comfort and safety, why not sort out those niggling problems soon after you've moved in and sent out the change-of-address cards? Adding value as soon as you can will give you a *Top Gear* experience, rather than suffering the equivalent of breaking down in an unloved banger.

Your home is your refuge from the world, where you spend time with family and friends, relax with a cuppa and the newspaper, maybe even fire up the barbecue on hot summer evenings. Doesn't it make sense to care for your private haven?

If you can't afford to sell right now – perhaps you are saving for the next step up the property ladder, or this is a stopgap before you move to a more desirable area – I suggest you make the best of what you have. This is not just a book about how to generate cash when you dispense with your property. It is also about how to create a sense of place and a good way to live no matter how long you plan to stay. Besides, families expand and not everyone can move up the ladder to a bigger house exactly when they want to. Rather than fretting about making the upgrade, there are ways to improve existing space and even fashion more space where you currently are.

PHIL'S TRADE SECRET

The trick with any improvement is to make it suit the property. The price bracket of fixtures and fittings must match the price bracket of the property. If you are living in a modest, two-bedroom terrace in the lower-to-middle end of the market, there is no point installing posh brand-name taps in bathrooms. Instead, use the substantially cheaper 'look-alikes' that are available. However, if you are doing up a luxury house at the top end of the market, then use the real thing. Buyers forking out higher sums will not expect skimping on items like this. Equally, do not overdevelop. Carrying out a major basement conversion in a small house with a petite sitting room and only a couple of bedrooms could make it bottom-heavy. A house has got to feel balanced and the rooms need to be in proportion.

THE SPACE DILEMMA

Lucy Webster, who works in London as a travel journalist, and her product-designer husband Nigel have a dilemma shared by a number of other young couples.

'It took us ages to scrape enough together to get a mortgage on our first flat just outside Sutton in Surrey,' she says. 'But with our parents helping a bit towards the deposit, we bought a lovely first-floor one-bedroom flat in a Victorian terrace that we thought would suit us for ages.'

But two years after purchasing the £194,000 flat with their £10,000 wedding present subsidy from the Bank of Mum and Dad, Lucy, now 35, discovered she was expecting their first child.

'Panic set in. How on earth would we squeeze a new baby, let alone all its paraphernalia, into what we saw as our cosy little starter home? I sat down and wept,' she says.

Luckily, Lucy's tears were soon wiped away. Nigel is a highly creative thinker, with great awareness of how to use space. He could see the benefits of adapting a generously proportioned area off the main landing, used to house the couple's books, DVDs and home computer, into a small bedroom for the baby.

'There was a window already there, admitting a good deal of light,' Nigel, 38, explains. 'So I took some measurements, made some preliminary sketches and took them down to our local builders' merchant. The guys there were really helpful and gave me advice – like the best way to block off the area and add a door without wasting too much space – as well as a list of recommended builders.'

One of the suggestions was to use a sliding door that met health and safety regulations – in case of fire you would need to be able to shut the door from the flames – while not pushing into the room and taking up space. The shop also suggested storage that would slot neatly under baby Nathan's cot – and later, bed – as well as a fun, brightly coloured wire rack system that easily screws on to walls. 'You could hang different-sized shelves and baskets that were totally adaptable,' adds Nigel.

The cost of the new nursery, including the flexible storage system and decoration, was a reasonable £3,500. Nathan, now a lively two-year-old, loves his room, and the new home office has been tucked into a corner of the living room, where it looks like it has always been.

The Websters saved some cash by sanding and oiling the wooden flooring and painting the room themselves.

'The local builder we employed said this will really add value when we do move on, as the new owner can use this as a study or a small guest room,' Nigel points out.

Yet value has also been added for the Websters themselves. 'We have been able to cope and live here for a lot longer than if we hadn't carried out the work,' says Lucy. 'And it has given us breathing space – literally. We have been saving up over the last few years and hope to buy somewhere a bit bigger, maybe with some outdoor space where Nathan can run around.'

A local estate agent recently valued the flat at £225,000. If the Websters get close to the asking price for their home, they will have covered the cost of the new room and made a bit of profit on top.

Even more important, however, they rectified a problem immediately and are still enjoying their first home. Living with a baby in a constricted place has turned into a snug and inviting experience, rather than a nightmare.

Says Lucy: 'Although I know we need more space as a growing family, I'll miss our flat. I have lovely memories of painting Nathan's room late at night – me with my bump and Nigel with a takeaway menu, ready to order a curry when we downed tools. We've been really happy here, and you can't always replicate those feelings, which have nothing to do with money.'

CHAPTER TWO

The Basics

Make your property stand out without spending a fortune

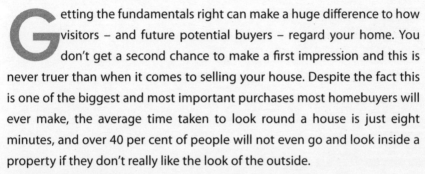

Getting the fundamentals right can make a huge difference to how visitors – and future potential buyers – regard your home. You don't get a second chance to make a first impression and this is never truer than when it comes to selling your house. Despite the fact this is one of the biggest and most important purchases most homebuyers will ever make, the average time taken to look round a house is just eight minutes, and over 40 per cent of people will not even go and look inside a property if they don't really like the look of the outside.

Research shows that most of us spend more time choosing new shoes than we do choosing our next house. It seems crazy, but apparently we spend less than 10 minutes deciding where we are going to spend the next decade or so of our lives, and anything up to an hour fretting over whether the brown lace-ups are preferable to the slip-on Italian loafers. So if you are thinking of selling your home, presentation counts. Encouraging prospective purchasers simply to step through your door is your first challenge.

Getting Them over the Threshold

Getting your house ready for viewings is like preparing yourself for a blind date. Appearance is everything because 'gut feeling' is going to kick in immediately. There is a kind of Lynx-effect 10-second rule, where, just like the instant impact of that aftershave, there is a very short time span in which buyers will decide whether the house is right for them.

Obviously, a beautifully presented frontage makes a significant difference to houses – as well as to lonely hearts! Fresh paint, combined with a neat garden, painted railings, clean glass and polished brass all give a good first impression to those deciding whether to venture up your path. And it doesn't cost much to smarten up the front of your home. Giving your house or flat a facelift needn't cost more than a few hundred pounds. However, if you are about to sell, then before you embark on a snazzy new look, remember the importance of mass-market appeal. Keep it neutral and understated – avoid anything that is too 'out there'. True, most people can overlook personal touches that don't grab them, but let me give you one of the most valuable pieces of advice I have to offer: do not seek to stamp your individual mark on your home when the time comes to sell. The correctly priced, 'blank-canvas', well-presented properties are the ones that sell first.

What else can you do to get prospective buyers through your door so that they can see how beautiful your home is on the inside? Simple. Walk up and down your street – and maybe a few of the surrounding streets as well – to get an idea of how the best houses look. The aim is to make your house look as good as the most suitable houses in the area. Whatever you do, you must match the most attractive houses in the neighbourhood.

PHIL'S TOP TIP

To find out what 'best in class' houses look like in an area, I get on my bike and take photographs of those that look most promising. You can pick up great ideas from your neighbours' handiwork and the photos will remind you of what you can achieve.

Kerb Appeal

To work out how the front of your house needs to look, start at the beginning. Put yourself in the place of the buyer walking up to the property for the first time. Maybe the buyer has already looked at several properties, is tired and hungry, but decides he might as well look at this one too now that he's here.

The buyer wants to move to an area that is well cared for by the community, so your path must be neat and inviting. If the drains at the edge of your pavement or leading up to your path are crammed with leaves and litter, it would be good form to clear them. Even if some of this is the responsibility of the council, it will do no harm for you to do your bit along your side of the street on days that viewings are carried out.

If you are laying a new path, I recommend you select something like slate or slab that is simple to look after and will scrub up quickly with a brush or hose.

Making a Grand Entrance

Some country-dwellers like driveways and pathways made from gravel as it is a good deterrent – you certainly hear any intruders approaching as they crunch down the path – but keep in mind that it tends to scatter everywhere and needs to be swept up frequently. You will have to invest in re-gravelling the path every few years. But I think it can look fantastic and is a good way to be alerted to any visitors (expected or otherwise). Friends of mine with a gravel drive and path hold a bi-annual 'gravel raking day', where they get loads of fresh gravel delivered and about 20 friends help them rake it over the areas that need it. Then we are treated to hot drinks and snacks to say thank you for helping. It is a good cost-effective way to spread the new gravel along the drive and paths.

If you have a fence, it should be in good shape. Now is the time to mend any broken slats and re-varnish or oil the wood. A tin of varnish costs under £10 and the wood will appear warmer and richer once a coat or two has been applied.

If railings surround your property, any broken ones should be replaced and painted. Specialist companies sell aluminium and metal railings usually coated in black primer from about £250 per section. Black is the traditional colour, although you can opt for grey or dark green. I would avoid any outlandish hues, which could appear garish and detract from the house itself.

The front of the house needs to look smart. A lot could depend on the neighbour's house, particularly if you are in a semi-detached or terraced house – and you might even want to talk to your immediate neighbours about a group approach to tidying up. Some people paint their houses the same colour so there is a sense of continuity. In a positive version of keeping up with the Joneses, your neighbours' homes looking as stylish as yours makes the street a more enticing place to live. It also shows you get on well with your neighbours, and there are economies of scale when several of you share the costs.

If you have a hedge out front, it must be trimmed and low enough to allow light to come into the house; an overgrown high hedge will make the property appear gloomy and depressing. Potted plants are not expensive and a bit of colour on or next to the doorstep – some lavender or bay trees are ideal – is a gardener's green welcome mat. Fragrant blooms, such as roses or honeysuckle, can add romance, but remember to plant flora that is in keeping with the house. Roses, clematis and overflowing hanging baskets might look appropriate swathed across a pretty country cottage, but a more modern townhouse would benefit from neat arrangements of fuchsias and miniature conifers in window boxes, olive trees – increasingly popular now that our climate is warming – and large pots with holly and box trees, which can be easily shaped and have the advantage of being green all year round.

I favour brick houses over painted properties. They require less maintenance and are cheaper in terms of upkeep – you don't need to paint the entire exterior every few years. But you do still need to paint window frames and sills – unless you opt for uPVC windows, of course – so they look fresh and clean.

If you are in a flat, you might want to talk the rest of the residents into giving the communal areas a bit of a makeover. A dingy shared entryway might put viewers off. If your fellow-residents aren't keen, then perhaps you or your builders could give the carpets a good shampoo and put a coat or two of paint on the walls of the communal lobby – but you must get the freeholder's permission before carrying out any work.

If your building is looked after by a management company and you are paying service charges to have the communal areas tended, the firm should do so on a regular basis. This might not coincide with the sale of your flat, however, and not all management companies are as rigorous as they might be when it comes to cleaning and decorating. It is worth talking to the company to see if the main areas can be spruced up before people start viewing your flat. If you don't get anywhere with them, doing something yourself – with permission, of course – might be the best course of action.

PHIL'S TOP TIP

If you painted the outside of the house only a few years ago, you might get away with just freshening up the ground-floor level as this is the storey people notice most. Slightly worn paintwork higher up might not be as glaring to the eye as the patch right in front of you.

Putting Up a Good Front

The condition of the front door is very important. At the very least, freshen it up with a new coat of paint. Sadly there are no official statistics on the most attractive front-door colour, although it is widely acknowledged that darker, sombre colours such as navy, grey and black are preferred. I too favour something elegant and fairly neutral, such as classic black, but if it suits the surroundings I would also consider a white, a grey or a pale green.

Polish and shine the knob, letterbox plate and lock, or invest in new door furniture if you can afford it. A smart doorknob costs around £35, while a bronze or brass letterbox plate is just under £25.

Choose door furniture to match the age of the house. A lion's head knocker from about £40 will suit an older building – there's one dating back to the 1770s at 10 Downing Street, the official residence of the First Lord of the Treasury. The famous entrance at Number 10 has two identical doors that are swapped over whenever they need a spot of maintenance. A great idea, but maybe one that is not practical for us all to adopt!

A house name or number should be attractive and easy to read. Decent quality stainless-steel house numbers cost from £5. You can source modern fonts, too, which cost from £25 for a 55-millimetre number. A plate combining house name and number can look inviting and would cost around £50. I recommend a black plate with white reflective text and numbers for night visibility.

PHIL'S TRADE SECRET

Ask your estate agent how he thinks your house looks. There is no harm in asking the agent direct questions – but be aware that he might avoid telling the truth if you haven't given him your business yet.

Agents know the local area well and operate on 'comparables'. This means they compare like-with-like when they value someone's home. Basically, they would gather up the details of several properties similar to yours (if you own a three-bedroom semi-detached home, they would find other three-bedroom semis) and compare the prices, eventually coming up with a price for your home.

Do ask them how they came to the conclusion that your home is worth an amount lower or higher than a neighbour's place. If it is considerably lower, question why. And if it is appreciably higher, make sure they aren't just trying to flatter you to get your custom.

Here are some good honest questions to ask your agent:

- 'What are the weak points of the house?'
- 'What can I do to make it more appealing?'
- 'Are there any changes you suggest I carry out?'

Help the agent do his job by putting straightforward queries to him, listening to his advice and then carrying out the recommended work.

CASE STUDY

WHAT A DIFFERENCE THE DOOR MAKES

'I hated my front door and wanted to make a bit of a statement,' says Melanie Crawford, a 37-year-old geography teacher from Bristol.

Living in a row of terraced houses, Melanie realised options for her main entrance were not as open as they would be if she was off the beaten track where her handiwork would not be so fully in the public eye.

'There were no restrictions as to what I could do, but I felt my front door wasn't mine alone. It is part of the overall streetscape, and although there are several brightly coloured doors further up, down at my end of the street colours are more muted. Besides, I was worried what might at first be seen as fun and radical could become quite annoying,' Melanie explains.

Talked by a designer friend into taking a quietly classy line with more longevity – 'A wise decision,' adds Melanie – she opted for a dark charcoal hue.

One tip her designer mate came up with was toning down a black door by diluting the black with red or purple. Just like there are off-white shades, there are a number of ready-mixed off-black paints you can buy too, including black-blue and aubergine-black.

As well as grey-black paint, Melanie also treated herself to a chic Victorian-style brass doorknob, in keeping with the period of the house, costing £63, and new brass door numbers at £13 each. And she rounded off her new street-smart frontage with two large pots of fresh white Michaelmas daisies for a total of £60.

Caring for Your Property

I'm a great believer in maintenance. If you can get into the habit of regularly maintaining your home, it will make life so much easier when you come to sell it, as well as making it better to live in while you are staying put.

- It is crucial to clear out blocked gutters and fix cracked pipes and drains. These cause problems with damp and look unsightly hanging precariously off your house or next to it.
- Keep water out of the parts of the house that aren't supposed to get wet. Get up a ladder and replace split tiles, keep a watchful eye on pointing (mortar that has been placed between bricks to hold them together) and paint the exterior to keep the damp out.
- Remove heavy moss from roofs, particularly in the spring and autumn.
- Inspect painted metalwork every couple of years and renew it when it is in danger of starting to crack and peel.
- Tackle frost damage and slippery algae growth on stone and brick steps and garden paths.

If the house looks like it is well maintained from the outside, it inspires confidence that there will be no problems once you get inside. Cracked drainpipes, for instance, indicate there probably will be overflow leakage, easy to spot once you have crossed the threshold. So why should a buyer bother going through the main door at all?

A good way to get an objective view is to ask an honest and straightforward friend what he or she thinks. You can also take a photograph of the front of your house. Seeing your house captured by a camera can illuminate its good points – and its weaknesses.

PHIL'S TRADE SECRET

If there is no exterior picture of a house for sale on its brochure or on the website, it could mean there is something wrong with it. Sometimes you are shown the back view of the outside of the house rather than the front – in which case, perhaps the owner is hiding a flaw, such as the house is in dire need of exterior work or it is subsiding. Or it could be on a busy road, next to a noisy pub or restaurant or in a shabby terrace.

Equally, if there are no internal pictures, it generally means the inside of the house is in a bad state and there is no advantage in showing any photos of its unloved rooms. If no one can supply decent pictures, then a canny buyer reckons he can save some time and not view the property at all – unless, of course, he is after a bargain-basement wreck.

So, keep this in mind if you are selling. If you aren't able to come up with some decent photographs, you will be driving away a good number of buyers, while those who still want to view your home are likely to be after a 'bargain'. People equate bad interiors with a wreck that they expect to get for a knock-down price.

First Impressions: Make the Most of Your Hallway

It is ironic that the hallway, not typically the best bit of a house unless you are lucky enough to own a grand country mansion, is the first room someone encounters. Do not have the pram, bikes and a big pile of trainers clogging the entrance. The hall generally is a fairly limited area, a complicated place where people tend to hover before they venture into the house properly, so it needs to be light and welcoming.

There are various tricks to widen and brighten a narrow or unprepossessing hall. You can hang a large picture or mirror on the wall. A mirror attracts light and can make a constricted space appear larger. If you surround it by a frame painted in a bright colour that matches the décor elsewhere, so much the better because it will tie the hallway in with the rest of the house.

Another sleight-of-hand is to hang a series of small framed mirrors or even a trio of larger mirrors side by side to show some thought has gone into the decoration of this first vital interior space. If you have a period house, consider a period mirror. There are great finds in junk and charity shops and at car boot sales. You could probably pick up an old mirror from around £10.

Paint the hallway in a light shade to make it appear more open, or wallpaper it in a warm colour, such as pale yellow or green. In a period house with a dado rail – also known as a chair rail, this is a strip of moulding running around the wall of the room at about the height of an old-fashioned chairback – you could wallpaper the bottom half below the rail in the traditional fashion. If some of the dado rail is missing or damaged, buy replacement sections – a 200-centimetre piece costs around £4 – and nail them up.

One simple fix is opening up a 'boxed-in' staircase. I did this myself in my house and it is quite simple. All you need do is take off the wood panels surrounding the staircase and open up the space. You can probably carry out this work yourself, or get a builder to do it for you. The trick is to be careful you don't damage the staircase itself when you rip off the panels. It is a job worth doing, however, as you will end up with a beautiful staircase, which is the focal point of the room. After oiling or varnishing the handrail and balusters – the vertical infill pieces between the handrail and base-rail – the new staircase will admit more light and look very smart indeed.

Update the Stairs

A friend who bought a Sixties house brought it into the 21st century by cutting off the rather twee and dated round balls at the top of the newel posts. He also removed the wooden balusters, updating them with sections of glass bolted on with stainless steel. It only cost about £600 for the materials – a good deal cheaper than replacing the entire staircase – giving it a sharp, contemporary look.

Lighting is important too. A well-lit approach to the main door – for example, a halogen floodlight that switches on automatically when someone enters the detection area costs about £20 – and warm lights inside the hall itself put a visitor at ease, particularly when arriving after dark. A hanging pendant light from about £50 looks especially good in the hallway of an older home, and modern versions are available for 20th-century properties.

Low-level lighting along the bottom of the wall that can carry on up the stairs is an inconspicuous but effective way to illuminate an area. If the lights are on a dimmer switch you can lower them in the evening, creating a convivial atmosphere as well as a 'night light' of sorts if someone wants to fetch a glass of water or find the lavatory in the middle of the night.

If there is enough space, I recommend putting a nice piece of furniture in the hallway. A beautiful console – a small table designed to stand against a wall – can look very smart and gives you somewhere to place the post and the contents of your pockets when you arrive home. You can even put a small lamp on the table that will emit a warm glow or, if there is space, have a tall standard lamp in a corner.

But remember: one of the most common methods of burglary is sticking a wire through the letterbox and hooking up keys to gain access, so be careful you don't leave your keys or other valuables in a vulnerable position in the hallway! You can buy a letterbox guard which will prevent this.

Speed-buyer Checklist

Put yourself in the shoes of a 'blind-date' buyer by asking the following quick questions:

- Is this the right location?
- Do I feel safe in this street?
- Does the house give off good vibes?
- Is the house well cared for?
- Do I like the approach to the house?
- Would I like to live here?
- Can I be bothered to take a look inside?

If the answer is yes to all of the above, then the prospective buyer is likely to ring the doorbell and you are one step closer to a sale. If he is wary and doesn't want to waste his time going any further, you have lost a good chance to sell.

If you have old original tiles in your hallway, it is well worth repairing or replacing any that are damaged or missing. Even just cleaning them up could be a good idea. People will notice and comment on them as soon as they come through the door.

Think about practicalities, such as where people will hang their coats – in a cupboard or on a stylish coat-hook? A traditional twist-style coat-rack would cost about £20 and a wall-mounted oak three-arm hook £30. You might want to invest in an umbrella stand – a rattan umbrella basket from £35, a funkier leather one from £130 or a very practical combined coat-hook/umbrella stand at £110 – and a mat from £5 upward where people can wipe their feet or remove wet footwear.

Introducing a line of vision – what people will look at from the entrance – is a clever way to guide people into your home. When designers talk about 'flow' – how you move people from one room to another – this is what they mean.

In my own hallway I removed a pillar so you can see out to the back garden from the entrance. As well as giving a good view and leading visitors towards the living room and garden beyond, it also gives the hallway more light. However, do not start knocking down pillars until you carry out a structural survey and get advice on propping up the house, if need be, with a steel beam or similar.

Some period houses have stained-glass windows at the top of the front door or in the hallway itself. If the glass needs restoration, you can hire a craftsman, which shouldn't cost more than a few hundred pounds and I think is money well spent. Normally they remove the panel, take it away to renovate and reinstall it. Or you could attend a course – a weekend course at a stained-glass or arts centre costs around £250 – and have a go at repairing it yourself.

PHIL'S TOP TIP

Key features that people can talk about, such as lovingly restored floor tiles, re-sanded original flooring or a beautifully preserved stained-glass fanlight, will get your house noticed. Buyers might view half a dozen or more properties in a day, so anything that stands out will be remembered.

Period Features

I believe that, generally, you shouldn't rip out period features. If your house still has original features of some character, such as dado rails, stepped skirting boards and ceiling cornices, they can be a strong selling point. Additionally you need to be careful not to tear anything out if you live in a listed building. You could be hit with a substantial fine and even a criminal record if you remove period features that should remain.

But if something has gone, then it's gone. If your house no longer has whatever was fitted into it in the first place, better just accept it doesn't need it. I do feel strongly, however, that whatever you do has to suit the age of your house. Trying to force a pastiche piece of stained glass or an older fireplace into a modern flat could look ridiculous, like mixing a long-frock-and-bonnet costume drama with an episode of *The Bill*.

Blending old with new can work in some cases, of course, as long as you show respect for the integrity of the house. Mixing contemporary with older furniture and features in a period house looks fantastic if you have a flair for introducing the new to the old. But trying to force older features – or 21st-century remakes of older features – into a modern house rarely does.

Quick Fixes

You do not need to spend a lot of money to get the basics right. Here is where to concentrate your efforts to add value:

- Try washing walls and woodwork first rather than repainting them; shampoo carpets rather than replace them. Consider hiring a specialist cleaning company for any of these tasks. It is incredible how good professional cleaners can make your house look for the outlay of a few hundred pounds.
- Get your curtains dry-cleaned – prices from around £40 depending on size.
- Sweep paving stones and the patio and remove weeds from cracks. Hire a pressure-washing kit (from about £50) or call in the professionals. Jet-washing can turn black, grimy paving into golden stone again.
- Clean the windows to let in as much light as possible. It might make sense to employ a professional window-cleaner from about £30.

- Fill in cracks. Even if you have no major structural issues, buyers equate cracks with subsidence, or worse.
- Change cupboard doors and handles in the kitchen to bring the room bang up to date.
- Update light switches and sockets. A shiny chrome version, instead of a cheap plastic one, costs just over £5.
- Re-grout tiles in bathrooms.
- Replace the splashback – the area on the wall behind the taps in kitchens and bathrooms, generally tiled or in another material. A neat trick is to paint a colour on to the back of a glass splashback – a great way to brighten up a neutral room.
- Get rid of the shower curtain and put in a glass screen from just over £100, or a shower door from £125.
- A new shower-head, from £20, is easy to install and immediately lifts a bathroom.
- Buy an up-to-date set of taps costing about £20 or more. A new sink is not expensive either (from £15) if yours is stained or chipped.

It does not always matter if everything in your house is not brand new. I went round one elderly couple's home that had not been decorated for a long time. It was wonderfully spotless. The bathroom and kitchen, probably the two most important rooms, were incredibly clean. This made the whole place welcoming and charming.

Remember, too, that fixtures and fittings need to match the price-bracket of your property. There is no point putting expensive gold taps into a mid-market house. A potential buyer will feel they are being asked to pay a premium for things they wouldn't necessarily have chosen for themselves, and things they weren't looking for when they decided to move.

The Need for Space: Good Storage

Most people decide to move because they have run out of space. They are concentrating on the amount of room they are going to get, rather than gleaming new fittings – unless you are at the very top of the range, of course, when people expect everything to be done for them.

One young couple with a small child and another on the way warmed to one particular terraced house. Who were the owners? Another young couple with a baby and the next one on the way. The way the house was laid out and how the space was used was crucial, with the buyers easily able to imagine living there. Of course, they had similar lifestyles, which helped, but being able to see how they could use the space if they lived there was very important. Having 'flexible' spaces – a home office with a bed so it could also be a spare room, for example – is appealing to a large number of buyers.

Storage – much ignored due to the fact it is not as sexy as an Italian shower or snazzy new kitchen – is massively important. A lot of first-time buyers don't think about it until they run out of space. I believe you can never have enough storage, so make sure your home has storage you will be proud to point out in an almost nerdish way. Women tend to think more about storage than men, I find, and men should certainly think about it more.

Any chance to convert a cubby-hole into proper storage should be eagerly taken. The area under the stairs is ideal for golf clubs, suitcases and skis (and more besides: see opposite). I confess I look in cupboards and storage places when viewing, so it is not good enough to hide unwanted junk in these places.

Clever storage is crucial for your sanity, especially if you are living in a Lilliputian-sized home. There are a number of nifty and affordable storage ideas for the home these days. Under-bed storage for a child's, or for that matter adult's, room costs only about £12, hanging tidies £13, a stackable shoe shelf £9, a hanging store for newspapers and other daily clutter – no more rummaging round the back of the sofa for the remote control – £10, basket tower kits to store clothing around £60, and a pantry storage unit for spices and bottles around £140.

Storing books and files on square shelving can make a room look more contemporary and can partition off part of a room. Fuss-free filing – two smart-looking boxes for papers that normally end up piled on the kitchen table, cost £10 – is necessary for anyone with home office space, which means most of us these days.

Use 'dead space' – hallways and corridors – to create more room. If there is space to slip in a desk or bookshelf, you are saving room in another part of the house. Forgotten 'dead zones' include high ceilings where you can install hanging racks (or 'laundry maids'). You can hang towels from them in bathrooms, clothes in bedrooms and stuffed animals and other possessions in children's rooms. In kitchens, they are ideal for airing laundry.

Another good notion is hiding shelves for 'secret' items, such as jewellery or other prized small possessions, in recessed windows. A friend's inventive builder secreted hidden shelves into the sides of her sash window when he repaired it and gave her a 'secret drawer' behind a skirting board.

I have also seen builders put up bookshelves above and round doors. I have even seen bookshelves on the back of large doors, but you must make sure the doors are strong enough to support the weight of the books and have a small lip along the bottom to hold the books in place when the door is shut. This works best with doors that aren't opened and closed frequently.

Freestanding storage that isn't built in gives you great flexibility. I know one family that bought five *armoires* (a tall French cupboard or wardrobe, sometimes ornately decorated) from French junk shops, one for each of their four small children and one for the parents. No matter how often they moved or their rooms were converted, every member of the family felt reassured by their *armoire* that held their clothes and personal possessions. They looked good too after a fresh coat of grey-white paint.

PHIL'S TOP TIP

I am baffled by how many people ignore potentially useful space under the stairs. It could easily be converted into a bathroom, study alcove, brilliant storage cupboard or just somewhere to put the broom and hoover. With space at a premium in most British houses, try to get this under-stairs area to earn its keep.

I despair when there isn't a cupboard in a house tall enough to house an ironing board and bulky items, such as a pushchair and hoover – and I've seen many, believe me, that seem to have omitted storage space for these essentials. A logical place is under the stairs, which is close to the main entranceway and usually not far from the kitchen.

It is fairly ambitious turning under-stairs space into an extra bathroom, but it can be done if the area is large enough. Period houses with generous spaces are more likely to accommodate a bathroom here. Reckon on paying about £1,000 to £2,000 to get the work carried out.

A small office can be tucked neatly under the stairs if you can carve out enough headspace (a lot depends on the configuration of your stairs and the adjacent room and whether you need to knock a wall down between the two areas).

Now that so many of us need a home office, a spot to do the home accounts or for children to do their homework – approximately six out of ten British households now own a computer – this could be a good investment. If you need to remove the wall to open up the space, this could add to the overall cost – which could be in the region of £3,000 to £5,000 – but you will undoubtedly use this 'instant study' and it should make your house stand out compared to the neighbours' when a 'For Sale' sign is hammered up outside.

Pushed for Space? Hire a Self-storage Unit

If your home is too small to accommodate all your belongings and you are tired of tripping over rollerblades, musical instruments and piles of books – and as Britain has the smallest new homes in Europe according to a study this might well be the case – then paying around £125 a month for a lockable self-storage unit is a sensible option. Viewed as 'the spare room', you typically have 24-hour access to your storage room or cage, depending on the size of the space you choose.

Some people simply keep unused items or articles, such as a favourite childhood chair they can't bear to throw out, or collections of china that are not required very often, in their storage unit, while others treat them as an off-site 'lifestyle space' where they create a library, practise a musical instrument or keep their fishing equipment.

Hiring a storage unit could be a godsend when you come to sell your home too. You can store pieces of oversized furniture, some of the children's toys and exercise bikes when clearing out your house before viewings. Losing some of your clutter will make your house look bigger and lighter, and you can always pop up the road to the storage unit when you need something.

Is De-cluttering the Answer?

The most common advice offered by a number of home makeover experts on television and in magazines is to de-clutter – a posh way of saying you should offload what you don't need – in order to make the best of the space you live in and to help sell your home when you put it on the market.

This is sound advice, which not everyone finds easy to accept. People can be very sentimental about their goods and chattels, I find, but once you are brave and take the first steps towards getting rid of superfluous items, you will be really glad you made the effort. In fact, the only complaint I hear from people who've taken the de-cluttering route is that they wish they had chucked out their old junk years ago, and even that they want to throw out more unwanted stuff.

When your house is packed full of clutter, nothing looks good. A good start is to sort your belongings into three piles: to throw away, to keep and a 'maybe' pile that you can revisit. Perhaps you are keeping clothes you hope will fit you again once you embark on that ever-elusive diet, or old gifts you don't really want but feel it a shame to throw away.

Now is a good time to sell items online. If you can't be bothered to do this yourself, check out companies that will collect your goods, sell them and take a commission, typically 20 per cent. You can give away things for free on Free-cycle (www.freecycle.org), an online community where you match items you no longer need with people who want them, or take them to charity shops.

It is worth finding out if your local council offers a furniture removal service. Some will take away larger items, such as sofas, armchairs and beds, which are redistributed to someone in need in the borough. In some places this is free; other local authorities charge from £30 to collect. Still, not a bad price if you take into account what it would cost for you to hire a van or pay someone else to take your unwanted furnishings away.

Another satisfying way to clear clutter is to hire a skip. You can order a skip from a number of specialist firms. The process is straightforward: the firm delivers the skip, you fill it up and it is collected a number of days later. Skips cost from about £75 to £170, depending on their size.

PHIL'S CONTACTS BOOK

- Recycling services in the UK, www.enviroyellowpages.com.
- Freecycle, www.freecycle.org, where you can give away or collect items for free.
- www.allyourjunk.com, 0800 032 8972 – London-based company that will take away your junk and rubbish for recycling for a fee.
- National Association of Estate Agents, www.naea.co.uk, 01926 417794 – for recommendations of good local agents to talk to about how a home should look in your area.

CHAPTER THREE

DIY

When to wield your hammer and when to call in the pros

DIY – doing it yourself instead of hiring someone else to do the job – can be tempting on many levels. It saves money, you can carry the work out in your own time and it can be rewarding when you admire your handiwork at the end of the project. However, you must make sure it really is worth all the effort. Sometimes you will be better off leaving bigger or more risky jobs to the experts.

With high Stamp Duty taxes when you move home, removal costs, solicitor's fees and all of the disruption caused, there is a strong argument for 'improving, not moving'. DIY is on the up: you can add £2,230 to the value of your home after spending £990 doing a little home work yourself, says a recent study. Research also suggests that over 130,000 households recently started home renovations costing between £25,000 and £50,000, with 50 per cent of homeowners making improvements to their property. In a depressed market, many people choose to sit tight and improve their homes rather than move house, putting money into kitchens and bathrooms and redecoration instead of relocation.

But you need to know what you are doing, especially when it comes to skilled trades work. A study by a leading insurance company reveals that over 5.2 million people in Britain have carried out electrical work in high-risk areas such as bathrooms, kitchens and gardens, sometimes invalidating their home insurance by doing so. I recommend taking out extra building insurance and having accidental damage cover in place before getting out that drill and causing unintended harm to yourself or your property. Or, if you know you are aiming beyond your level of expertise, it might be time to call in the professionals.

Get it Right, as DIY Could Devalue Your Home

Not all DIY undertakings add value to a home. Experts warn that some DIY enthusiasts might actually be reducing their home's value. I believe bad DIY puts people off. Immediately, people viewing a bodged property start to expand their worries, wondering if what looks terrible on the surface is even worse underneath. 'If the sink isn't grouted properly, will I have to re-plumb the entire house?' A survey highlights some of the key DIY projects that detract from, rather than add to, your home. These include:

- Cheap new flooring
- Bad open fireplace restoration – for instance, choosing the wrong mantelpiece, not putting in a decent fire basket and not installing a quality fire surround
- Converting a garage into the wrong room, particularly a bedroom or gym

It's not only about the standard of the work. There is also the matter of taste. What appeals to you might not appeal to others. It is a good idea to talk to local estate agents and builders in your area to get a sense of which projects work well for your kind of property and in your street.

You must take into account that almost every house has a 'ceiling price' – a price it is unlikely to rise above, no matter what work has been implemented. In some cases, you might devalue your home by converting a garage into another room when the majority of possible buyers prefer to keep the garage. I guess the distinction here is doing the DIY work properly, but also making the right DIY choices. There is no point in embarking on a DIY project that you might like the idea of, but others think is a waste or pointless.

Equally, you need to get a feel for what purchasers want and how much you should realistically be doing at your level in the property market. If you spend many hours installing expensive wooden flooring, you want to be pretty certain this is what prospective buyers are keen to have. If they express a preference for carpeting instead, you will have wasted a good deal of energy and cash. If, however, you feel you will get a good deal of enjoyment out of a particular feature, by all means install it. But you might need to think about updating or reversing it when it comes time to sell so it appeals to the majority of buyers or at least to your target purchasers.

Beware of the NERDs

This brings us to an irritant I have witnessed too many times. At least 7 million UK households suffer from the plight of NERDs. These are homes with Never Ending Renovation Dramas, and there is nothing worse than seeing half-finished DIY schemes that are unlikely ever to reach a conclusion.

More than 1.7 million Britons have been living with a NERD for over a decade, a depressing statistic if ever I've read one. According to a report, 2.8 million homes have uncompleted kitchen refurbishments and another 2.5 million have bathrooms where work has ground to a halt.

My advice is only to take on projects you can realistically complete. If you try to build something of Taj Mahal proportions and then flounder midway, you will have to endure living with the messy aftermath of some-thing you were probably not up to in the first place. And a potential buyer will run a mile.

A good halfway position is to take on the tasks you can handle, while seeking help from professionals for more daunting or specialist jobs. Doing it yourself doesn't always mean you really have to do everything yourself. There is no shame in getting a bit of help from your friends, or the profes-sionals for that matter, when you need it. And if you are living with a NERD, you might want to consider calling in skilled tradesmen to finish it off. It could do a lot for domestic harmony too.

Learning the Tricks of the Trade

There are a number of good courses on offer for DIY buffs. For those who live in period houses, there are courses run by the Society for the Protection of Ancient Buildings (www.spab.org.uk, 020 7377 1644) on topics such as how to mix lime mortar. For more general skills consider the Building Skills Academy (www.buildingskillsacademy.co.uk, 01635 522007), which runs handyman courses for DIY workers and DIY courses tailored for women. A weekend course for beginner women builders costs £299, covering anything from plumbing and tiling to carpentry and general DIY skills. For queries about DIY projects and general building work, you can contact builder and writer Jeff Howell (www.ask-jeff.co.uk). He unmasks dastardly practices as well as handing out advice on how to accomplish building tasks.

And remember, fashions and expectations change over time. Ten years ago, people would ask if a house had central heating and double-glazing. Now these improvements are accepted as standard and the ante has been upped. People expect quite sophisticated home offices, en-suite bathrooms and state-of-the-art double garages. These projects can be quite a challenge – we are talking about more than hanging a towel rail here – but if you get them right, you will gain great satisfaction, which also will be enjoyed by the next owner.

Top 10 DIY Tips

1. Manage your budget sensibly, working out the figures before you start.
2. Be safe – ensure you know how to use equipment and you're wearing the right kit.
3. Use the right tools for the job.
4. Shop around DIY stores and online to compare the cost of materials.
5. Do not be afraid to experiment with smaller tasks; a lot of DIY disasters can be painted over.

6. Avoid the latest fads that might only appeal for a few months – opt for a classic overall look, introducing what is in vogue now through accessories that can be updated.

7. Do not take on more than you can handle; bringing in the professionals for key jobs might make sense.

8. Check out whether you need planning permission and consult building regulations.

9. Do not overspec – do not go beyond the specifications that make sense for your house and area.

10. Be realistic about how long everything will take and how much it will cost.

Improvements That Are a Good Investment

I always think you need to be in the right frame of mind with plenty of patience and, ideally, a reasonable amount of time to be good at DIY. Having the right tools is crucial. I sometimes joke that you need a grand's worth of tools before you can save 20 quid, but there is some truth in this. There is nothing more irritating than starting a job only to discover you have the wrong-sized screwdriver or need more drill bits. I spent ages putting up a shelf recently, and halfway through the job found out I didn't have a spirit level. Any hope of getting the shelf straight evaporated quite quickly without this relatively inexpensive but vital tool.

However, DIY can be fulfilling and satisfying. It is wise to do one job at a time and finish it off properly, or your partner will threaten to leave you. The old adage that it is easier to take something apart than put it back together again certainly applies here. It will be unsafe and disruptive if you start tearing up parts of your house, leaving them in chaos for ages before you get round to completing any one task.

If you are determined to drag out your tool kit and get stuck in, some projects give a good return on your money – with some profit on top when you decide to sell.

- **Central heating** – New central heating that has been fitted correctly always pays for itself. You will need to spend about £1,000 to £3,000 but could stand to add £5,000 to the value.
- **Double-glazing** – Installing double-glazing can be of huge benefit in keeping heat in and noise out. It doesn't cost a great deal – anything from a few hundred pounds to a few thousand depending on the size of your house and how many windows you want glazed – for the return benefits you will receive. I believe this definitely adds value to your home, probably £10,000 or more, as long as it isn't done too cheaply. Pay for the best double-glazing you can afford.
- **Bathrooms** – Unless you are a Seventies *aficionado*, ripping out that avocado suite and wildly colourful tiles might be advisable. I think you might nearly double your money if you splash out on quality tiles, clever lighting and cabinets with big mirrors to make a small bathroom appear bigger. This is a job most people do not want to do themselves, so find it a relief to see the work has already been done. The cost is from £2,000 to £20,000, adding as much as £25,000 or more to the value for a top-end bathroom. At the other end of the scale, even spending a small amount updating a bathroom – from £500 upwards – can add at least 3 per cent to the value of your home, according to mortgage lender GE Money.
- **Kitchens** – Branded kitchens go in and out of fashion, so be careful what you choose. Remember those homely units with wheat sheaves that went down so well 30 or so years ago? You do not want buyers snickering at your style errors, so select timeless units that will not date. The kitchen really is the heart of the home – people spend the bulk of their time here – so do not stint on appliances and worktops. Perhaps spending a bit more on tiles or a good fridge/freezer will pay off in the end. Depending how far you go, you can shell out £3,000 to £30,000 (although some top-end kitchens cost double that amount), but you are likely to add

anything from £2,000 to £40,000 to the value of your home. A lot depends on the quality of the units and materials you install, but I would reckon a good mid-range kitchen, with good tiling, a nice worktop and smart appliances, would cost about £10,000 to £20,000 and you are likely to add £25,000 to £30,000 to the value of your home. And although you can't always put a definite sum on it, a good kitchen does help sell a house faster. Getting the layout right is crucial, so concentrate on getting the appliances in the right place – you don't want to walk miles between the fridge and the cooker, for instance – and properly planned storage space.

- **Extensions and loft conversions** – Converting the loft does not come cheap – estimate £20,000 to £40,000; nor do extensions, typically costing between £10,000 and £30,000. Yet experts think a well-executed loft conversion or extension can net you around 25 per cent of the cost of the project in profit. If you spent £20,000, for instance, you could be adding about £5,000 (a quarter of what you spent) onto the value of your home. As most people move to get more space, I reckon you will recoup your money and then some.

- **Conservatories** – A lot depends on what kind of conservatory you plump for and how well it is integrated with the house and garden. There is nothing worse than a cheap-looking conservatory plopped on to the back of a house. However, a good conservatory that seamlessly blends in and offers extra usable space to the ground floor will add value. Expect to get your money back at least for a decent conservatory costing £5,000 to £30,000. And for top-of-the-line conservatories, you might get 10 to 20 per cent more value.

- **Redecorating** – Simply getting out a paintbrush to spruce up the paintwork is thought to add most value to a home, according to a recent study. Offering you the highest return on outlay, a thorough redecoration job could add up to £5,000 in value for an investment of only £100 to £1,000. A botched paint job will not do your house any favours, however, so if you worry about your prowess with a roller this would be a good time to call in a professional.

GOOD DIY

Michelle and Barry Horton turned a love of DIY into a friendly and distinctive family home. 'Our son had left home a few years ago, so we started hatching plans to sell up and downsize to a smaller place in France,' explains Michelle. 'But our three-bedroom house needed some attention, and with a limited budget, we realised we'd have to do a good deal of the work ourselves.'

Luckily, Michelle, a former schoolteacher, had recently retired and Barry only worked two days a week as an accountant. 'We had plenty of time to carry out all those jobs we wish we'd done when we bought the house 17 years ago. It was quite shameful in some ways that we hadn't got on with it, but life somehow always got in the way of our plans,' says Barry.

The Hortons bought their semi-detached house in a quiet village south of Manchester for £82,000. A solid-looking two-storey house, it required a fair bit of work, however, including installing central heating, rewiring, re-plumbing and knocking through the kitchen and snug.

'As we didn't mind doing a bit of DIY on the weekends, before we stopped working fulltime we had already restored the wooden floors, redecorated the living room and dining room, levelled the ground outside and planted a small orchard and kitchen garden,' says Michelle, now 61.

A dab hand with a power drill, Barry was eager to have a go at some of the rest of the work needed in order to attract a buyer. 'The problem was we hadn't finished everything off and let the work drag on, so this was our chance to get the house totally in order ready to sell.'

The Hortons spent over 18 months adding on a new porch

— Michelle discovered she had a talent for bricklaying — revamping the new kitchen, putting in central heating and laying a patio. They hired the services of a kitchen-fitter friend to install their new units, an electrician to sort out some of the wiring and sought advice from a local builders' merchant about the best way to tackle putting in the central heating and plumbing in the new bathroom.

'We did get some things wrong initially, like not putting in French doors or good-sized windows in the kitchen, which had the best view of the garden and surrounding countryside,' admits Barry. 'As this was one of the main selling points of the house, we cut down on the number of kitchen units going into that side of the room and put in a large window instead.'

Another mistake was not focusing on one particular job until it was complete. With several tasks started all round the house, and none of them completed in a hurry, it was not the best way to tackle the work required. 'It drove me mad,' Michelle confesses, 'and it was really depressing not feeling we were making any headway. The crunch came when I broke my toe on the edge of a floorboard that hadn't been secured properly and that's when we changed tack.'

The breakthrough came after the couple hired a local builder to give them some help and advice. First he worked with them on a plan of action outlining which jobs to do in which order. He also was hired to help with some of the tasks, such as installing the central heating and bathroom fixtures and fittings.

'The extra cost for his work at about £500 was worth every penny,' notes Barry. 'We still saved I reckon several thousand pounds by doing the rest of the work ourselves. However, at one point Michelle did say if she had to sand one more floor she would go mad.'

Tips from the Hortons include:

- Invest in the best tools you can afford, or rent decent equipment.
- Do not tackle anything that is beyond your ability.
- Carefully keep track of costs on a spreadsheet.
- Preparation is all – there's no point painting a wall that hasn't been filled and sanded properly.
- To achieve a professional finish on a budget, use own brand paints for the undercoat and first coat and then apply higher-quality paint on top.
- Become friendly with the guys in your local builders' merchant, who can offer good advice and names of skilled workmen in your area.
- Once you discover a particular talent, go for it – Michelle turned out to be brilliant at tiling and bricklaying, while Barry displayed a flair for basic plumbing and decorating.
- Get the infrastructure right – it is more important to spend money on a new boiler than on a plasma-screen TV.
- Keep all the receipts and guarantees for the work so potential buyers can see what you've done.

A local agent valued the Hortons' finished house with all their handiwork at just over £465,000. Building costs for the whole project are estimated at around £85,000 in total.

They had over a dozen viewers the first week the house went on the market and accepted an offer at £455,000 a month later. After selling the family house they worked on so hard, the Hortons are now hunting for a house in the south-west of France where they hope to retire.

'If we hadn't been bold and eager to learn new skills and carry out some of the work, we wouldn't have found a buyer so fast,' reckons Barry, whose new challenge is brushing up on his French. He also believes their English DIY experience will make the couple less afraid to renovate a French property in the future.

PHIL'S TRADE SECRETS

Do

- opt for the elegant and timeless;
- pay attention to detail – hastily finished work looks scruffy and amateurish;
- play to your strengths – if you are good at carpentry, lovingly hand-crafted stairs or cupboards will be noticed;
- use the best materials you can afford.

Don't

- add personal touches like saunas or sunken baths;
- do anything too fussy like stencilling or wallpaper borders;
- skimp on supplies – buy those extra few tiles rather than struggle with damaged ones;
- buy cheap paint – you probably will have to apply more, so you won't save money anyhow.

Getting a Professional Look

Making DIY work appear as professional as possible is the key. If something looks 'hand-made', you want it to be for the right reasons. A well-turned piece of wood that is admired by all is preferable to a wonky bit of timber that attracts embarrassment rather than approval. Here are some tips from the pros:

- Extend kitchen units right up to the end of a wall instead of leaving an amateurish and space-wasting gap.
- Blend colours in a room with a chosen main feature, such as a fireplace or eye-catching sofa.
- Create a mood with neutral and warm highlighting colours and well-planned subtle lighting.
- Don't be afraid to engage specialists when you need them – the pros do it, so why shouldn't you?

- Use reclaimed bricks that blend in with older ones – they might cost a bit more, but the overall look is well worth it.
- Attention to detail sorts the men from the boys – use the right-coloured mortars and finish all details properly.

PHIL'S CONTACTS BOOK

- The Society for the Protection of Ancient Buildings, www. spab.org.uk, 020 7377 1644. There are tips and advice on the website and SPAB runs courses on how to apply lime mortar and other tasks relating particularly to period buildings.
- Videojug.com has short films showing you how to put up shelves, remove a radiator or tile a wall.
- The Building Skills Academy, www.buildingskillsacademy. co.uk, 01635 522007.
- For information on how to tackle DIY projects, contact builder and writer Jeff Howell, www.ask-jeff.co.uk.
- www.ultimatehandyman.co.uk – free help and advice covering many DIY tasks. You can post a message on the forum and forum members will help.
- www.diydoctor.org.uk – free advice and help for self-builders and DIY enthusiasts.
- www.diyfixit.co.uk – free help on DIY jobs and advice on how to improve your home.
- www.diynot.com.

CHAPTER FOUR

Extensions

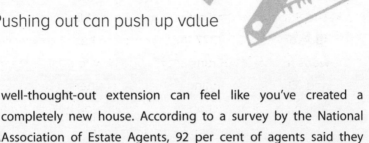

Pushing out can push up value

Awell-thought-out extension can feel like you've created a completely new house. According to a survey by the National Association of Estate Agents, 92 per cent of agents said they believed that adding an extension can increase the value of a property.

When agents were asked to specify how they would add worth to a home, 41 per cent said they felt the best idea was to add an extension. Seventeen per cent favoured the installation of a new kitchen, 4 per cent upgrading the exterior and another 4 per cent adding a conservatory (a kind of extension itself). With sellers keen to increase the value of their homes (and this eagerness increases in a less certain market when home-owners lose confidence), it's good to know that a well-planned and well-built extension that creates additional living space could increase the value of a property. It could also add to the joy of living in your home, as we are almost all greedy for more space in Britain.

The way I look at it is this: it is cheaper to build space than to buy it, so chances are you will be quids in. Square footage equals money – the more you have, the better. If you have a three-bedroom terraced house with one bathroom and you manage to turn it into a four-bedroom home with two bathrooms, you are making the place more sellable as well as adding value in monetary terms.

Of course, an extension could be a walloping great addition that substantially changes the layout of your home or a simple add-on that just gives you a bit more space in one section. But it will cost money to achieve. So before you embark on the project, think carefully about what you need, how you live and how best to artfully attach the extra room you require.

As all of you will have worked out by now, it is cheaper to build an extension yourself than to buy a house with one already done. Generally, the seller of the house – advised by their estate agent trying to get the highest amount possible – will have tacked on to the price the cost of the work carried out to build the extension and added in a profit margin.

Adding Space

Extensions can provide more space: an extra bedroom or bathroom, perhaps, which can make life for a family much easier. Or you could extend the existing kitchen, a vital component of any home. A new conservatory is another favourite project, which adds space and also provides a lot of pleasure for those looking for somewhere to sit in the summer. Now that conservatories are less rustic than they used to be – most can be used all year round and have proper heating and lighting – they are becoming much more part of a house, rather than a 'lean-to' extra. The best conservatory, I believe, is one that does not feel bolted on and looks like it was originally there. I have friends who have a splendid dining room in their conservatory where we've enjoyed many relaxing meals. With the lights dimmed inside, you can see the stars at night and feel you are eating outside – but without the chilly winds and annoying insects.

Sometimes, rather than extend, you might be able to use the space you already have in a more practical fashion. I'm a great fan of knocking down walls to open up space. British homes that were built in the Victorian era have plenty of small rooms – apparently, it was a status symbol to have a large number of rooms – rather than fewer, larger spaces. We live differently today. Rather than constantly going up and down a crazy number of stairs to miniature rooms where you can't even fit a cat, let alone swing it, we prefer more open and lateral spaces that the whole family can enjoy together. Mothers like to be close to their children in a play area or room, and teenagers might hang out in a snug watching TV while Mum and Dad read next door.

Extending just for the sake of it without thinking through what you are doing can be a big mistake. I have been in many cavernous extensions that are soulless and even pointless. If they don't blend in with the logic of the house and are not used in the right way, they can be a waste. I keep talking about the need to have good 'usable' space and this certainly applies to extensions. For instance, just tacking on an extension to the kitchen that isn't big enough to take a sofa and some chairs as a space to watch TV in, or even hold a desk for a home office, just creates more frustration. The space needs to be usable, not empty space that isn't adding to or improving how you live.

PHIL'S TOP TIP

Treat planning an extension like you would a holiday. You would look through brochures to choose where you want to go and then start gathering information on the currency, temperature, good places to eat, activities in the area and maybe even how to say some common words in the local lingo.

The same applies to planning an extension. You need to look through brochures or research on the Internet to decide what sort of extension you could have, and it is important to gather as much information as possible. It helps to learn the lingo as well to interpret the phrases builders, planners and architects use, so you can communicate with them about what you want and what you can do.

Benefits of an Extension

One of the major benefits of an extension is that it can allow you to add what I call 'no-nonsense' space, which is practical and sensible. This could include a proper kitchen, extra bathroom, home office, utility room or garage. No-nonsense space might include a bedroom as well if you and your family are stretched at the seams.

A braver move would be to change the entire layout of your home when you add on an extension, but this might also be a clever thing to do. Designers talk about the 'flow' of a house, which means getting the right ambience through a house leading from one room to another. This could be the opportunity to get this right if you are revamping the internal arrangement of space.

I think an extension that simply brings delight to your life should be applauded too. We work terribly hard and should remember that our homes are sanctuaries from the outside world. An extension providing some form of escape, be it a small gym, mini-library, steam or hobby room, will give you pleasure and, in many cases, add value later on when you sell. Creating new spaces, rather than adapting what you already have, can be very exciting. They could even move out into your garden and take the form of a garden room, studio or, for the truly inspired, an amazing treehouse for children, adults – or both.

Getting the Size Right

Work out carefully how much room you require for your extension. If you are keen on building a games room with a snooker table, you need a certain amount of space to be able to move around the table and pot balls. Equally, if you are adding on a media room with a large plasma-screen TV, you need to be able to sit far enough back to see the screen properly. If you are adding on a bedroom, will it have a double or single bed and can you fit in an en-suite bathroom too (which could add more value)?

Working out size doesn't always mean you need gargantuan spaces. You can neatly tuck in a small home office if all you need is enough room for a desk and chair and maybe a few shelves above the desk. A utility-room extension needn't be massive if all you want is a sink and somewhere to put a washer and dryer.

Before looking at all the alternatives, keep in mind you must try to come up with a plan for an extension that suits the house. I once visited a house in Croydon, Surrey that had had a gigantic extension, doubling the size of the interior. The owner was keen to get as much money as he could when he sold the house – hence the enormous extension. He valued his completed house at £400,000, twice the amount of the house next door that was only half the size and sold for £200,000, which made a kind of sense. However, his very large house didn't really fit into the street or the area, where nothing else approached his price. If anyone had that amount of money, they probably wouldn't have wanted to live in that street. No buyer could be found willing to pay such an eye-watering sum.

Normally, a really good extension adds about 10 to 15 per cent to the value of your home, but if it is done badly or is totally out of proportion to the rest of your property, it can actually detract from its worth. So, be careful you extend to the degree that is right for your house, and your area, or you could lose out when it is time to market it.

My best advice is to look closely up and down your street and note what other people have done. This gives you some idea of what is typical in the neighbourhood and what planners are generally happy for people to do. This doesn't always apply, mind, as a new planner might arrive with different views from his predecessor, but it does give you some indication of what is allowed in your area.

The Possibilities

You can extend your house in four directions:

- up
- down
- to the side
- to the rear

Depending on the footprint of your house and the size of your land, you need to work out the best way to add extra space in keeping with the look of the house and without reducing your garden too drastically. An estate agent in west London has told me he is getting increasingly worried about the number of people extending into the garden and cutting back on its size. Remember, outdoor spaces are precious, particularly in cities and large towns where they come at a premium. Having a huge extension jutting out into what was once a pretty little town garden might have the opposite effect when it comes to adding value.

The loft conversion

Eking out more room from the roof space is a popular kind of extension. Loft conversions are relatively easy to carry out and can add considerable value to your home. But do remember that you have to work out where to store everything that previously had been slung up into the loft. Loft conversions are covered in detail in Chapter Five.

The basement conversion

Digging down below to create a whole new floor in the basement is increasingly popular, especially in prime areas where the price per square foot is high. A basement conversion can be disruptive and expensive, mind, and might not be for everyone, but it can be a significant way to add value. Basement conversions are covered in detail in Chapter Six.

The side return

The Victorians came up with a number of ingenious ideas, including a coherent railway network and great sewage system. The side return – a covered passage from the kitchen door, which was typically at the side of the house, to the garden – was probably regarded as a good notion at the time but is somewhat less useful today. This rather poky and dark space served a purpose once – it is believed this is how Victorians sheltered themselves from the elements when visiting the outdoor loo – but such a use is obviously no longer relevant.

You can convert the side return into usable space with a glazed side extension after knocking down the side wall of the kitchen or sitting room and pushing a new wall out to the garden boundary. The roof can be vaulted in a Victorian style or made of convex glass, resulting in a bigger light-filled room.

A small side extension costs less than £25,000, including all the building work, wiring, plastering and a radiator. A larger two-storey side extension to a big house could cost as much as £100,000. Costs can be cut down if you share the work with your neighbour, who could be interested in having his side return converted at the same time.

You might not think you are gaining much extra space by incorporating this bit on the side, but extending the side return can make a real difference. Some people opt to put the dining area in the side return, while others install a play area for children, or a snug with a sofa and a couple of armchairs. The amount of square footage gained might not appear to be that signifi-cant, but the improvement to usable space is huge. This is one of my favoured value-added options that makes a big difference to how the room functions.

CASE STUDY

THE SIDE EXTENSION

Rakhee Connell and her husband Jared, a 42-year-old IT consultant, have extended the kitchen sideways in their house in Norwich, Norfolk, turning what was once a narrow room into a big open space.

Rakhee, who is 39 and a part-time physiotherapist, says the side extension has created a wonderful extra area. 'We have created a dining area under the glazed roof and we also decided to have a conservatory added on at the same time. The company we hired, which specialises in conservatories, did both jobs for us.'

The main advantage, according to the Connells, is more light is admitted. 'Most Victorian houses tend to be on the gloomy side and with the vaulted glass roof giving a feeling of height this makes the whole room brighter,' explains Jared.

Opening up the side return cost £16,000 and the couple feels it was money well spent to lose an unused, dingy spot, turning it into a family dining space. The conservatory cost about another £20,000.

'It's really improved our lives, giving us a decent amount of space for the whole family to relax and eat. We have two children, Rajah, who is four, and Narinder, 18 months, who love playing nearby. There is plenty of room for Rajah to ride his trike around and Narinder to stack her bricks,' Rakhee says.

The family do not intend to move from their four-bed terrace, bought two years ago for £315,000, quite yet. They see the value primarily in terms of improving their lifestyle, rather than their finances.

A local estate agent estimates, however, that by adding on the side return and conservatory, the Connells' home is likely to be worth over £360,000. 'It also will make it a lot easier to sell when they want to move, because their house will stand out from the rest in the street,' the agent suggests.

Adding a Conservatory

A conservatory is one of the most popular and straightforward options when it comes to extending a house – and is in the top three home 'must-haves', along with a new kitchen and bathroom.

Before you go ahead with your conservatory, however, you need to think about whether you really want to have a full-blown conservatory or whether a smaller version, such as a sunroom, will do. There are even 'mini-conservatories' or mini-bay extensions that help grow a room for those with restricted space. These miniature versions, which measure 1.2 by 2.2 metres and have room for a couple of chairs and a small table, cost about £3,000, as opposed to £10,000 for the average conservatory.

Under new planning regulations that came into force in October 2008, a conservatory is treated the same as any other extension under planning law (see the restrictions outlined in Chapter Fourteen), no matter what materials you decide to use. The planning rules apply largely to the dimensions of your addition, where it is located on the house and how close it is to the boundaries of your property. In most cases, you will be allowed to build a conservatory without having to seek permission and any reputable builder or specialist conservatory firm should be able to advise you. However, do not take their word for it if you are doing anything complex or unusual. It is worth checking the rules with your local authority (go on to the local council website and find the planning section).

A conservatory should be in keeping with your house. There is nothing worse than seeing a fine house with a conservatory that sticks out like a sore thumb. There are a number of styles, from Georgian and Victorian through to gable – with a steep pitched roof lending extra height and light – and lantern – a period version with two tiers that has a ceiling in the shape of a lantern.

The size will depend on how you are going to use your conservatory. Will you just want a quiet spot to sit in the warmth, so you only need space for a couple of chairs and side tables? Or do you want to fit in a large table to feed your guests in a less formal dining-room setting?

Some people like to work in a conservatory, although it would have to be kitted out with the right communications connections for a computer and phone. Also, you would probably have to get blinds installed to block out bright sunlight shining on your computer screen.

The finished look of this new addition to your house is very important. To avoid 'the lean-to effect', you want the conservatory to either slip in comfortably with how the rest of the house looks, or to make a statement of some kind that might be brave but should always be aesthetically pleasing. Conservatories can be made from all sorts of materials: wood, brick, uPVC, aluminium, glass and steel. Some companies and builders will recommend a blend of materials – for instance, wood on the inside and aluminium on the outside. This might cut down on maintenance costs, but you need to be careful the look of the conservatory isn't compromised. It is good to save money, of course, but if you then regret how this extension looks, you might find yourself wishing you'd forked out the extra for the materials you wanted in the first place.

The roof is likely to be made of glass or, in lower-cost versions, polycarbonate sheeting. Great strides have been made in the sort of glass you can buy. One kind is 'self-cleaning' glass, where most of the dirt or debris runs off easily when it rains. Another is toughened glass, which is resilient to bumps and knocks and also usually reduces the amount of heat gathering inside, which means you don't get too hot, and helps it stop escaping when it gets too cold ('the greenhouse effect').

Personally, I wouldn't be too mean. I would avoid cheaper plastic or polycarbonate roofs. They can look rather nasty and are not all that well insulated. You can end up scorched in the summer and freezing in winter. Conservatories can be a great haven for those who like spending time out of doors but need some shelter in the dead of winter. You can sit in some comfort out of the cold, but still see the stars and feel you are in touch with nature on the other side of the panes of glass.

Getting coated, self-cleaning glass might cost several hundred pounds more, but is well worth it in terms of maintenance. You won't be forever clambering up ladders to clean the roof, which means you'll be safer from accidents as well as free of hassle. Also, if you can afford hardwood, go for it. It's more attractive in most instances and sturdier. If you tie in bricks and hardwood with the rest of your house, it will be less jarring visually. Conservatories are the one extension that can really look like an extension, and you should aim for them to seamlessly match the rest of the house.

PHIL'S TOP TIP

Don't lop too much off your garden – a family needs enough room to get out and kick a ball and run about a bit. It's a good idea to stake out the space the planned conservatory is going to take up, then you can see how much of your garden is left over and whether it is in balance with the house. Losing too much garden could detract from the value of your house, so don't get carried away. Conservatories need not be big, hulking additions, after all.

A good designer's trick is to lay down newspapers where you imagine a sofa and chairs might go, and you can do the same to get the right-sized furniture for your conservatory. If you buy

> *furniture that is too big (a common problem in rooms inside your*
> *house as well as in extensions), your conservatory will appear*
> *crowded and you won't be able to move about easily.*

Adding More Rooms

Maybe the most ambitious expansion of all, but adding an extra room or rooms can really boost your living space. As most people count up the number of bedrooms, bathrooms and reception rooms when they buy a house, offering an extra room or two that is well planned and well finished could certainly bump up the price of your home.

Equally, if you have a growing family or work from home, having more rooms will make your life a whole lot easier and cut down on family arguments or discontent. If you ever had to share your bedroom with a messy, noisy sibling, then you'll know what I mean. Creating more and good living space will always help sell a home too. Closely identify what is missing and what would make your life – and a future buyer's life – better before you proceed.

CASE STUDY

ADDING ROOMS

When a Cotswold farmhouse wouldn't sell, the owners found out why and made some changes.

About 18 months ago, the Hollands put their 3,000-square-foot (279-square-metre) five-bedroom farmhouse on the market at £1.25 million. Along with a three-bedroom cottage and four acres of paddock and garden, you would think the house would shift quickly.

However, it started to languish on the market. Interested buyers lined up to view the house, but felt it lacked a good bedroom layout and large reception room. Ironically, the main reception room in the accompanying cottage was larger than the living room in the house.

So the owners decided to add some extra rooms and give the buyers what they were asking for. Just over a year later, the thoughtfully extended 4,000-square-foot (372-square-metre) house was back on the market with a large new ground floor drawing/dining room and an en-suite master bedroom and dressing room above. Along with the extra floor space, the price went up accordingly to £1.5 million, to cover the building costs of nearly £100,000.

Making key rooms bigger gives the property an added dimension and added value, says the estate agent who helped with the Hollands' sale. 'You are turning a modest farmhouse with a cottage into a splendid country house with a cottage.'

This is an example of a homeowner taking expert advice to enhance a house and help sell at a good price. It might seem baffling that buyers felt the property lacked space, as the place was awash with rooms before the building work was even planned or carried out. However, people expect a good-sized living room in a country farmhouse where they imagine everyone gathering for Christmas and other major occasions. If it is too small and out of balance with the rest of the house, it doesn't fit in with what people expect from a decent-sized rural property.

The original 16- by 14-foot (4.9- by 4.3-metre) drawing room is now called the sitting room and the extension has become a spacious drawing room of 25- by 24-feet (7.6- by 7.3-metres), with doors opening on to the dining room. Above, the new master bedroom suite with a fitted dressing room and smart en-suite bathroom is closer to the ideal a prospective purchaser would have in mind when buying a family house in this area.

Marcia Holland, a 48-year-old health practice administrator, says they were careful to match the new rooms to the older Victorian house.

'Some people go hunting for animals, but I went hunting for beams,' she explains. 'During my search, I also found round bricks and slate for the fireplace, so it doesn't look too glaringly new.' The Hollands also put in wood skirting and architraves that look similar to what would have been in the house originally.

Costs were kept down with members of the family carrying out some of the work themselves. Marcia's husband Kevin, a 50-year-old lighting designer, helped drive a small digger to get rid of some of the soil and Marcia sourced most of the materials, ordered them and kept track of the budget.

The family is moving on with their children, Jeff, 15, and Louisa, 13, and Marcia says the extension has been 'lovingly done for us, and not just to sell the house. This is not a quick bodged job. We selected good oak flooring over less-expensive laminate and put in wood detailing above the windows'.

Marcia and Kevin also have planning permission in place to build a tennis court on their land. An outbuilding has been converted into a small gym and new owners could turn it into a home office or a studio if they preferred.

'We wanted to use the best of the space we have and offer flexibility as needs change,' says Kevin. 'There is a large games room above the garage and a separate 2,000-square-foot (186-square-metre) three-bedroom cottage, ideal for visitors or for an office if you work from home.'

After only three weeks on the market, the re-launched house with its roomy new extension sold for close to the asking price. 'We covered our costs, managed to make a bit on top and sold the house for what we felt it was worth,' points out Kevin. 'And guess what the new owners like most? You guessed it – the master bedroom suite and the new living room.'

> ## PHIL'S TOP TIP
>
> *If you have become the heir to someone else's extension and it is not to your taste, do not despair. You do not necessarily have to spend a great deal of money to sort it out. You can lift up the carpets, and if there is decent wood flooring below, it is easy to fill it in, if need be, sand and oil it. Or you could replace unattractive windows, update the lighting and repaint the walls. Rethinking how you use the space could improve your home as well. An unloved dining room might make a good playroom. You could even consider knocking a wall down to open up the space further.*

The Garage Conversion

There is some debate as to whether you are adding much value to a home by converting a garage, but I think in some circumstances it can add worth. With many of us not actually parking our cars in our garages any longer, why not use the garage as an extra room? This is particularly so if you have an integrated garage that isn't separate from the rest of the house.

It is important to really work out how best to use the garage, however. A number of modern houses typically have the garage on the right hand side and the house on the left, with the main door in the middle. It is simple to create a room in a garage, but it might end up being a bit awkward in terms of layout. A garage that is off to one side like this seldom works as a dining room, as it is too far from the kitchen. Equally, I'm never convinced such a garage works as a playroom either, as again it is too far from the main core of the house. However, a home office or den for teenagers that is slightly separate from the rest of the home could be a good option in these circumstances.

You need to find out what is allowed in your area. Some local councils are happy to let you convert your garage into living space, while others are not. The planners might not like too many cars parking in the streets and would prefer them to be hidden away. If you have neighbours who've undertaken this kind of conversion, talk to them to get a feel for what they have done, and talk to the planning department too. Check out the council's website for regulations and advice.

I have a friend who lives in a street where the garages have been used for a multitude of things. The planners are fine about the conversion of the garages as long as the external appearance isn't altered. This means you need to keep the same external windows and make sure the integral garage still blends in with the rest of the building. My friend has converted his garage into a state-of-the-art kitchen, while a neighbour uses his as a utility room and for storage. I favour my friend's approach, which involved moving the kitchen from the back of the house to the front. This has freed up the space overlooking the garden at the back, which has been opened up into a terrific living room/dining area.

Compared to creating a whole new extension, this can be far less hassle and you might not even need planning permission. Even if you do, it should be reasonably straightforward. A garage conversion should cost less than a whole new extension as well: about £10,000 upwards, depending on how many structural changes need to be made.

You need to make sure you still have somewhere to park. If there is room on your driveway, you can put your vehicle there. If not, you need to ensure there is space for street parking. You could lose value if you convert the garage but the street-parking alternative is difficult or nigh on impossible.

If the garage isn't integrated into the house and you need to exit your home and go outside to get to the garage, this might be viewed as a nuisance by some. If the garage is going to be used as an office or games room, this might not be regarded as a problem. However, if you convert your garage into a bedroom, having it separate from the main house could put some buyers off when it is time to sell on. You might be able to link the garage to the main house if it is separate. This is something you are likely to need planning permission to carry out, so get advice from an architect or the council before you go ahead with this plan.

Garden Buildings

Putting up a new building in the garden is a clever way of gaining more space. Effectively a posh version of the shed, this is becoming popular with those wanting a retreat where they can work, garden, relax and even house a teenager, nanny or guests.

A number of specialist companies have sprung up that will dig out the foundations, put up the structure, sort out any electrics or plumbing and decorate for you. The building can be a simple wooden erection or a more contemporary and striking structure. One young designer has come up with a 'pod' unit that resembles an egg.

Typically, you don't need planning permission for a garden building as long as you aren't putting anything up that uses up more than half the garden space or overlooks the neighbours in an intrusive way. But if your property is listed or in a designated special area, you might need to consult the planners and seek permission in order to build a new garden structure.

Depending on where you live, converting an outbuilding might be a clever option. Some local authorities encourage this practice, particularly if your outbuilding becomes your place of employment and it leads to work being created in a rural area. If your home is listed and the planners are not enthusiastic about you adding on an extension, you might be able to get some of what you want by changing the outbuildings instead.

The costs to erect a garden building vary according to size. A rough estimate is from about £10,000 to £30,000 for a kit or 'ready-made' structure. You could save a few thousand pounds by carrying out the work yourself, but you need to add in your time and work out whether you have the expertise for such a project. Hiring an architect to draw up plans and produce drawings will cost from about £500 to £1,000.

The advantage of putting up a kit home is you can dismantle it and take it with you when you move, whereas a more permanent structure would have to stay behind. Of course, this doesn't add value when you sell the property on to the next owner, although if he is keen on the kit home remaining and you are prepared to leave it behind for him, you could negotiate a price. Also, if you run a limited company and you use your building as an office, you can reclaim your VAT on the premises, but you would need to check this with your accountant.

Prefab Sprouts

Another way to win the space race is to think about investing in a prefab. This might conjure up rather nasty images of post-war huts, but these days prefabricated buildings are anything but cheap and tacky. Instead of spending months getting architects to draw plans, battling with planners and putting up with builders traipsing all over the place, the 'ready-made' prefab supplied at a fixed price could save you a great deal of trouble and money.

If you fancy a glass dining room off your kitchen, for instance, you could have a full glass box room in kit form delivered and erected for just over £20,000 in a matter of weeks. A brick and glass version would be even cheaper than the totally glass one. More traditional prefabs that match the existing look of your home, and that could form a new playroom or office, are available too. Prices start at about £18,000 for a 3- by 3-metre brick, stone or wood extension. This might keep planners and your neighbours happy, who could be concerned about anything too modern in your area.

A neat trick is building up rather than out, with an upper layer being added to your home in less than a day (although you will need planning permission for this upwards manoeuvre). A small-scale rooftop extension of this sort was carried out for Carol Thatcher, who had a studio and chic bathroom installed on her flat on London's South Bank in under 24 hours.

Other prefab arrangements include a utility room, kitchen extension or a home office. Now that the technology has changed, the panels are lightweight and easy to carry through a house, making the kits especially helpful to owners of terraced houses where access has typically been tricky. Many see the prefabs as the next stage on from garden rooms – who wants to have to troop outside to go to the home office or extra bedroom, after all?

The main advantage is how quickly prefab kits can be put together on site and the up-to-date, properly insulated materials meet all the building regulation standards in this more eco-friendly world. Also, everything comes from one place, so you are not waiting for different workmen to arrive with materials from different sources.

Contemporary prefabs are popular and as long as your plans aren't too gargantuan, you shouldn't need planning permission. But if your house is listed or in an area reckoned to be special, you might need to consult your local planners. Check out www.planningportal.gov.uk/house to discover the latest rules and regulations.

Planning Permission for Extensions

Under new Government regulations that came into effect in October 2008, it should be easier, in theory, to add an extension to your house. An extension is considered to be within 'permitted development' – what you can do to your property without having to seek permission.

There are a number of limits and conditions, including no more than half the area of land can be covered by additions or other buildings. This is dealt with in more detail in Chapter Fourteen.

PHIL'S TRADE SECRET

Be nosy and check out what your neighbours have done. Talk to them and ask which local builders or specialist companies they used. They might even let you take a peep at their new extensions, or a builder or firm might get permission to take you round to see their handiwork.

As well as working out the positives from past experiences in your area, ask your neighbours what they would do differently if they could build the extension again. I find that this 'I wish we had done' information is as important as the work that was actually carried out. A good builder learns from each project and implements changes next time round to make the next house better, and you can benefit from this inside knowledge.

A Fine Balance

I do keep coming across strange extensions. People say, 'I can get an extension on to this,' but just tacking something on can make the house go higgledy-piggledy. I've even seen houses with several extensions that have been put up over the years with different materials and no evidence of an overall plan. It's not a good idea to make a house bigger just for the sake of it. Often, people think that if they have added a massive kitchen/diner on to their house, then they should put in a massive kitchen. It can be difficult to live in those very big spaces though. They might be great for a party, but you need to think quite hard how you will use such an airy space the rest of the time. 'Dividing' it up with furniture or maybe even a few steps taking you to a different level to define a new area can be a good idea.

This is not to say you should always play safe. One carefully conceived glass extension in my street looks very cool and stands out from the crowd. When my neighbour sells the house with this sharp-looking extension, he should attract a number of interested buyers. If you are extending, say, the kitchen, then maybe it is a good idea to do something a bit more striking.

One of my pet hates is seeing people use the wrong bricks on extensions. Don't leave this decision to your builder, who might want to save money and go for the cheaper and less-attractive option. You can buy reclaimed bricks that might cost a few pounds more but will look a great deal better.

Accessing the extension is an important consideration too. To keep the right balance and flow, you want any outside entrances to be in the right place. Getting the extension to flow into the garden and the garden to flow into the extension on the house is crucial and, if you get it right, it will add value to your home.

One piece of advice I can pass on is to put in lintels strong enough on a glass extension to take sturdy blinds, even if you are not installing the blinds yourself. Not everyone likes to live in what can feel like a goldfish bowl, and giving a buyer the option to add blinds easily will be noted. Or install blinds from the outset. The motorised versions are very sexy and work well on double-height or tall windows. At the touch of a button, the blinds slide up and down. These are not cheap, however, and can cost several thousand pounds.

PHIL'S TOP TIP

If you cannot afford to do everything you want right away when extending your house, why not tackle it in stages? The best course of action is to hire a good architect, or other expert, to work out a master plan and then break it up into two or three parts. This way, you ultimately get what you want, but maybe not all of it immediately. This is probably a better option than doing something on the cheap that you might regret later.

PHIL'S CONTACTS BOOK

- www.planningportal.gov.uk/house – this Government website is a valuable resource, listing all the regulations linked to planning and building work. There are even interactive homes – a detached house, terraced house and an eco home for the future – which you can click on to learn about the planning guidelines for different parts of each kind of property.
- www.channel4.com/4homes and www.bbc.co.uk/homes – two useful websites that supply free advice on how to improve your home.
- www.estimators-online.com – a website that will work out the true cost of your extensions for a small charge.

CHAPTER FIVE

Lofts

Turning your roof space into real space

Converting a loft can be a relatively pain-free experience in most instances and has an instant impact by opening up the space in your home. A good loft conversion can add 15 to 20 per cent to the value of your home for a cost of about £10,000 to £40,000, depending on where you live, the size of the conversion and the materials you use. Build costs in London and parts of the south-east can typically be one-third more than elsewhere in the UK.

So, what can I do?

Under planning regulations brought into force by the Government in October 2008, most of us do not need permission to convert the loft because it comes into the category of 'permitted development' – what you are allowed to do within the regulations without having to seek permission. Unless you are tampering with the external appearance of the house, have side-facing windows overlooking the neighbours or you are in a listed building, you should find it quite a straightforward process.

As long as the conversion doesn't exceed 50 cubic metres for a detached or semi-detached house, you can go ahead. However, if you live in a conservation area or other special area such as a national park, you will need to apply for permission. There is more information about the planning process in Chapter Fourteen.

Lofty Ambitions

One in five of us appear to be eager to convert our lofts, according to a study released after the new Government rules came into effect, with property owners in Wales and the north-east keenest. Thirty-one per cent of those questioned said this would be their home improvement of choice. Such sentiments are supported by the Royal Institution of Chartered Surveyors, which reckons a loft conversion can add £10,000 or more to the value of a property. This also ties in with the current mood of 'improve, don't move'. Since the average cost of moving house to gain more space is £40,000 to £50,000, a good loft conversion of £30,000 looks like better value. Besides, maybe you love your home and don't want to move, no matter how tight for space it is.

An advantage of converting the loft over a ground-floor extension is you do not have to sacrifice green space in your garden. This can be a real boon to a family desperate for a decent amount of outside space, or even a single person or couple keen to hold on to a coveted patio or a smaller garden.

Loft Basics

Before you eagerly start your climb up to the stars, it is worth noting that not every loft space translates easily into extra rooms and extra value. If the ceilings are too low and you aren't allowed to raise them up any higher (planners normally take a dim view of altering the external height or appearance, remember), you need to assess how you can use the area or whether the taller members of your family have to get used to stooping every time they use this space. In this case, the loft might be okay for storage but not much else.

Before you lose what could possibly be, depending on the size and accessibility of your loft area, the best storage space in the house, really think where you will put the skis, suitcases, golf clubs, collected memorabilia and all the other stuff you have accumulated in your loft. You will need a cupboard or other storage place big enough to accommodate what normally gets pushed up there. Also, keep in mind that you will lose some space on the level below when you build up the floor and put in a decent staircase to the loft.

A particular bugbear I have is when access to loft spaces isn't as clever as it should be. Very narrow and steep staircases can be dangerous, and older people and families with young children viewing your house when it is up for sale might take against them. The same could apply to spiral staircases, which might look pretty winding upwards in a graceful arc but aren't always practical. Have you ever tried to cart furniture and other awkward items up a spiral or narrow staircase? You're far better off fitting a proper one with a protective balustrade.

Your loft conversion could be simply a place for you to mess about with a train set, accessed by a humble flip-down ladder. But a temporary staircase, rather than a more solid fixed one, means the loft won't be counted as a 'liveable' space when it comes time to sell – and therefore, will be worth less.

What Is 'Liveable' Space?

The official definition of 'liveable space' is 'where you intend to use the room as a normal part of your house, including spare bedrooms which may be used infrequently'. If you decide to create a liveable space in an existing loft space, it is likely to require alterations. Some of these could have a negative effect on the building and how the occupants will use it if not thought out carefully, well planned and undertaken in accordance with the current legislation. If in doubt, consult an expert, such as an architect, surveyor or specialist loft conversion firm.

Estate agents love houses that have had the lofts converted. These rooftop extensions are very commonly carried out these days and represent good value for money in most cases.

Yet, not every loft is ripe for revamping. Before you consider converting the loft, decide whether the extra room or rooms you create will be 'liveable', or what I call 'habitable'. By habitable I mean rooms with strong floor joists to support people and furniture (as opposed to space that is only suitable for storage). You also need to put in proper insulation, safe access from the staircase to the conversion and fire doors to meet building and safety regulations.

Sound insulation is another consideration, particularly at the top of the house where noise between the loft and the rooms below can be irritating. This might make you think twice about putting a teenager partial to punching out blaring music at strange times of the day into the new loft room. Despite decent sound proofing, some noise will still percolate down. You don't want to disturb the neighbours either, so think about insulation to cut out noise that could find its way through the adjoining wall to their house too.

If you can produce a 'liveable' room in the loft – and this will be one that passes fire regulations and can be awarded a safety certificate – then you are adding real value to your home because you have increased the number of usable rooms. To increase enjoyment of your loft, it is advisable to do the job properly, to put proper floorboards down and build a really good solid staircase. Then this area can be turned into a terrific office, playroom or even an extra bedroom, sometimes with a small adjoining bathroom.

Even if you don't need planning permission to proceed, you will have to get the nod from a building control surveyor. Once all the work complies adequately with building control regulations, you will be issued with a completion certificate. I believe it is vital to get the paperwork signed off at the end of the project, so you can show it to the buyer's solicitor when you sell. A major concern is safety in the event of a fire, so that anyone in the loft can escape and also, if a fire breaks out in the loft, it can be contained. It is worth checking what the current regulations are so you can make sure you stick to them. It is crucial you get this fire safety certificate. When you sell your house, you need to prove to the buyer that you have a liveable space in the loft that passes this test.

> ### PHIL'S TOP TIP
>
> *Keep in mind that just because you can stand up in the loft space, this doesn't necessarily mean you will have proper head height and will be able to turn it into a 'liveable' room. Insulation and joists will need to be added during the building work, which will take away some of the headroom. A six-foot (1.8-metre) space, for instance, might end up as only a five-and-a-half-foot (1.7-metre) space after insulation and joists have been installed. Older houses are usually easier to convert than homes built from the late Sixties on, because they have steep pitched roofs and clearer open spaces. It can be more complex to convert the roof space in a newer home and, therefore, can cost more.*

Let There Be Light

Windows to admit much-needed natural light are crucial to loft conversions. There are a number of different types of windows available, and what you do is likely to be influenced by the sort of house you live in and what has typically been allowed in your street. I say typically, because rules are not always rigid and what has been allowed in the past might not be allowed now – or vice versa.

The windows you choose to put into your loft have a strong influence on how the exterior of the house looks. Matching your house to the rest of the street is important, and can even give you ammunition to get the conversion you desire if you do have an issue with the planners. However, no planning department has to let you do something just because your neighbours have been allowed to do it. Precedent doesn't always count – planning policy can change, remember – although it certainly can help your argument if you do have to appeal against a decision.

Mansard or mansard roof

A mansard is where extra space is formed by part of a new roofline coming out of the existing roof in an 'A' shape. Mansards are common in terraced houses in big towns and cities in Britain. If you look up as you drive past rows of terraces, you'll see how they have been created from the roof spaces. It is fairly easy and inexpensive to convert mansards.

Dormer

A dormer or 'Heidi window' is spotted frequently on chalets, or bungalows when there isn't enough height running along the entire loft space. Sometimes, dormer windows are introduced if you want to add extra height for a purpose, such as needing enough room to stand up in a shower or over a sink or while using a staircase.

Roof lights (or skylights)

If you have enough head height already, you can save money and hassle by simply installing roof lights, also known as skylights. There are a number of these on the market, from triple-glazed polycarbonate domes through to skylights that come with automatically opening smoke vents wired into the fire system. Some are 'fixed' – you can't open and close them – and others are manually or electrically hinged. Roof lights are easy to fit and are set in flush to the original roof. They're ideal for barn conversions – planners don't like windows to jut out and ruin the look of the exterior – and the best-known brand is Velux, although there are a number of other versions. The advantage of being able to get away with just roof lights – although a lot depends on the configuration of your roof and what looks right on your particular house – is that they are great fun and not all that costly (they start at about £60).

Whatever sort of window you select, keep in mind that you will have to clean them. If you end up with the fixed variety, this could be tricky. Having easy and safe access to the roof to clean them regularly could be a good idea. Using self-cleaning glass, where most of the accumulated grime and debris washes off when it rains, can save you time – and money, if you are paying a window cleaner to make your windows sparkle.

You want to make sure you are buying heat-reflective glass so you don't suffer from heat exhaustion in your new loft conversion. On a hot and sunny day, the windows will attract the sun's rays and it could become quite stifling in a loft without such glass. Also, consider how you will open and close your new windows. If they are set into a high roofline you might not be able to reach them. There are a variety of devices to help you get to them, from the cheapest, a long metal pole with a hook, to more expensive automated methods where you hit a button on a switch or remote and the windows open and close themselves.

Converting Loft Spaces in Flats

We tend to equate loft spaces with houses, but you can gain a lot of desired space if you live in a top-floor flat. If you are a first-time buyer, converting the loft in your flat is a classic way to add value. You need to make sure the lease to the flat actually says you own this top-floor space. The freeholder – in property law, the freeholder is the person who owns a freehold building – owns the roof, so you may find yourself having to pay for the rest of the attic space. This could cost a few thousand pounds, depending on how commercially minded the freeholder is.

Another interesting option is buying the 'air space' on a flat roof. This means you own the area on top of the building, where you could add an extension. This could be very valuable, if you think in terms of the square footage you are gaining. One fairly straightforward way of filling in this newly acquired 'air space' would be to have a prefabricated unit lifted up by a crane and positioned on the roof. A prefab would be at a fixed cost, in the region of £10,000 to £30,000 depending on size and quality.

TERRACE LOFT CONVERSION

Vinny Morgan, a 43-year-old university lecturer, hankered after more space and decided the best way to get it was to convert the loft in her two-bedroom terraced house in Leeds.

'I have my niece Rita living with me while she trains to be a doctor, and what was my home office is now her bedroom. I thought it made sense to use the roof space as a bedroom with an en-suite, giving Rita her own space and much-needed bathroom and I get to reclaim my office,' says Vinny.

Vinny bought the mid-terrace house five years ago for £94,000. 'It was in good nick and I was lucky, because the previous owners had added a really good conservatory. I have enough living space downstairs, but really needed the extra bedroom and bathroom upstairs.'

Vinny lives in a conservation area and had to get planning permission. She hired an architect recommended by a friend, who provided detailed drawings and took photographs to send to the planning department. There was some discussion about what sort of windows and materials Vinny's builders would be using, but other than that, she was granted permission to carry out the conversion.

'It certainly helped using an architect with experience in this area. He had worked on several loft conversions in my street and in the neighbouring roads, which made it easier when it came to fighting my corner to get the windows we wanted. Rather than be fobbed off with smaller windows, we were allowed something grander once the architect pointed out that my neighbours had been allowed to put something similar into their roof spaces.'

Vinny was given three quotes by different builders suggested by the architect and she choose one that had just completed a similar project up the road. The job cost £14,000, which included a state-of-the-art power shower, oak flooring and extra noise insulation.

'Rita loves her new space, as it gives her more privacy and there are no more queues for the bathroom. I've got my office back too, which is a lot better than trying to work from a corner of the sitting room,' adds Vinny.

A local estate agent believes Vinny has added real value to her home by converting the loft so successfully. 'She has spent that bit extra on quality materials, particularly in the bathroom, which a buyer would notice straight away. She could probably get about £120,000 to £125,000 for her house if she sold it now.'

Bats in the Belfry

If you discover bats in your loft, you mustn't harm them or disturb how they access their roost. Bats are an endangered species. It is against the law to kill or hurt a bat. All is not lost if you find bats in the attic, however. You will be able to carry out the work to convert your loft, but only after you get in touch with the Bat Conservation Trust (see Phil's contacts book on page 73).

Cash in the Attic

Always think of how best to balance your home when you are trying to add value, in terms of the pleasure you are getting back and what you might gain when you sell. A loft can convert easily into an office – I work from the top of my house and love it – a spare bedroom, TV room or a bedroom for a teenager. Be careful of the noise factor though. As I've mentioned already, teenagers rarely live a quiet life and booming music or late-night phone calls could percolate below to the irritation of the rest of the family.

It might make good financial sense to convert a three-bedroom house into a four-bedroom one by converting the loft. But it might not be quite as logical to convert a six-bedroom home into a seven-bedder – unless you have an unusually large family, perhaps. In this instance, the house becomes top heavy with more bedrooms than living space.

One thing I would never do is put a playroom into a loft. Small children do not want to be pushed away to the top of the house while everyone else is on the lower floors. It is dangerous and lonely for young children to be banished to the roof space. Besides, it will turn out to be a waste, because they will never use it.

PHIL'S TOP TIP

If there is room for a bathroom in the loft, then put one in. This will up the costs of the work, but it could add to the worth of your home. I don't believe every bedroom needs a bathroom, mind, but a four-bedroom house with only one bathroom is definitely at a disadvantage when it comes to selling. A family house ideally should have two bathrooms. By installing an en-suite into the loft conversion you solve a potential problem.

Moving On Up

Depending on the configuration of windows in your loft, try to make the best of the wonderful views you enjoy at this level. A fabulous loft conversion with a splendid master bedroom and bathroom with great views of the city or countryside, for instance, can be immensely valuable. You can be your own king of the castle and feel happily tucked away from the rest of the world.

Another good use is as a relaxing family room or area for entertaining. Guests can join you and partake of those views too, which could be great fun while you are in situ and a good selling point when you decide to move on.

PHIL'S CONTACTS BOOK

- Bat Conservation Trust, www.bats.org.uk, 0845 1300 228, for advice and help for builders and homeowners dealing with bats and bat-related problems.
- Federation of Master Builders, www.findabuilder.co.uk, 0800 015 2522. A useful resource if you want to track down a builder in your area with experience in converting a loft.
- www.localserviceguide.com – provides questions you can ask your builder on loft conversions.

CHAPTER SIX

Digging Deep

What lies beneath could be buried treasure

D igging up the garden used to mean preparing the vegetable plot or weeding flowerbeds, and conjured up images of a burly chap in a checked shirt leaning on his shovel. Now it has come to represent a chance for homeowners to embrace an underground extension, typically in 'cash-rich, space-poor' urban areas. But it could also be a simple matter of getting the best from an existing basement without spending huge sums.

Digging deep means you can use every nook or cranny discovered below the earth. The remains of a wine cellar or storage area can be transformed into an extra room – or rooms – in your home. Most people think you need large reserves of cash to turn these spaces into something more usable, but this is not always the case. For as little as £1,000 you could start making use of underground space. The other misapprehension surrounding basement conversions is that you have to spend a fortune on finding a way to admit natural light. Although natural light is important for certain rooms, such as a kitchen or a playroom, this is not always the case for other spaces, like a larder or utility room or even a mini home cinema.

Equally, artificial light sources are becoming more and more advanced and might do the trick, which means not having to spend extra money on expensive light wells (see page 80). Installing enough artificial light in the right places can solve many lighting problems, and it is worth considering paying for a consultation with a good lighting expert. This could save you enough to pay for the session with the expert several times over.

Artificial Lighting

Despite improvements to lamp design over the years, artificial light is generally considered a poor substitute for the real thing and tends to get a bad press. However, artificial lighting has come a long way since the incandescent lamp was invented in the 1870s, and new lighting techniques are being produced all the time to meet the demand for higher-quality artificial lighting now that so many of us spend our working lives indoors.

Clever new methods include hybrid solar lighting. Here, daylight is captured by a solar collector, usually positioned on a property's roof, which looks a bit like a satellite television dish. Sunlight is then distributed through the house using optical fibres. Another process is the Solatube. This innovative daylight system captures light from the rooftop and pipes it through highly reflective tubing to where it is needed.

Daylight lamps and bulbs are a far cry now from the harsh fluorescent lights of yesteryear. Vita-lite bulbs, for example, generate warm, ambient light that is more relaxing than earlier cool white lighting systems.

PHIL'S TOP TIP

Get ideas for underground conversions by looking at what major property developers are doing in more expensive projects. There is no copyright in design concepts for building projects, so look around and talk to builders, architects and estate agents to gather all the information you can and get suggestions on what you might be able to do to your own property. I've seen a nine-metre-deep hole behind an investment banker's west London home that will house a 16-metre swimming pool, spa with a Jacuzzi and treatment room, vast kitchen and parking for six vehicles. Other lavish underground projects have included a ceiling high enough to accommodate a boxer in his ring, and a squash court and double basement with the space to spring off a high diving board into a pool (yes, really!)

Not many people can afford to go quite this far when planning their own underground spaces. It is interesting, though, to see how much you can do if you really want to go ahead with such adventurous designs. The examples I've mentioned are rather grand demonstrations of how shifting some soil and sticking in some solid joists and decent lighting can provide you with a whole extra storey to your house, especially valuable in our crowded cities.

CASE STUDY

IDEAS FROM THE RICH AND FAMOUS

An upper-scale house builder dug out the lower quarters of a mews house in Grosvenor Crescent Mews, Belgravia, one of the most exclusive areas of London, to come up with one of the most lavish basement designs ever created. The end product wouldn't look out of place in a James Bond film.

Although not many people can afford this house's media room, bar, library, steam room, gym, study and dramatic nine-metre waterfall cascading down from the first storey to the underground Zen garden, you can sneak ideas from such a project.

Luxury bunker space doesn't come cheap – this particular house is on the market for an eye-watering guide price of £8 million – but you can borrow bits of this extravagant reconstruction and try it out on your own soil. You may not want to find the space for a Zen garden, but is this somewhere the laundry room or treadmill can go, and what space could you create in the rest of the house by adding new areas for storage downstairs?

The Beauty of Going Underground

Even for country dwellers with many acres to ramble over, every square foot counts. As planners and conservation bodies want to keep the bulk of houses within certain parameters – normally, they allow building within the confines of the footprint of the house – an ambitious basement extension is a good way to create extra space. Be aware that ceilings will need to be at least three metres high to create decent-sized rooms.

When talking to planners, architects and builders, draw up a list of the sorts of questions you might need to ask. These include:

- Where can I build underground?
- When do I require planning permission?
- Do I have to remain within the footprint of the house, or can I go further under the garden itself?
- Do I need to worry about the water table?
- Is drainage likely to be a concern? What are the options and what suits my property best?
- Subsidence could be an issue. Is it in this case? If so, how can I ensure my house won't crack and be affected by the underground works?
- What is my local authority's stance on this?

- And is there an eco-friendly way to do the work and keep everyone happy?

The beauty of well-planned underground development is that because it is beneath your house or garden, no one will realise that anything has occurred. Equally, the external look of your property isn't damaged. Good architectural drawings should help any planning application, if required.

Mega-basement projects, the archaeological digs of the property world, are not for the fainthearted, however. You need to pay from about £300 a square foot and employ a battery of expensive specialists – surveyor, engineer, damp-proofing expert, builder, and perhaps a solicitor – to carry out the work.

But once you take into account estate agent and solicitors' fees, Stamp Duty (about 7 per cent of a house's value) and removal costs, it could make financial sense to build a floor underground rather than move to a bigger house that could cost substantially more than the underground work. Many people are choosing to remain in their homes longer, so this could be a good opportunity to expand, rather than decamp to a new place.

What is Stamp Duty?

Stamp Duty Land Tax is a tax levied by the Government on homeowners when they sell their property. New thresholds introduced in September 2008 meant that if you bought a property costing £175,000 or less, you didn't have to pay any Stamp Duty. However, this tax break was abolished on 31 December 2009.

Now, if you pay £250,000 or less for a home, you have to pay 1 per cent of the purchase price. If the price is £250,001 to £500,000, you pay 3 per cent of the purchase price. And if you buy a home priced at £500,001 or more, you pay 4 per cent in Stamp Duty.

For more information, go to www.direct.gov.uk.

You simply might like the area where you live and don't want to uproot if you are settled happily there. There might not be many larger houses in your favourite spot, and rather than decamp elsewhere you can stay put. Or, it might not be the best time to sell up just to acquire that extra bedroom or a playroom for the children.

Due to the expense of moving, some would rather make a larger leap up the property ladder at the right point, rather than make several interim moves that each gain only small amounts of extra space. Back in the Eighties, people moved every seven years on average; over the last decade we moved once every 16 years. It is believed we might remain in our homes even longer in the near future – up to 25 to 30 years. As moving house is the fifth most stressful life event, adding on to your property can be preferable to dragging out the packing cases. By digging down you stave off that move, or perhaps even do away with it altogether. A solid basement conversion could turn your house into 'the forever house' – the house where you will spend the largest portion of your life, a concept both emotionally and financially appealing.

Light Wells

Rooms that do not need windows are best suited to being hidden under the surface of the earth, although you can also work wonders with light wells admitting natural light to brighten up an underground space. Light wells reduce the need for electric lighting, can add a central space within the building and provide an internal open space for windows to give an illusion of having a view outside. A light well is a shaft in a building that is open to the outside at the top, so daylight and fresh air can be admitted through windows set into the side of the shaft.

Light wells emerge above ground for most basement conversions, but do not take up much space in a garden and are not particularly obtrusive. They can make a huge difference to the basement, allowing natural light to pour through the glass dome or plate above.

Digging In

Shifting soil can be one of the most costly parts of getting your basement. In towns and cities, soil often has to be painstakingly hand dug and lugged away because it is difficult to get permission to use large machinery. And even if the local authority says yes to a digger, there may not be enough space for one on site, which means back to paying plenty of workers to dig by hand and fill up bags.

You can cut costs on your project by helping with the 'grunt work' – digging out mounds of earth, bagging it all up and transporting the bags off site. I know one couple who actually enjoyed helping with the underground work at their house in Oxfordshire. They learned how to operate the small digger, which removed a good deal of the debris and soil, and sourced all the materials and fittings themselves. They saved thousands of pounds and enjoyed being involved in the project.

One country dweller came to an agreement with the local estate (his cottage was in a village on the landowner's patch). He paid only a couple of hundred pounds for the use of a trailer to take away the soil and for the estate worker who drove it. The head of the estate was only too happy to have the soil placed next to a footpath to fill in an unsightly ditch, so everyone was happy and money was saved.

Access to and from your new underground space is important too. By law, a fire escape of some kind is pretty much obligatory. A rule of thumb is if your house has three storeys or more, it will need a fire escape.

When I dug out our basement recently, I decided to put the fire escape at the back. The light well I installed has a small door, railings you use to climb up it and a metal grill you can pop open to exit safely into the garden.

The owner of the house next door, who also has a basement conversion, has chosen a more permanent mode of access. He has installed a staircase that goes down from the garden to the basement, a good idea if you want a separate entrance. This may suit a nanny, granny or even a lodger, who can come and go as they please.

There are also ways of getting great ideas for damp-proofing, lighting systems and, most importantly, the layout, without spending a fortune. I find one of the biggest turn-offs for potential buyers is bad layout. This means properties that don't have a good balance between living rooms and bedrooms, or awkward layouts that include unusable dark areas and nooks and crannies. Buyers look for usable spaces and imagine how they can best live in a place.

PHIL'S TRADE SECRET

Look at nearby properties for sale or rent and see what they've done with the basement. Viewing a few places and examining brochures – agents' websites are a good first port of call for brochures you can download – will offer up good suggestions. You will find most developers and agents will share information with you.

Small hotels come up with novel design solutions too. When you are next on holiday, take a look around the basements or lower ground floors in hotel complexes to see how they use this space. Often it is about breaking up a large space into small 'rooms' rather than just adding on a vast expanse. Hotels are good at producing inviting corners where you can imagine holing up with a cuppa and a good book. Keep this in mind when planning your smart new bunker.

Phil Goes Underground

My rule of thumb for a really successful extension is one that feels like it has always been there. You don't want people coming round and saying, 'Oh, you've dug out your basement.' It should feel like just another level in the house that doesn't appear any different from the rest. Recently, I converted the basement of our semi-detached late Victorian house, digging down under the house and right under the garden.

The first question I asked was: will this work for me? If the amount you will be adding to the value of your house is less than about £300 a square foot – the cost of the work to go under the earth – then it is not worth it in monetary terms.

I thought it was worthwhile financially, but value is not just about pounds and pence. You need to factor in the hassle factor of uprooting yourself and your family to move to a new home with more space, which could be the equivalent of your basement dugout.

It took a year to do our basement conversion, and there were economies of scale because we decided to do the work at the same time as the neighbour. As well as sharing some of the costs and bringing down the price a bit, it was also of benefit to the builder. For instance, to call a tradesman out to just do a few hours' work at one house might not look to him like good value, but if he can work at both houses and fill a whole day with work it starts to make sense.

The other decision I made was not just to dig under the house. As we were going through all this upheaval, we might as well carry on burrowing under the garden as well. I knew we would never own the nicest house on the street, but if we could create something people took note of, we would be adding real value. Someone up the road might have better fixtures and fittings, but ours will have a better underground space.

The real motivating factor for the basement project was to gain the key thing our house was missing: a playroom for our two young sons. We also were keen to have a decent utility room, a spare bedroom and bathroom and extra storage. You can never have enough storage – and now we have tons. Our boys will get bigger, and the bigger they get, the bigger the toys they will acquire. And I have the biggest toys of all, naturally, so we needed to create a home for life. Something else we achieved was adding height to our kitchen by dropping the floor down two feet when we dug out the basement.

To make the most of your investment, I think you need to ask key questions. What are you trying to achieve? What rooms are you trying to create? There is nothing worse than a wasted opportunity to best use space, so think how you will use the space now and in five years' time. Also, think of how a purchaser from the target market in your area might use the space.

It is good to be flexible in your thinking. I can imagine our playroom will make the most amazing cinema one day. And as well as putting in a loo and shower, I had the plumbing run into two other parts of the basement too in case we – or the next owners – want to add another bathroom or a small kitchen at some time in the future.

You can make basements light and bright – we've managed this by putting in glass bricks and a light well – but some basement rooms actually benefit from being in darkness. You could build a darkroom, for example, if you are into photography. A cinema room – somewhere snug with fun chairs or sofas and some freshly made popcorn – does not require light either, of course.

It cost £200 a square foot to dig out our basement and £100 a square foot to fit it out. We added an extra 1,700 square feet (158 square metres) to the basement and 300 square feet (28 square metres) on to the kitchen of our house, originally measuring 2,200 square feet (204 square metres).

We moved out for a year, although I thought we would only be out of the house for nine months. Major building projects often take longer than you imagine, so be prepared to double how long the work might take. You can live in your house while the builders work around you if you want, but it might be cheaper and quicker in the long run if you can afford to rent elsewhere while the work is carried out.

I would advise hiring an experienced person, because it is very serious playing with load-bearing walls. You do not want your house to tumble down just for the sake of saving a few quid. I started by getting a quote from a slick basement specialist company that was very together and organised. The price was very high, but I knew it would be stress-free – as far as a big scheme like this can be stress-free. I then compared this quote with one from a local builder, which was about a third less. In the end, I hired the local builder. Everything took a bit longer and maybe things did not run as smoothly as they might, but I was aware that was the decision I had taken, along with the neighbour who was sharing the work and the costs.

I had to get planning permission from the local authority for my subterranean extension. It is also necessary to have a visit from the building control department, who make sure you have carried out the work to their criteria. If the work is satisfactory, you will receive a completion certificate. It is important to get this certificate to show to the new owner when you sell your house. If you don't get it, it could slow up – or even halt – the sale.

After receiving planning permission, I faced the decision to completely wreck the ground floor, taking up all the floorboards and sending a digger in to excavate the basement. The other choice was to keep the floor intact and get a few blokes to dig the soil out with shovels. This would take a good deal longer and cost more, but we could conceivably remain living in our house. But I am glad I opted to send in the digger and rent elsewhere for the duration of the work.

I had to reapply for planning permission when I decided to dig under the garden as well as the house – digging under the garden hadn't been in the initial application – which added on another room of about 14- by 6-feet (4.3- by 1.8-metres). I also wanted to excavate under the side return, gaining an extra 4 feet (1.2 metres).

I cannot emphasise enough that this is a big commitment. Digging out a basement involves a lot of structural work and you have to be happy with the people doing the work, ensuring no corners are cut. Do check out some other projects carried out by the builder before engaging him or his company. And if you have any concerns at all, now is the time to raise them.

I get a lot of queries about the safety of big basement schemes. The Royal Borough of Kensington & Chelsea in London, concerned about the effect of so much soil being removed and how this could impact on drainage and subsidence, carried out an independent survey. It did not reveal any problems, however. Three basement conversions were carried out at the same time in my street, which worried people, but everything is fine.

Drainage is quite a big issue. The builder who did the work on our basement installed a cavity drainage system that originally came from America and is now used here in the UK. It has 'egg crate' plastic – it looks like egg crates on a plastic roll – that runs around the inside walls and is joined with plugs or special tape. It is not wholly waterproof, but follows the path of least resistance. Basically, water always finds a way in somehow and this cavity drainage system goes along with this premise and then deals with it. Any water that trickles in goes into a drain around the perimeter of the house. A little sump tank with a battery backup system then pumps up the water. It is collected into a 1.8-metre sewage tank, which also holds any rainwater that might have found its way into the earth – and the edges of the basement conversion – along with anything from the basement toilets and any other moisture. The two vortex pumps used are not noisy and an alarm goes off if one fails. Even if you were away for three weeks or so and a pump stopped working – say, there was a power cut – it would take some time for the 1,000-litre tank to fill and overflow, so all should be well.

I could invest in a backup generator for the whole house if I was feeling a bit nervous about drainage and damp problems and wanted even more protection. But this would cost about £1,000, could be noisy and I don't think it is really necessary with so many failsafe systems in place already.

Our underground endeavour was quite messy and caused a bit of damage to the outside of the house, so we had to redecorate afterwards. The good news is the builders completely sealed the upstairs off, so this part of the house was not too badly affected. Be warned, though – there is a lot of knocking and banging and you will get cracks that you will have to deal with.

There were times I turned up and was quite horrified by the chaos. A digger even drove into our bay window at one point! Renting another place for a year was immensely expensive, but there is something to be said for not having to clear up at the end of every day.

One thing I did to keep the peace was to take a case of wine to the neighbours at the beginning of the project – and again at the end. They renovated their house the year before we did our work and we lived through that, but I still felt it polite to make up a bit for all the noise and dust they had to put up with throughout our project.

A Quick Guide to Underground Development

Why bother digging down?

Adding extra space to your property is always a good thing. Throughout Britain, but especially in the cities, space is at a premium. Most of us long to have more space for a family room, open-plan kitchen, study, teenager's den, nanny/granny flat, or somewhere for guests to stay. It can be fairly straightforward to dig under the footprint of your house – and even go underneath the garden – to create a more spacious home. But, and this is a big but, you should work out whether all the effort and cost will be worth such an ambitious amount of work. Look at other homes locally with this extra below-stairs storey and do your maths. Some authorities are becoming less enthusiastic about giving consent for going down and out and have fears about potential negative effects this may have on the substructure of buildings. So, make sure you get a proper report confirming the roots of neighbouring trees and any other potential hazards won't be an issue.

Is it common?

It has grown in popularity over recent years. With the associated costs of buying a new bigger house, staying put and adding more space is an attractive notion. One of the early excavators was Sir Andrew Lloyd Webber, who joined up his two homes in London with underground tunnels. Another is David Cameron, who created extra space by adding a basement extension. But a posh new basement is no longer just for famous folk. Families desperate for more room are paying builders and specialist basement conversion companies to reap the benefits of digging down.

Will it work for me?

Some townhouses and terraced houses are tricky to support and can't be underpinned – supporting a structure by propping it up from below – singly. If your house is being held up to a degree by the rest of the terrace, going down could prove to be more problematic, and in some cases impossible.

It is important to get the right advice in the first place to avoid disasters. Make sure you engage the services of an experienced architect, quantity surveyor (if required) and/or specialist conversion company. It might be worth talking to someone at your local builders' merchant, who can recommend suitable people.

Check out other projects in your area, but don't engage anyone without getting good references from homeowners they have worked with previously. Ask if you can contact some who will let you take a look at the work and answer questions about the builders. Local website forums have comments from satisfied – or disgruntled – customers as well. You can find these through local sources – ask your neighbours or tap in 'builders' and the name of your town or area into an Internet search engine and see what comes up.

Remember, it is more difficult and expensive to dig down through houses with solid floors, compared to timber suspended floors, and if you want to excavate under a leasehold flat you will need to get permission from the freeholder – the person or company that owns the building – before you start any work.

It is advisable to agree everything with neighbours, who might need to sign a party wall agreement – an agreement between you and your neighbour where a shared wall adjoins the properties. Communicating with everyone can nip any impending rows in the bud, saving you time and money. You could offer to pay for their surveyor when settling the party wall agreement, and replace any trellis or plants disturbed during the work.

Keep in mind that what happens to this 'shared wall' is of concern to your neighbour as well as you. You could even propose to the neighbour that both of you get similar work done at the same time. This would cut down on the costs for you and the neighbour, and the disruption factor would be minimised as you are in the same building boat.

Make sure everything is planned at the outset. Contact the planning department at your local authority to get permission sorted before you speak to the neighbours. A useful Government planning website is www. planningportal.gov.uk; look at your council's website too. Then, you can hand over copies of any permission granted and other relevant documentation to the neighbour, if he has any concerns. Hiring a good architect to do the drawings and help fill in the planning application could be money well spent too.

People are understandably sensitive about what is happening below ground as more and more basement conversions take place. A friend of mine returned home one day to discover that her neighbour, who was digging under the garden to create extra rooms, had dug under her garden too. It took several meetings with the architect and builder – and a threatening legal letter from her incensed solicitor – to get them to retreat from her garden. So, beware.

How much do I need to pay?

Converting an existing basement is cheaper than doing the whole job from a standing start, as a good chunk of the cost is tied up with digging down and carting away the soil. Expect to pay on average from £200 a square foot to convert something that is already there and £250 to £300 a square foot upwards if you are starting from scratch.

It can cost more in London and the south-east, but if you work out how much house prices are per square foot (£1,000-plus a square foot in some areas), you could end up in profit when it comes time to sell. And in a competitive market, the extra space you have created will make your house stand out and sell faster than one further up the road without the expansion.

Won't water come flooding in?

Damp can be an issue, but modern damp-proofing methods ensure a gap remains between the wall and a special waterproof membrane. Any water can escape between the two, into channels and sumps where it is pumped away (see page 85). This cavity drainage system works well, although it needs to be checked and maintained and you need to replace the pumps about every eight years. It is good to have a backup system too – a battery backup kit, for instance, in case the pumps fail.

Planning permission

Normally, you don't need planning permission if you are converting an existing basement. You will need to seek permission, however, if you are altering the appearance of the exterior – adding a staircase or light well, for instance – or if you are living in a listed building, a conservation area or an Area of Outstanding Natural Beauty. If you are doing something that affects the 'change of use', you need permission from the planners too. For more information on planning guidelines for basement conversions, check out Chapter Fourteen.

What if my property is listed?

In listed period houses, rooms are often quite small, and the listing means sometimes you can't touch architraves – decorative strips of wood or plaster round doors or windows – or even doorknobs, which makes refurbishment difficult. Digging down could actually enable you to produce large contemporary spaces: a playroom or a family kitchen for example, without breaking listing regulations.

CHEAPER THAN MOVING?

Michael and Carin loved their detached three-bedroom cottage in the Park area of Nottingham, just outside the centre of the city and close to the historic castle. The only problem was the lack of space when their second child, Thomas, was born. With frequent visitors from Carin's homeland of Australia and a small living/dining room, they needed more space. But what to do when they couldn't afford the step up the property ladder to a larger home?

'The price differential was too great to move somewhere bigger,' says Carin, a 29-year-old psychiatric nurse, 'and we were tripping all over one another. Our older son, George, who is four, was driving us mad. His toys were strewn all over the place – what we would have given for a playroom for him – and relations between ourselves and guests were a tad strained on occasion.'

Michael, who is 35 and a surveyor, picked up on the idea of digging down to solve their dilemma. After consulting with a few architects, one came up with plans that were suitable and within their budget. They ended up spending just under £40,000 – £10,000 more than originally intended, but their choice of finishings bumped up the cost – and added a playroom, spare bedroom and bathroom with a separate entrance from the back garden.

They were able to bring a small digger on to their land, which cut down the cost considerably, and the local authority happily took the soil off their hands to use in the gardens and grounds of the Park.

'Spend money on the best experts you can afford,' advises Michael. 'With caves and underground caverns below the land in this part of the city, it would have been a disaster to not check things out properly and then hit something we weren't expecting.' Their architect, who had experience in basement conversions and dealing with the council's planners, was certainly worth his £3,000 fee.

Local agents think the expenditure has already matched the increase in value of their home, and in the long term they should make a profit. Besides, there is a lot to be said for improving the way they are living now, let alone adding up how much their home could be valued at when it comes time to resell.

'We are so happy to have the extra space,' says Michael, 'and our neighbours now want to do something similar. They believe it shouldn't be hard to get permission, because we got it quite readily.'

It would have cost an extra £60,000 to £75,000 to buy a home locally with the extra room they required, so this option was at least £20,000 cheaper. Plus the couple had the added bonus of getting the plan they wanted, rather than someone else's design if they decided to buy a different property, and they didn't have to go to all the trouble of moving.

PHIL'S CONTACTS BOOK

- Royal Institute of British Architects (RIBA), www.architecture. com, 020 7580 5533. Includes a directory of more than 4,000 UK architectural practices registered by RIBA.
- Royal Institution of Chartered Surveyors (RICS), www.rics.org, 0870 333 1600.
- www.planningportal.gov.uk.

CHAPTER SEVEN

Kitchens

The heart of the home

Research shows the kitchen to be the most popular home renovation project in the UK, with Britons spending on average £4,344 refurbishing them. Many experts would agree with this choice, saying that if you're going to do just one thing to spice up your property, put in an excellent kitchen. Well, yes … and no.

The kitchen has had a serious makeover over the last few years. These days it's more than simply a room where you boil a kettle or grill fish fingers for the children's tea. It has changed from a utilitarian place to the multi-functional 'heart of the home', a favourite hub for family life. You're just as likely to find the space in a modern kitchen being used to complete home-work, browse on the computer or shine a pair of shoes, as you are to find someone actually getting on and doing some cooking.

In addition, the kitchen has become a magnet for must-have accessories. People lust after top-notch kitchens gleaming in glass and steel, or want to be soothed by handcrafted wooden country kitchens that transport them back in time. Fans of celebrity chefs aspire to recreate the professional's workspace at home, decking out the family space in hardwearing alumin-ium and utensils to satisfy their inner serious chef.

But although a kitchen can sometimes make or break the sale of your home, it is not always the best investment to make. Because it is such an important room, often one of the first things new buyers do after signing the final contract is to rip out the kitchen and replace it with the one they really want.

So why bother installing a new kitchen in the first place? Here's why I think it might be worth the effort:

- Kitchens don't come cheap, and there will always be some buyers who breathe a sigh of relief knowing they don't have to spend a fortune straight away to replace a worn and tatty kitchen.
- A kitchen is normally the hub of your home. People tend to lean against the counter, sip coffee at the table and generally feel homely, so it could lure a buyer in.
- Storage is always a big issue in homes. A good, well-planned kitchen can attract those worried about where on earth all their belongings will go.
- As a 'key' room, the kitchen is the blueprint for how the rest of the place is laid out.
- Today's kitchens have become elevated to brilliant objects of desire that can be serious and entertaining at the same time.
- Where do you spend most of your time at home? Most people would answer: in the kitchen. So, if you spend most of your time there, then it should be one of the best rooms in the house. Or as good as you can afford to make it.
- Research shows that women buyers put the kitchen at the top of their property wish list. Estate agents tell me that unless the woman in the family rates the house, which often comes down to the kitchen, there is no point trying to go ahead with a sale.

Yet, is it really worth it? If it is such a hassle installing a brand-new kitchen, shouldn't you just let the next owner get on with it and do it himself? Well, a new kitchen nearly always adds a certain amount of value to your home. Most estate agents will say that kitchens really do help sell houses. Experts suggest that replacing an old kitchen can increase your home's value by 5 per cent or more, depending on the sort of kitchen you choose and the bracket your property – low, middle or top-end – falls into.

Overspending in general doesn't make sense, but you might find yourself paying a bit more for a kitchen if you see this as the 'main room' in your house and are eager to create a space that you and your family will enjoy. The average amount people in Britain spend on a kitchen is £7,000 and you can get some smart-looking kitchens in that range from a number of suppliers these days.

A clean, clear and light kitchen will offend no one – so this is what you should aim for if you want to make this room attractive to future homebuyers. This could just mean sprucing up your existing kitchen, to be honest, which isn't going to cost anything, or not very much. Giving units a good scrub with soapy water and touching up small nicks and scrapes with matching paint (call the manufacturer of your kitchen – you'd be surprised how many of them will supply tiny pots of paint for only a few pounds or even for free) might be all you need to do.

Worktops are important. If yours look worn, you could replace them. Buying new ones will cost far less than renovating the whole space, and this alone can make the room feel a lot fresher. There are some fantastic heat- and stain-resistant surfaces now that come in a variety of colours and they don't cost the earth. You can get decent worktops these days for anything from a few hundred pounds rising upwards to several thousands of pounds.

Cracked tiles are a no-no, as are missing door handles, torn linoleum and very dated appliances. Getting a handyman in for a few hundred pounds – if you can't do it yourself – to replace tiles, lay new linoleum or repair what's there, and add new handles to units and doors can make the whole room look nearly new. I have seen homeowners do nothing more than replace the handles on their units with something more fashionable and up-to-the-minute and create a huge difference. In one home, the basic units were a lovely taupe colour. Replacing the old yellow handles, which looked a bit Eighties, with sparkling and stylish red ones rejuvenated the whole kitchen.

Getting rid of old units is also an option, but a good halfway house is talking to companies that specialise in replacing unit doors. After all, why replace the entire kitchen when it just needs a change of face? New doors can cost as little as £20 and drawer fronts £7.50, depending on size and quality. There is a good choice of colours and styles too – contemporary, classic, Shaker or Linea, for instance. Most of these companies supply all the accessories you need at competitive prices, from knobs and hinges to handles and worktops.

Do not make the mistake of ripping out an 'old' kitchen if it has period value. A lovely warm Edwardian or groovy Seventies kitchen could have extra value of its own, so think twice before removing it. Original period features, such as a beautifully crafted sideboard, cornices and a stained-glass dome in the ceiling, are hugely attractive to most buyers. If you are lucky enough to still have these in your kitchen, hold on to them. Remember, even if you decide to remove a period kitchen for whatever reason, you can sell it to a specialist shop or on the Internet. One couple I met actually held on to their old kitchen and stored it in an outbuilding in case a buyer might want to reinstall it one day.

Recipe for a Good Kitchen

The first rule with kitchens is they should be appropriate to the house. If your house is minimalist and clean-lined, the kitchen should match this style. Fitting a kitchen that doesn't suit the property is a big mistake – do you really want a retro Fifties kitchen in a brand-new apartment, for example? Yet you can get away with installing an up-to-the-minute kitchen in a period house if you know what you're doing. The Italians are brilliant at this, placing the latest stainless-steel kitchen next to a frescoed wall in a converted *palazzo*, but not everyone can get this look right. You might want to pay for a consultation with a good designer or architect, which shouldn't cost more than a few hundred pounds, to get their ideas on what would look best.

As clichéd as it might sound, the kitchen really is the heart of the home, so be generous with the amount of space allocated to it. A pokey, narrow kitchen might be okay for a tiny studio flat, but if at all possible try to have an 'eat-in' kitchen – estate agent-speak for a kitchen big enough to hold a table and a few chairs.

The majority of people in the average-sized family want enough space to cook, sit and eat, plus store all their food and utensils. Kitchens often need room to house appliances too – a dishwasher and maybe even a washing machine and drier – if you do not have a utility room, bathroom or cupboard to put them in.

It's worth considering reducing the size of a dedicated dining room or even knocking it into the kitchen to create a bigger kitchen and eating space. But before you start pulling down walls, talk to a couple of local estate agents to determine what buyers really want. If they are wedded to dining rooms on your patch, it is advisable to leave the dining room as it is. Open-plan kitchen/dining rooms are also popular, and this could be the better course of action.

Bring Back the Hallway Dining Room

Unfashionably perhaps, in these days of open-plan living, I'm quite partial to a dining room, and I'm a real fan of hallway dining rooms. It probably comes from my childhood. I was brought up in a house in Kent that had a fabulous dining room in a large hallway right in the middle of the house, which you had to walk through to access other rooms on the ground floor.

If you have a hallway space big enough for a dining table, I would seriously consider plumping for a hallway dining area. It was immensely enjoyable to use and it was a great place to entertain. However, you could lose a chunk of value if you don't use it for 320 days of the year, and it mustn't become a dumping ground for clutter.

Is Open Plan a Good Plan?

More Britons are knocking down internal walls to satisfy their yearning for open-plan living. A study shows that 2.9 million rooms have disappeared, with a further 2.1 million thought to be about to go under the hammer in the near future.

The main casualty is the now little-used dining room, increasingly a cold, dusty space that is more likely to hold piles of paper and other unstored junk on the table, rather than your best crockery and tempting bowls of food. It is the most popular room to knock through, with 590,000 dining-room walls pinpointed for demolition, the study says. If this trend continues, it is believed the traditional formal dining room could be extinct in a decade or so.

Normally, if you knock on a wall and it sounds hollow, it is likely to be a plasterboard partition and game for pulling down. A lower thudding noise means it is probably a load-bearing brick or concrete wall, so be careful. It is crucial to consult an architect or surveyor if you are uncertain and *before* you start to knock down any walls.

Open-plan living appeals to a large number of visitors and, when time comes to sell, to buyers. There is something wonderfully appealing about a central space where everyone gathers to do homework, draw pictures, play with toys on the floor, work on a computer, listen to the radio, cook, have a drink, read a paper while enjoying a cup of coffee, clean shoes, watch television and maybe even fix a bicycle.

The days have pretty much gone where the hostess cooks alone in a kind of gourmet gulag, while her partner and guests enjoy drinks and canapés in the living room. Entertaining is less buttoned up these days, with guests often helping to peel vegetables and having a chat while a meal is being prepared. I like the idea of a seamlessly stylish or friendly multi-purpose place that is flexible in its use. And so do people I take round to view homes.

Open plan doesn't mean a cavernous space that hasn't been thought out properly. You want to break up the area into separate sections. You shouldn't feel exposed and open to the elements in an open-plan scheme. A well-planned open-plan kitchen has small, subtly defined areas for eating, relaxing and entertaining. Good lighting can help delineate the different sectors, and inexpensive dimmer switches starting at £7 each are open-plan living's best friends. Softening the mood in a comfortable snug or breakfast bar where you are enjoying a drink with friends can make all the difference to the look of a particular part of the room.

PHIL'S TOP TIP

I have seen many a bachelor pad where a massive loft space is pretty much empty with only a lonely-looking armchair and telly in one corner. This is open-space living at its worst. The trick is to think about your big open space and work out how best to chop it into smaller spaces that effectively become 'rooms' in their own way.

You can define these areas by laying down a carpet in the corner that might be the snug, placing a cabinet or bookshelf to separate a living room from the rest, or even by using lighting or plants to screen off a family room, kitchen or dining room. Different sorts of flooring can 'create' a kitchen (tiles or linoleum), living area (wood or limestone, maybe with a rug on part of the space), or a utility room (hard-wearing tiles, rubber or easy-to-clean linoleum).

When it comes to remodelling or adding a kitchen, think of who might want to buy your house one day and how they will want to use the kitchen. If your area is very family-dominated, you will need a kitchen that is roomy enough for children to play, do homework, sit and eat meals and gather round to socialise. A corner for a computer could be invaluable and good, family kitchens often lead on to a terrace, garden or some kind of open space. If you are lucky enough to have this outdoor space, and no matter how small it is, try and link it to the kitchen if you can.

Some Important Considerations

Here are some questions you need to answer before beginning work on a new kitchen.

Can I put in a kitchen without getting permission from anyone?

As long as your home is not listed, you can remodel your existing kitchen. If it is listed, you might need to be a bit more careful, particularly if it affects how the exterior of the building will look. A Grade-II listing means you cannot change the 'special characteristics' of the building and this applies to the inside as well as the outside, according to English Heritage. If you are unsure what you can and cannot do, talk to the local authority's planning department. They usually employ a listed-building specialist, or have a planning officer who can guide you. You will not be charged for the advice, although some planning departments prefer you to submit an application and drawings, which could cost a few hundred pounds or more, before they speak to you. The local authority's website is a good first port of call, offering planning guidelines and information. Usually, the planners will not allow the removal of any features relating to the period when your house was built. This can include fireplaces, cornicing, skirting boards, beams, panelling and original doors and cupboards. Sometimes, this can even include later additions – such as features added in the Sixties – depending on when the building was listed and what the planners believe is crucial to the building's integrity and history.

My house isn't listed. Does that mean I don't need planning permission?

You might need permission from the planning office if you want to move the walls, change the drainage, alter the appearance of the house from the outside or develop a separate self-contained property by adding a kitchen and some other rooms.

If you live in a conservation area – a zone where special regulations on building and development help maintain the historical and architectural characteristics of the area – you might need permission as well. This usually relates to the exterior of the house, so adding an extension, a large sliding door to access the garden from the kitchen or replacing windows could require permission. If you are not sure, contact the council and check before starting any work. A good local architect or estate agent will be able to help too. Try to find an architect who has experience working in the area so he knows what a planner is likely to let you do. Contact the Royal Institute of British Architects (RIBA), www.architecture.com, 020 7307 3700, for a list of qualified architects.

Building regulations – do they apply?

Sometimes you do need building regulations approval. If you change the current drainage system or introduce a new one, install a ventilation system or make any drastic changes, such as turning a different room into a kitchen, you might need to have the work inspected before you receive a building regulations certificate. Moving gas pipes or cookers can be dangerous and work should be carried out by a recognised and registered CORGI, or similarly approved, gas fitter. Do not take chances when it comes to gas and electrical work – someone could be hurt, or even killed. Employ a fitter with the right qualifications and level of knowledge. Having details of this work, with the proper certificates, to hand will impress buyers and make it easier to sell your property. The buyer's solicitor will want evidence the work has been carried out according to the building code and supplying the certificates will certainly speed up the purchasing process.

What Sort of Kitchen?

Deciding what kind of kitchen to go for is mainly down to personal taste. But you should try to incorporate the best look for your particular property without putting off future buyers. The best starting point is deciding who will use the kitchen and what will be most important to them. Ask who the target audience is that might be interested in buying your home one day – and using your kitchen.

For instance, a family keen on cooking, playing games and chatting around the table might come up with a kitchen quite different to a young professional who believes cooking food should remain firmly in restaurants, envisaging this space more for mixing cocktails and heating up the odd pizza.

If you are putting in a kitchen to help sell your house, it is advisable to go for the broadest audience possible. This needn't mean making the room too bland and sticking to beige walls and units. A room so unassuming it all but disappears might not be the best way to get a buyer's attention. A clean, warm, inviting space with a hint of colour – there are some terrific whites with tinges of yellow, light blue, green and grey – that does not impose your taste too much could be the look to aim for. Beware of anything too glaring or *outré* that could distract people trying to imagine what it might be like living there.

The key to a good kitchen is to think about what sort of person you are and how you want to use the space. If you live in the country with a large family and a dog, for instance, it sounds like a friendly wooden country kitchen with tiled or stone floors that are easy to mop up might fit the bill. If you are a couple that loves to entertain in your city flat, something sleeker – maybe glossy white or black units – in an open-plan set-up so guests can mingle could be a good choice.

The Kitchen Work Triangle

Everyone talks about making the best use of space, but what does this really mean? A good rule of thumb is to use the 'ergonomic triangle' or the 'kitchen work triangle'. Ergonomic means the applied science of equipment design to maximise productivity and reduce operator fatigue and discomfort. The ergonomic triangle in the kitchen is the best way to use the space sensibly while cooking and carrying out other activities in this room. As probably the most-used room of the house, a kitchen that is efficient will be a good place to spend time in.

The kitchen work triangle is thought to be the most researched and applied ergonomic principle and is at the centre of nearly all kitchen designs and layouts. A good kitchen work triangle places the three most common work sites the right distance apart to cut down on traffic in the key work zones.

The three main zones are:

- cold storage work site (refrigerator)
- cleaning and preparation area (sink)
- cooking work site (stove)

If the three points of the triangle are too far from each other, you will be trawling back and forth when trying to cook a meal. I have seen a lot of kitchens where the fridge is at least a dozen steps from the work surface, which seems pretty daft to me. On the other hand, if the three points of the triangle are too close to one another, you have a small, cramped kitchen with very little workspace. A recipe for divorce or disaster, in my opinion. You don't want to be always fighting your partner for elbow room. The trick is to minimise the space spent walking between the fridge, sink and stove in a bigger kitchen. And – possibly even more of a challenge – not to feel like you are in the diminutive galley of a ship when trying to do things in a smaller kitchen.

Work out the triangle in your kitchen – or whatever shape links the sink, cooker and fridge – and the routes between the points. If you have to go a long way round in an illogical fashion from the stove to the fridge, then the layout may not be using the space as effectively as possible. If you are having difficulties with the layout, a session with an architect or designer could be a good investment. A free or low-cost idea is to use online planning tools, where you can try out different sorts of arrangements on a plan the size of your kitchen. This can give you a good idea of what looks good and what fits into your space.

PHIL'S TOP TIP

Popping into a specialist kitchen shop or into a large DIY shop with a kitchen department can be quite illuminating. Trained kitchen advisers can come up with good ideas for how best to use your particular space. Most will visit your house to measure up your kitchen and sketch ideas on to a plan. Normally, this service is free. Some will charge you about £100, or maybe less, if you want to take the plans away with you.

Extras

Try not to be too taken in by tempting 'extras' that are unnecessary. A friend was talked into buying a second small sink for the central island in her kitchen, which she has never used. She is even thinking of putting a board over it so she has extra counter space. A shame, as it didn't come cheap in the first place.

Think about what you use most of the time – a kettle, toaster, microwave and blender, perhaps – and where these smaller appliances will go. If you will find it easier to have them on the counter or worktop most or all of the time, is there enough space without the room looking cluttered? And will you actually use them?

We often buy kitchen toys, such as fondue sets, fizzy drink makers, deep-fat fryers, waffle irons and electric popcorn makers, that spend more time gathering dust and taking up valuable cupboard space than they do being used. We are eager to buy these gizmos, it seems, but seldom get round to plugging them in and turning them on.

It is a good idea to take stock of what you use most and how often. If you do use your toaster every day, it might pay to get a decent-looking one that can take pride of place on your kitchen counter. Consigning those ludicrous purchases to a charity shop or online auction site will make room for what you really need and like, helping you design your kitchen more efficiently and making your life less cluttered as a result.

The Space Race

As I said before, you want enough space so more than one person can use the kitchen at a time. Kitchen experts suggest dividing the kitchen into different 'active' or 'dynamic' spaces. Well-divided kitchens save time and trouble, and make the space much less stressful to be in at meal times. Live or active zones include:

- food storage area
- china, cutlery and glass storage space

- washing/cleaning space – typically, a sink and maybe a dishwasher
- preparation zone – where you chop and prepare food, the 'engine room'
- hot spot – the cooking space, which can include the hob, oven, microwave, pots and pans and other cooking implements

The Quick Once-over

Although sorting out different zones is important for you to get the best out of your kitchen, when you are selling a viewer often spends only seconds going round your kitchen. Here are my tips on how to present your kitchen in its best light for a quick once-over:

- Arrange a couple of stylish stools along a breakfast bar.
- Clear off the counter tops, hiding away as many portable appliances as possible, leaving behind just a kettle and toaster.
- Get rid of messages on the fridge and any other surface clutter.
- Hang colourful towels on the oven door handle, unless you have a minimalist kitchen where you should conceal as much as possible in cupboards.
- Put fresh flowers in a vase on a counter or table for a splash of colour.
- Turn the lights on so the room looks light and bright.
- Line up a few good cookbooks on a shelf, or leave one open on a worktop to draw viewers into wanting this lifestyle.
- Polish taps and clean the tiles or splash-back.
- Clean the stove and oven thoroughly yourself or call in a specialist cleaning firm to give them a good going over.

Storage

With storage a problem in many homes, it is important to get this right. A kitchen consultant or builder specialising in kitchen refurbishments is certainly worth contacting. Get them round to your house so they can work out the way to get the maximum amount of storage space in your new kitchen. I can't tell you how many times I've seen really fantastic houses utterly let down by their dismal lack of storage. I have a bit of a thing about storage. It improves so many things. Having somewhere to store things means having less clutter about the place and a better sense of order in general.

Make sure cupboard heights are right. If everything is too high off the floor, you won't be able to reach the essentials, although putting some items you don't use every day up high can be a sensible solution. There are terrific corner 'lazy Susan' units – sometimes they are called 'magic corners' – that swing out and around, filling hard-to-access corners neatly, and new, wide drawers that hold an immense amount. Take a stroll around kitchen shops and get ideas from their displays.

Some ideas are gimmicky, however – do you really need that £300 posh coffeemaker in its nifty little storage slot? You may want it, but is it worth the price or can the space be used by something essential instead? And will you really use it all that often once you get it home?

PHIL'S TOP TIP

Storage solutions needn't be complicated or expensive. You can buy fun-looking glass jars with smart metal lids, for example, and pour items you use every day into them. A jar of interesting pasta shapes and one with golden grains of light brown sugar can look quite attractive lined up along a shelf. A smart metal hanging rail with hooks to hold utensils can be practical and aesthetically interesting too.

Which Kitchen Should I Go For?

The shape of your room will dictate what sort of kitchen you can install. The trick is to get as much in as possible without it appearing to be crowded. If there is too much clutter, you won't be able to move around, and you want a certain amount of breathable space.

- **Corridor kitchen**: this is a kitchen in two facing strips, an option if space is limited. You can get a surprising amount in if you plan it well. One tip is to buy appliances, such as dishwashers, that are not full-sized, so they take up less space.
- **U-shaped kitchen**: another option if space is limited. This works well if you want to tuck in a small table and a couple of chairs at one end of the U to create an 'eat-in' kitchen, which certainly adds value when it comes time to sell. Estate agents like putting an 'eat-in' kitchen on sales particulars, which suggests the kitchen is big enough to hold furniture. But don't try and create an 'eat-in' kitchen if it is so small it means uncomfortably wedging in the table and chairs, as buyers will see through this.
- **L-shaped kitchen**: the more traditional shape and a good idea if the kitchen has to fit into a corner space. Again, you usually can tuck a small table and some chairs up at one end.
- **Island kitchen**: all the rage in larger open-plan set-ups. A central island provides another workspace, extra storage and often you can pull up stools and turn this into a breakfast bar or a place to enjoy drinks when friends come around. I have seen houses where the island has been added later when the kitchen has expanded. As long as you can match the units tastefully, this is a good solution to making your kitchen fit a growing family.

Work Surfaces

There is a multitude of choice here, from the very grand and expensive to the low-grade and not very hardwearing. My advice is to go for something that is resilient to water and small children, heatproof, easy-to-clean and good to look at.

Granite looks good and is durable, but you will have to re-seal it every few years. Wood adds warmth and homeliness to a kitchen, but it scratches easily and you need to be careful with water and hot pans or it will mark. Quartz is increasingly popular with people who fancy granite but can't be bothered with all the high maintenance – but it isn't cheap.

Laminate is definitely less expensive and a good option for a lower-budget kitchen. It can become damaged easily, however, and can look cheap if you buy the wrong sort. Newer versions of laminate work surfaces are coming on to the market that are more hardwearing and less prone to gouges and scratches. A good tip to sort out the good from the bad is to get in some samples and test them. Put hot objects on them and scratch them to determine which are most resilient. A good kitchen fitter or shop should advise you on what is best.

The latest trend for celebrity chef stainless-steel kitchens is great for people who really like to cook. They are stylish and incredibly utilitarian – heatproof, waterproof and easy to clean. They can scratch easily though and all that rubbing with baby oil to get rid of smudges – the recommended method – might get a bit tiresome. They don't come cheap, either, so although they look great on television, you need to find out if your budget is enough.

There are also new fun materials for work surfaces that are worth looking into, such as Zodiac, a granite-type material that is matt in finish and without all those bling flecks of gold that put some people off.

Throughout the process, think clearly about how you will use the kitchen and what matters to you most. Choose the kitchen that reflects your person-ality – you might want a gloss finish or bright reds or groovy monochromes – but keep in mind anything too outrageous might put off buyers when the time comes to move on. Often something a bit more standard and timeless is sensible, and won't put off buyers who might not have the same love of bright colours or cold-looking steel, but could easily customise a more neutral kitchen to better suit their tastes.

How to Get the Look on a Budget

You don't have to pay vast sums to end up with a fantastic kitchen. One friend of mine bought a perfectly good dark, laminate kitchen from IKEA, and ended up with change from £1,000. In order to make it stand out, she hired a carpenter for two days for about £150 and he put beading around the kitchen and made sure everything fitted neatly. It looks great and the money for the extra fitting work really paid off. This could be a good route to take if you buy a flatpack kitchen that you want to look more professional.

You can also just change certain elements in the kitchen if you are strapped for cash. As well as replacing the door fronts, why not:

- Replace worn flooring with tiles or a stylish laminate.
- Spice it up with a plate rack or hanging rails for utensils.
- Paint the walls.
- Put in a new blind – a wooden Venetian blind to match a wooden floor looks smart and friendly, and at the same time is easy to clean.

CASE STUDY

KITCHEN-LESS HOMES

If you fancy unwinding with a glass of something chilled in an open-plan kitchen, or whipping up Jamie Oliver's latest seared carpaccio of beef recipe, then avoid visiting writer Laura Barlow's Manchester flat. Expansive open spaces with central islands, quartz worktops and inviting stools lined up along the breakfast bar might be what most people aspire to for their kitchens, but not Laura, who has wrenched out the heart of her home – the kitchen – from her fourth-floor flat.

Laura has succumbed to this New York trend – doing away with the kitchen completely. 'I am never in, so I never use the kitchen,' says Laura, 32, 'although I always keep a bottle of wine in the miniature fridge in case of social emergencies.'

Now, Laura's 'not kitchen', as she calls it, functions as a study with former kitchen counters holding the computer and printer, while specially created doors hide the washing machine and fridge. She has held on to the kettle and microwave, although she admits the latter has become little more than a place to store her vitamin pills.

Most agents believe this new American 'kitchen-less' trend applies mainly to overworked 30-something single people who want a weekday pied-à-terre, while they live on takeaways or eat out. To me, killing off the kitchen sounds like a particularly unhealthy way to try and add value to your home, and I'd say is best avoided, especially if you're expecting mum or granny to pop round for a cup of tea and slice of cake.

Depending on where you live and how big your home is, this could be a way of deterring, rather than attracting, more mainstream buyers. If space is terribly limited it might make sense not to have a full-blown kitchen, but you certainly should check with an estate agent in the area before you start ripping out a kitchen. And I suspect most agents would tell you to leave the kitchen where it is, or at least have a kitchen of some kind, to appeal to the majority of buyers.

PHIL'S TRADE SECRETS

- Go to kitchen shops and book a consultation for free or a small fee. A kitchen designer or consultant will come round and do a plan for what could work in your kitchen. There are no obligations attached to the consultation, so it doesn't matter if you don't like what they come up with, and maybe you could use some of their ideas to help you formulate your own design.
- Websites offer great kitchen suggestions. The larger home stores that sell kitchens have kitchen planners you can

download. You can drag and drop in different styles of kitchen units and play about with ideas.

- Look at particulars in estate agents' windows and get inspiration from the glossy photos of the kitchens. You might even look around a few show homes on new developments or attend Open Houses – special viewing days for certain homes on the market – to glean ideas from developers or homeowners.

PHIL'S CONTACTS BOOK

- Guild of Master Craftsmen, www.guildmc.com, 01273 478449 – choose craftsmen, such as builders, kitchen fitters and carpenters from this national register.
- Federation of Master Builders, www.findabuilder.co.uk, 0800 015 2522 – the federation lists approved builders and has information and a free sample contract you can download from the website for building projects.
- CORGI (Confederation for the Registration of Gas Installers), www.trustcorgi.com, 0800 915 0485 – organisation of approved gas installers if you are looking for someone to put in your gas appliances.

CHAPTER EIGHT

Bathrooms

Lose the ghastly avocado suite and make a big splash

O nce upon a time a bathroom was a frosty, unheated room where you had a speedy wash and quick brush of the teeth, eager to escape from the damp chill. Maybe if you were lucky you managed a quick dip once a week in a hot bath. Back then, of course, there wasn't much comfort to be had in lingering too long in the bathroom, so any bathing rituals were more of a scurried scrub before the next member of the family took over your now cooling bathwater.

Something remarkable has happened over the last decade or so, with bathrooms becoming sleek and even sexy places to hang out. Gone are the uninviting, draughty rooms of yesteryear where we performed our decidedly practical daily ablutions. Today, they have been replaced by welcoming and sensuous spaces that would rival any luxury spa. And the miracle that has been wowing those at the top of the market is trickling down to the mid and lower levels, benefiting many of us keen to transform our bathrooms.

I knew we had turned a corner a couple of years ago when I picked up a brochure at the launch of a new development by one of Britain's mass house builders. Alongside glossy photographs of the latest kitchen, elegant dining room and lustrous sitting room, there was a funky must-have bathroom, with a deluxe egg-shaped limestone bath, magnificent marble and a hi-tech shower, that doubled up as a steam room. Funnily enough, the word 'bathroom' wasn't even mentioned. Instead, the phrase 'water therapy' was prominent on the page.

Now, calling a bathroom a 'water therapy' zone can be put down to marketing hype. As builders try new ways to shift their product, they will come up with notions like this to get us to part with our cash. But they also are picking up on what we want in our homes, which means comfortable, warm, energising and also relaxing bathrooms.

Research shows that we now spend far longer in our bathrooms and regard them as mini-pleasure palaces rather than just somewhere to have a swift wash. I think this modern trend a good thing, and if you have a nice bathroom, it helps sell your home. Life is busy and noisy, so we want somewhere to go that is a private, quiet sanctuary with no telephones, kids or TVs (although TVs are creeping into some bathrooms now).

A decent bathroom is important to our lives. Even if you don't go quite so far as the ambitious house builder with his 'water therapy' room, you should at least aim for somewhere that is clean and warm. A bathroom is where you start the day and end the day, after all – make it a good kick-off and a good space for winding down. If the bathroom – typically the first room you go into when you get up – is cold and untidy, you feel like just going back to bed again. Therefore, getting the vibe right to make this first foray a good one is crucial.

How Many Bathrooms Should I Have?

People expect more than one bathroom these days. For a family home with four bedrooms, it makes sense to have two bathrooms at least – including an en-suite to the master bedroom, perhaps – and I think one of them should have a proper bath. There has been a tendency to rip baths out of bathrooms and replace them with showers, but small children and older people usually find it easier and preferable to have a bath. Expanding choice, rather than taking it away, is a good strategy with items like baths.

People like to see numerous bathrooms in homes these days, but I think you can have 'bathroom overkill'. I see homes that are, if you'll excuse the pun, awash with bathrooms. Some homeowners have gone down the route where every bedroom has its own en-suite, with maybe an extra bathroom or two for good luck installed in the house as well. This seems a bit excessive to me – every bedroom does not need to have its own trendy en-suite. As long as there are enough bathrooms to satisfy the needs of the people in the house, this should be fine.

One good addition is a downstairs cloakroom, if you haven't already got one. Most people are put off at the thought of having to go upstairs to the bathroom, and putting one in on the ground level can be practical and value-added. No one wants to troop upstairs when coming in from doing the gardening, and visitors will feel more at ease as well.

Do Not Steal the Soap from Hotel Bathrooms – Nick Ideas Instead

Many of our ideas and expectations for bathrooms stem from the fact that more people are travelling to foreign places and picking up ideas from hotels and homes they are renting. I love spotting something new, or a good idea that is so simple I wonder why we haven't thought of it back home. For instance, a clever and eco-friendly notion I discovered while on holiday in France came from a small hotel that wasn't grand or over-the-top. The room we were in had a bathroom created from a loft space and some of the lovely oak removed during the conversion was put to good use as wooden steps leading up to the bath, attractive open shelving and a terrific window with an oak shutter that swung over horizontally when you wanted to keep the light out.

We can't all be the proud owners of the most up-to-the-minute bathroom admired while on vacation, but there is no need to be overly flashy anyhow. Borrowing upper-scale ideas and adapting them can produce a sumptuous look for those on a budget.

Bathroom Basics

If you are a bit strapped for cash, just go for a clean, simple bathroom that doesn't feel grotty and dated. Visitors – and potential buyers one day – will wince if they see black mould, peeling wallpaper and crumbling window-frames, so getting rid of damp problems and carrying out some standard maintenance is a wise move. There are some great products to clear mould, for example, which are easy to obtain from supermarkets or builders' merchants and cost no more than about £5 a tin. You simply spray the product on, leave it to soak for a bit and then scrub the mould or algae off.

Re-grouting and replacing your old tap with a new one can give your bathroom a whole new feel. There are a number of taps on the market now, many of them cheaper copies of expensive Italian varieties. Although I would argue it pays to go for 'the real deal' if you are designing an expensive bathroom in a multi-million-pound pad, there probably is no need to splash the cash in quite the same way in a typical family home.

You might want to update the sanitary ware in your bathroom, but bear in mind you don't have to replace all of it. If your loo and bath are fairly neutral and in good condition, you might get away with just renewing the sink. I reckon a loo is a loo and a bath is a bath but the sink is what sets the tone. There are some great sinks available now from a few hundred pounds upwards that make quite a statement and lift a whole room.

Re-tiling is another great way to add value. If you are going to tackle this job, make sure you don't stint on the number of tiles you use. If you can afford it, run the tiles right up to the top of the walls instead of just putting a few above the bath or using the minimum amount in a shower. First of all, it will look more generous – if you choose larger tiles running across the floor and up the walls the room will appear larger – and also, more tiles will prevent damp problems. If the tiles are very expensive, consider mixing them in with some that are lower-priced. If you choose the right tiles, no one will be able to tell the difference.

One warning when it comes to tiling: ensure you can get to the pipes in case something goes wrong. I have seen too many bathrooms where no one thought of being able to access anything beneath the tiles or the wall, which means ripping up the bathroom when you need to carry out repairs. Place a panel over a good, easy-to-reach point, potentially saving a great deal of money in the future, or get the sort of fitting that allows you access. Beware of groovy designers that come up with slick bathrooms but don't really want to think about how you will find the pipes in an emergency.

I speak from experience. There was a problem with the chrome plug in the main bathroom in our London home. It was the kind of plug operated by turning a knob to make it go up and down. The plug broke, but because marble is surrounding the bath there is no way to get to the plug to fix it. Rather than rip all the marble up, I have resorted to using a cheap plastic plug bought from the builders' merchant for 49 pence. Not as snazzy as our expensive and shiny original plug, but it will have to do for now.

PHIL'S TOP TIP

If you have a family with young children, a decent-sized bath is a good idea. A mixer tap, as opposed to individual taps for hot and cold water, is safer so they don't burn themselves. In addition, you might want to install a hand-held shower set into the bath taps. Most children hate having their hair washed while standing under intimidating wall-mounted showers and you can use the simpler hand shower or a wall-mounted version that detaches instead. They are inexpensive, starting from about £15.

Planning a Bathroom

The first thing you need to do is work out what you want to fit into your bathroom and how best to use the space. If you are in a small flat or starter home and pushed for space, the good news is there are a number of smaller smart-looking sinks, showers and even baths on the market now. This way, you can squeeze in what you need, but don't try to cram in too much or it will feel claustrophobic. Get a large sheet of grid paper with small squares to help you design your bathroom. You can do various sketches to scale of where the fittings might go after measuring the ones you fancy.

Don't forget about the extra space required, including at least 2.2 metres of headroom above the bath and enough room to manoeuvre round fittings. Also, I think it a good idea not to put the bath right up against the wall, so you have space for a ledge or shelf where you can put your products, candles and a radio, and lean your elbows.

Upgrading Your Bathroom

It is pretty straightforward and not too costly to install a new bathroom suite or move a bath or shower, as long as you don't have to alter the pipes. As soon as you start radically changing the pipe work and running it somewhere new, the costs can add up. Laying new piping alongside the existing pipe work is one solution that can save some pounds.

A skilfully revamped bathroom can add anything from 5 to almost 10 per cent on to the value of your home, according to estate agents, depending on where you live and what you've done. It costs about £1,000 to £4,000 to replace the average bathroom.

There is a trend for quite grand bathrooms, some the size of a large bedroom. If you can afford to give up this amount of space and it fits in with the balance of the rest of the property, this can add value. Usually, you find these imposing bathrooms in state-of-the-art bachelor pads and majestic millionaire mansions where space isn't a problem. I wouldn't recommend turning a bedroom in a smaller property into a large bathroom if you are doing this to help sell your home. Most people would rather have an extra bedroom than an oversized bathroom.

For the sanitary ware, there is a variety of materials, from porcelain to limestone, marble and copper, and just as many styles, including rustic rural, sharp contemporary and continental cool. Of course, a country-style butler's sink might look silly in a minimalist city apartment, while a groovy wet room could look out of place in a Cotswold cottage. You can blend old with new. One of the hippest bathrooms I've ever seen was in a restored Tuscan farmhouse. It had a brave blend of old colourful mosaic tiles and an antique bath with the sharpest modern Italian taps and shower. There is an art to mixing the old with the new and it can be fantastic when you get it right. Getting it wrong can detract from the worth of your house, so you need to know what you are doing.

I'm a great fan of wall-hung loos and sinks that are raised off the ground. This makes the room look bigger, maximises space and makes it easier to clean the floor. Keep as much clutter as possible off the floor and provide loads of storage above the sink. You can get neat units that go under the sink to offer even more storage – you can never have enough storage – but that are still off the floor, retaining that light and airy feeling.

Showers

There are a number of different kinds of showers on the market and I would choose one that has all of its working parts on the outside for easy access, not hidden underneath the tiles or wall. Otherwise, if anything goes wrong you will have to take off your new tiles and dig into the wall to repair the shower. Far better to change an external part instead of tearing up your newly decorated bathroom.

If you buy an expensive shower unit, make sure it comes with a guarantee, as it can be difficult to obtain individual replacement parts. If you can, test a shower in the shop before you buy it, particularly if you are parting with a good deal of cash for it, to make sure it's the right one for you.

Bath/shower mixer

A standard type of shower often found on a bath, the temperature can be controlled through the taps and the mixer produces a pressurised spray. This is an inexpensive way to get a shower as there is no extra plumbing involved (prices start at about £50), but the pressure isn't all that great and it can be tricky to adjust the temperature as well.

Manual mixer

A good-value (£60 up to about £250) wall-mounted unit, the manual mixer has a hose and spray and temperature-control system from a hot and cold water supply. You need to put the mixer at a reasonable height to get the right water pressure and hot and cold water has to be plumbed in.

Thermostatic mixer

This is effectively a manual mixer with a built-in stabiliser so the temperature of the water is self-adjusting – a good idea if you have young children or older people, because the temperature is not affected if water is being used at the same time elsewhere in the house. The cost is a bit higher, from around £130 to just over £500.

Electric shower

Water comes in separately from the mains, and this kind of shower provides its own instant hot water supply. This is terrific if anything goes wrong with the boiler, because you will still get hot water no matter what. The downside can be meeting the right mains pressure level to make the shower work adequately, and you will need to employ an electrician to sign off the job. Costs range from about £60 to £250.

Power shower

All the rage, power showers are connected to an electric pump or the pump that comes with the shower itself. You get a shower with terrific pressure, but most power showers do not work with combination boilers. If you are looking for something eco-friendly, a power shower will not be your top choice as it uses as much water as a bath. You need to pay about £250 to £750 for a power shower.

Big showerhead

It is worth investing in a big showerhead, but along with having a power shower, you need to make sure you have pipes of sufficient diameter to take the pressure – if they are too narrow at any point en route to the shower, the pressure levels will drop. In my house we have a big chunky pipe running from the boiler but unfortunately the piping is too small for the last four feet running to our bathroom, so there is not as much pressure as I would like.

Shower enclosure

When it comes to keeping the water where it should be – in the shower, for instance – you will need some kind of enclosure. I don't think shower curtains are all that practical. People leave the curtain hanging outside, whether on a bath or in a separate cubicle, which can cause flooding. Curtains tend to go all black and nasty after a period of time too. If you can't fit a shower door and have to use a curtain, buy one made from anti-mould material and think about washing and changing them regularly. Glass doors are more practical, I think, for baths and showers. Some are on the flimsy side, so it might be worth forking out a bit more to get one that is sturdy and safe. Prices vary depending on quality and design, but you can get something decent from about £50 or £60.

The Wet Room

If you want to witness your neighbours turning avocado with envy, you can consider installing a high-style wet room. A wet room is a specially tanked (waterproofed) bathroom with a drain plumbed into the floor. What is special about a wet room is you can use the shower without the worry of shower screens, curtains or any other enclosures.

There is something very indulgent about just being able to step into your wet room (the ultimate in walk-in showers, really), turn the shower on and point it pretty much anywhere and not be concerned about where the water will go. Wet rooms can cost anything from about £400 for a cheaper kit package through to many thousands of pounds for a top-of-the-range designer version. New products, such as pre-formed shower floors that gently slope towards the drain area and are placed directly on joists before being tanked and tiled over, are making wet room installations more attractive. Pre-formed floors cost about £500.

Top wet rooms boast super power showers with steam, chromatherapy (light therapy) and water jets for a multi-sensory experience. (A friend reports that he used a wet room recently that had an extra strong 'jungle' power shower with special thunder and lightning sound and light effects.) To complete the look, wealthy homeowners like to splash out on a quality finish, using materials such as polished plaster, remote-controlled lighting, surround-sound music systems with radio channels included and intricate mosaic designs.

Wet rooms are not suitable for all homes, though, and it is unlikely you will be allowed to install a wet room into a listed building. An alternative that won't blow the budget but will give the same 'wet room look' is to go for frameless shower doors and panels that look clean and minimalist.

I really love using wet rooms, but if they go wrong they go very wrong. You need to consider the benefits alongside the risk damage, and how they are installed is crucial. If a wet room starts to flood it could be quite expensive sorting out the problem and mending the damage. This is one area where I would get an expert. I would not even begin to try installing a wet room myself. Seasoned DIY fans might prove me wrong, but you really need to know what you are doing to make sure the room can drain properly and is completely watertight.

PHIL'S TOP TIP

As I love using a warm towel, I think a good heated chrome towel rail, starting at about £50, can be a stylish and useful accessory. A good option is to have the rail independent of the central heating and on a timer, so you can set it to be warm first thing in the morning and again in the evening. This makes sense in the summer, in particular, when the heating won't be on.

Other Bathroom Considerations: Carpets and Colours

Carpets are a no-no in bathrooms today. They get sopping wet, take ages to dry out and are considered unhygienic by many people. There is a great deal of other flooring available, including tiles, linoleum, marble and limestone. Choose something easy to look after and that is likely to appeal to the widest common denominator when you sell your house.

The choice of colours for sanitary ware and walls always causes a great deal of debate. I would opt for white or sandstone for the sanitary ware. A monochrome look is a classic, bringing a slightly retro feel that ties in with contemporary design. It doesn't offend anyone and it doesn't date. Avoid pink, blue or anything with dolphins. You can add colour through accessories, if need be, although I think there is nothing nicer than clean, white towels and not much else.

Baths in bedrooms

I'm not totally convinced by the vogue in freestyle baths popping up in bedrooms. This might look cool in a hotel, but I'm not sure it translates that well to a private home. When you get in and out of the bath, water spills everywhere and the bedroom floor would need to be made out of the right water-resistant material. Also, when it comes time to move on, this trend is unlikely to appeal to the majority of potential buyers.

Condensation and fans

You definitely need fans to get rid of condensation, which can be quite damaging, allowing mould and other bacteria to grow. I am happy with a fan on a switch that I can control myself, although others might prefer one that automatically turns itself on and off. Some fans have moisture sensors that switch on when they detect moisture or water in the room, and then switch themselves off later when it has gone, while others come on when the bathroom light is turned on and go off again when the light's switched off.

Under-floor heating

I really love a warm, cosy bathroom and under-floor heating is a great way to achieve an even temperature. Will it help sell your house? No one really knows. If you have a floor made of a cold material, such as slate or stone, under-floor heating will make it more pleasant to walk on, particularly when you are barefoot, in the winter.

There is a knack to getting the hang of operating under-floor heating that you don't instantly turn on and off. You keep it running gently, a bit like an Aga, and it can take some time to warm up and cool down again. Under-floor heating was considered costly a few years back, but prices have come down now. I deal with under-floor heating in more detail in Chapter Nine.

Windows

If you are lucky enough to have a window in your bathroom, take advantage of it and admit as much natural light as possible. With regards to window coverings, choose something that won't be affected by moisture and is easy to clean. I favour frosted windows – no one can see in, but you still retain a good deal of the light. A good buy is a roll of frosting you can stick onto windows that costs less than £20. Other good options are wooden shutters that look stylish and are not affected by moisture.

PHIL'S TRADE SECRET

There is a new, inexpensive range of wooden shutters made up of wider and thicker strips of wood that look far less flimsy than those with narrow strips. They are great value, starting at £90, and come in a good range of colours, as well as natural wood stains.

DESIGNER BATHROOM

Artist Kate Nolan inherited a very heavy, masculine en-suite bathroom with black marble tiles and gold taps when she bought her two-bedroom flat in north London 18 months ago.

'The bath was under the window and took up a great deal of space, which made the bathroom look quite small,' she explains. 'I decided to open up the space and get more of the light from the window to flow into the room.'

Kate, 33, hired a designer to help her create her dream bathroom. Although this might appear to be an expensive move, Kate reckons the designer's fee was set off by her being able to get all the tiles and sanitary ware at rock-bottom prices.

A rather nasty doorway was removed, and to provide Kate or her partner Alexander privacy when they want it, a sliding door was installed. 'I love it, because it doesn't take up any room like the old door did when it was open.'

Kate was lucky to have oak flooring running through the bedroom and en-suite bathroom when she bought the flat. She had the flooring sanded and oiled to spruce it up a bit – money well spent, she says, when you see the sheen on it now.

A traditional roll-top bath replaced the old one, the walls were painted a fresh white, and blue and white mosaic tiles lined the shower. Alexander, a graphic designer, sourced the tiles on the Internet, saving about 60 per cent of the price.

'The designer talked us into having double basins, which I thought was a bit naff at first,' Kate admits, 'but now that we have them I think they're great. I can keep all my stuff in the cupboard under my sink and Alexander has his things in the other cupboard under his. It is a bit like being in a hotel, but better really.'

Kate said the shower put in by the last owner of the house was only about a year old and still has two years left on the guarantee. The designer updated the showerhead to provide more pressure and a wider selection of sprays.

'I love the blue and white tiles. They have a Dutch feel to them, but look very modern too. The whole bathroom is simple and clean and with the lovely wooden floor there is a great feeling of warmth.'

To save her lovely wooden flooring from being splashed, Kate has some plain white cotton bath mats she bought on the High Street for only £15 each. They hang on a hook next to the shower and she can put them down when showering and then hang them back up again.

The entire job cost about £4,000 including the designer's fee. 'It was money well spent,' believes Kate. 'I have no idea if I will get my money back or whether the bathroom will add value when it comes time to sell, but we are getting so much pleasure from it meanwhile it has an added value all of its own.'

An estate agent in the area thinks Kate has added value to her flat. 'In this area, the sort of people who might buy, including professional and downsizing couples, would appreciate the materials she has used and the careful design of the space. I would think she's added about 10 to 15 per cent to her house by getting a proper designer to organise the job and put in high-quality items for her.'

PHIL'S TOP TIPS

- Invest in a demisting mirror so you can see through the fog to shave and put in your contact lenses.
- Position a mirror in place of a tile in the shower. I shave in the shower while looking in my little shower mirror.
- A large showerhead looks terrific and pulses out at high pressure.
- Put in enough storage so you have somewhere to put all those bottles and other things that accumulate.
- Taps in the middle of the bath will give your bathroom the 'spa look' and they won't jab you in the back, or opt for a bath that fills through the overflow so you don't have any taps at all.
- Double basins add some Hollywood style, as well as practicality in a busy household.
- Large tiles make the bathroom look bigger than it is.
- A heated towel rail and under-floor heating will give you a warm and comfy bathroom.
- Skylights can bring in more natural light if you can fit them in.
- New taps can update a bathroom and are inexpensive compared to redoing the whole bathroom.
- Do not forget to put in plenty of hooks for hanging towels and dressing gowns.

PHIL'S CONTACTS BOOK

- Association of Plumbing and Heating Contractors (APHC), www.aphc.co.uk.
- Kitchen Bathroom Bedroom Specialists Association, www.kbsa.org.uk – free advice and a list of over 300 independent specialists.

CHAPTER NINE

Flooring and Lighting

The subtle enhancements of good
flooring and clever lighting

Two key areas that can add a great deal to the enjoyment of your home, and also to its value when you decide to put it on the market, are flooring and lighting. When you think of adding value to a home, you probably imagine glamorous, attention-grabbing projects, such as installing a glossy new kitchen, media room with the latest flat screen plasma television and built-in sound system or maybe a gym fit for an Olympic athlete. However, I believe strongly that if you concentrate on putting in the best flooring you can afford and devise good lighting for different zones in the house, you will up the worth of your property considerably, without dwelling on how large the plasma should be.

It is hard to put a figure on how much these two enhancements will add to the value of your home, but they will contribute to the overall ambience. This is a subtle way of enhancing value, which will be appreciated by a new purchaser. And in practical terms, this duo will make your life a whole lot easier. By choosing the right flooring and lighting for the way you live, you will be able to get great pleasure from simply being in your home. For instance, if you lay solid flooring in the main living area of a family home, as opposed to carpets, you might find this saves worrying about stains from spilt drinks and muddy footprints. This has to be a lot more relaxing than hovering with a damp cloth and bottle of carpet-stain remover.

Equally, placing the right sort of lighting where it is required – good reading lights at desks and in seating areas in the living room, for example

– you need not strain your eyes every time you try to read a book, thread a needle or carry out other close work. Soft mood lighting, from the simple to the outright intricate, will soothe your spirits no end as well, turning a house into a haven.

FLOORING

Having the right flooring is very important. Even when money was tight, I have always spent a decent sum on flooring – and I've never regretted it. The good news is there is a tremendous amount of choice. Even on a budget you can pick up something fairly reasonable. You want to make the right decision, however, because once you lay flooring down it isn't easy, or cheap, to yank it back up.

My first bit of advice is that unless you are lucky enough to live somewhere that already has good flooring, take up a bit of carpet or some of the existing flooring and check what is lying underneath. A friend of mine who lives in a thatched cottage in Wiltshire was fortunate enough to discover some old wooden flooring underneath some nasty carpets he was desperate to replace. Some of the gaps had to be filled and the odd board had to be replaced, but by and large the flooring was terrific. His builders repaired, sanded and oiled the flooring and it looks marvellous. He had to factor in the cost of the builders' work and the extra boards purchased, but it was worth it in the end.

Another house I visited recently had some amazing original Victorian tiles all along the length of the main hallway. The owners didn't even notice they were there until they tore up the old carpet covering them, in a bid to spruce up the house before putting it on the market. They cleaned the tiles and they have hugely lifted what is otherwise a pretty dull house. Everyone comments on the tiles the second they come through the door, so do make the best of hidden gems like this if you have them.

But you might be stuck with old floors that have no merit whatsoever, and come with glitches, dips and bumps. It can be hard to lay some types of flooring, such as laminate, on top. When selecting flooring that suits you and your house, think carefully about how you live and what makes sense for your household. There is no point putting carpets in a house if a member of your family suffers from asthma or allergies. If you have pets, you need to have practical floor coverings or you will be forever mopping up and dragging out the hoover.

Here is a selection of floorings and the pros and cons for each.

Carpet

Pros: Easy and quick to lay, a good heat- and sound-insulator and you can hide dips or glitches that are below.

Cons: Dust mites can bother eczema and asthma sufferers, stains are hard to get out, carpets can look naff if not fitted properly and they are not ideal for areas with water or lots of traffic (kitchens, bathrooms and family rooms).

Laminate

Pros: Cheap to fit as you buy only exactly as much as you need. A good low-cost option to real wood and easy to clean.

Cons: Can look nasty when scratched and scraped, not easy to fit if your floors aren't level and if not fitted properly can look shoddy.

Vinyl/linoleum

Pros: Inexpensive, easy to fit and quite pleasant and warm to walk on.

Cons: If you buy a budget version the quality isn't great and if not sealed properly there can be damp problems.

Wood

Pros: Looks smart and timeless, very hardwearing, easy to mop up spills and can add value to a home.

Cons: Old flooring might need renovating, you need an expert to fit it, it can be expensive, wood can scratch and mark and not best for places that get wet (kitchens and bathrooms).

Stone/ceramic tiles

Pros: Waterproof, looks chic, lots of choice, hardwearing and fairly easy to keep clean.

Cons: Porous stone can stain, cold to walk on, need to clean and re-seal frequently (particularly limestone) and you need an expert to fit it.

Coir/sisal

Pros: Good for people suffering from allergies, looks natural and light and isn't too expensive.

Cons: Not all that easy to clean, hard to get rid of stains once there is a spill and not particularly hardwearing.

Costs

Flooring can cost anything from about £4 a square metre for budget-buy carpet or laminate, up to £200 a square metre for top-quality wood fitted by an expert. To get something that looks reasonable, you should budget about £40 to £50 a square metre.

Bathroom Flooring

Bathroom floors tend to get hammered, with a lot of traffic and any amount of water thrown on to them. Choose something that is hardwearing, water-resistant and practical. Whatever you choose should be totally waterproof.

You want your bathroom to be hygienic. Installing a surface that can be mopped and wiped easily will make the most sense. Wet floors can become slippery – avoid polished granite and marble and non-slip tiles if you have young children or older people living in your home.

I hate carpet in bathrooms, and so does most everyone else these days. Ceramic tiles work well in a bathroom, as does stone, slate, limestone and marble. Wood looks great, but it might not react well to copious amounts of water spilling on to it. You can protect it by sealing it, and always use bathmats to cut down on water getting onto the floor. There are some smart High Street buys now and you can pick up a stylish bathmat from £10 plus. Under-floor heating (see below) can be very successful in bathrooms – after all, there is nothing better than padding about on a warm floor in your bare feet.

When fitting bathroom flooring, try to get right under the bath. If there are cracks or gaps, water will find its way in and you will end up with damp. Tiles must be keyed (or attached) on to the right sub-floor. With all the heat and moisture that is given off in a bathroom, the grouting round the tiles will crack if tiles are not stuck properly on to a flat, dry sub-floor.

PHIL'S TRADE SECRET

People often think that if they are tiling the floor of a small bathroom, they have to pick small tiles. However, the opposite is the case. A visual trick employed by architects and designers is to choose large tiles because they make a room look bigger. If you use the same tiles on the walls and floor, it can make the room appear even larger still.

What is Under-floor Heating?

This kind of heating warms a room or even an entire building through a heating system under the floor. Generally thought of as a recent innovation, it has been used for centuries in different parts of the world. The Romans used it, and today the Scandinavians are particular fans.

Under-floor heating has become popular for a number of reasons. The advantages are:

- It is invisible.
- This form of heating is a good way to save space, with no bulky radiators taking up the walls and intruding into the floor area.

- Under-floor heating runs at lower temperatures than radiators, making it cheaper and more energy-efficient and cutting bills by 15 to 20 per cent.
- Each room has its own circuit and you can control the heat when and where you want with hard-wired or wireless programmable room thermostats.
- Heat is distributed evenly, reducing cold or hot spots in a room.
- Improved air quality cuts down on environmental triggers for asthma sufferers.
- There is more freedom for interior design with no pipes or radiators getting in the way.
- Ceramic and hard-finish floors feel warm and welcoming.
- When it comes time to sell, under-floor heating is a good feature to mention on the sales particulars. The next buyer will be grateful you carried out the work.

Under-floor Heating Options

There are two types: a 'wet' system and a 'dry' (or electric) one.

Wet under-floor heating

Warm water circulates through a series of coiled pipes in a special membrane that is laid in the floor at the time of construction. A screed is poured on top of a layer of insulation normally at around 100 millimetres then pipes from a continuous loop between two central manifolds are placed at a depth of 65 to 75 millimetres. Effectively, you end up with a sandwich with the insulation on the bottom, the screed with the pipes running through it in the middle and your floor covering of choice at the top.

The hot water running though the pipes heats up over time, producing a gentle heat. It can take five to six hours to heat and to cool down, so this is not a system if you are after instant heat. I would not recommend it for bedrooms, where you want to alter temperatures fast. A radiator system that can heat up in five minutes flat to warm a cool bedroom might be better.

A wet system is a bit more complicated and expensive to install than a dry one, because you have to run all the piping to and from the boiler and take floors up. You can, however, mix and match wet under-floor heating with radiators if you don't require under-floor heating in every room.

Dry under-floor heating

If you are retro-fitting (putting under-floor heating in after a house is built), then a dry, or electric, system might be an easier option than the wet system. You won't have to run any pipes to it and the system used is thinner (about 10 millimetres), meaning you don't have to dig as deep or put in a step taking you up into the under-floor-heated room.

Dry under-floor heating comes in the form of a cable system: a basic heating cable, flat cables or a kind of woven mat. The system is laid on top of the existing floor and you then cover it as you choose. Dry under-floor heating can be fitted as a DIY project, saving money on labour costs, but a qualified electrician must connect the cables or mats to the main electrical system.

Some people express safety concerns about having an electrical system in a bathroom. Although electrics and water are not a good combination, as long as your builder and electrician are experienced and know what they are doing, all should be fine. Make sure they have carried out this work before. Another good option is to check out firms that specialise in providing under-floor heating materials, as well as installing systems. They can supply qualified workmen to install the materials you order, so you don't have to source a builder and electrician separately.

I have noticed in some houses that it is almost impossible to find or operate the controls for under-floor heating. Put them somewhere accessible – not in the back of a cupboard that is hard to get to and where it is difficult to see anything. Equally, they can look messy mounted on the wall. Trying to keep down the number of switches and controls should be a primary aim.

Cost

Under-floor heating isn't cheap. You need someone to quote based on the size of the room or rooms where you want to install it, the right system for your house and your choice of new flooring. Some flooring products are recommended over others, such as engineered board – where you have three to six millimetres of character-grade hardwood on top of plywood backing – which conducts the heat better than solid hardwood. You might spend as little as £12 to £16 a square metre and as much as £30 a square metre for under-floor heating. The more rooms you fit, the cheaper it will be per room.

> ### PHIL'S TOP TIP
>
> *Under-floor heating is ideal for conservatories. Conservatories tend not to have much wall space to install radiators, making under-floor heating more practical and aesthetically pleasing. Remember that to comply with Part L of the building regulations, you must install controls that can switch off the under-floor heating when it is not needed so you save energy.*

Kitchen Flooring

You want something immensely practical and absolutely waterproof in a kitchen. A quality laminate or good tiles can be fine in a kitchen, although you don't want anything too hard. Otherwise, when you drop your favourite teapot it will smash to smithereens.

I find some stones and tiles quite cold as well. Under-floor heating can solve this problem, but sometimes we are seduced by the stone and marble floors we spot in buildings in hot countries. These cooler stones look fantastic in a sunny climate and are fresh to walk on, but I'm not sure if this always translates to a cooler climate. In the country, you might choose flagstones, terracotta or stone. Again, some of these can be a bit cold and hard, so think about under-floor heating and be careful with your precious china.

Wood is fantastic and can look fabulous, particularly if you have timber in the living spaces throughout the house and want to carry on running it into the kitchen. Wood can be quite forgiving, but you need to be careful about sloshing too much water about. It might be better suited to a home for a couple without children or a family with older children, although spills do wipe up easily and you don't need to worry about stains if you have accident-prone toddlers. If you drop a pan and a little dent is left behind, it doesn't seem to matter too much – the wood forms a patina, which seems to add to its character.

Maintenance is important. Regularly water-sealing or oiling kitchen flooring annually can be a good idea. Look after your flooring – there is nothing worse than grease or other marks ruining a new floor. Tiles can crack if you drop something heavy, while dropped objects tend to just bounce off linoleum.

Limestone looks great – it is light and large chunks of it are very chic indeed – but it is more fragile than you think. If you drop hot fat or tomato ketchup, it will be difficult to get the stain out. My neighbour's wonderful limestone floor is blighted forever from a tomato sauce spill and marks have been left behind from where she placed her Christmas tree. Cleaning and sealing your limestone floor every year can make a real difference.

PHIL'S TOP TIP

If there isn't enough wall space for radiators in a kitchen, under-floor heating could be the solution. However, make sure it is on a different circuit to the main central heating, so when the kitchen becomes too hot from cooking you can turn it off.

PHIL'S TOP TIP

Run any flooring right underneath the kitchen units, or at least under the kicking plates. If you have a gap, you will be driven mad by dust, breadcrumbs and other food morsels becoming trapped around the edge.

CASE STUDY

UNDER-FLOOR HEATING

Solicitor Will Chandler and his 35-year-old life-coach wife Alana decided to install under-floor heating in a Sixties house they revamped near Exeter, Devon. On the advice of their builder, they installed both wet and dry under-floor heating systems in the living/dining room and bathrooms.

'We put the wet system in the big living/dining room that we opened up by knocking a wall through. We also extended out a few feet and to the side, ending up with a really fantastic open modern space that is now 600 square feet (56 square metres),' explains Will, 38.

The couple followed a good tip handed on by an architect friend. Because the builders were already digging down to install the under-floor heating, he pointed out that they might as well go a few feet deeper to raise the height of the room. Typically, ceilings in Sixties houses are lower than those in period buildings, and by going down a bit more the room looks even bigger and lighter with higher ceilings.

'Not wanting to ruin the open plan and contemporary look with radiators and pipes, we chose under-floor heating and liked the idea of the wet system with its gentle heat,' says Will.

Will and Alana selected engineered board with black American walnut flooring on top that conveys heat well and won't shrink or buckle in the same way straightforward timber might.

The couple opted for electric under-floor heating in both bathrooms – their en-suite and in the guest bathroom. 'The builder thought this was more practical, because then we didn't have to cause more chaos installing extra pipes and ripping up more than we need to. It was cheaper too,' Will points out.

Altogether, though, it wasn't cheap to install the under-floor heating. The whole job, including the labour and materials, came to about £6,500. Was it worth the money?

'Every penny,' Will declares. 'It is so brilliant having a warm bathroom and it feels great walking on the heated ceramic tiles we put down.'

The living room is a favourite for Alana, who was brought up in a variety of balmy places, including Singapore, Hong Kong and the Caribbean. 'It is a bit like living in the Bahamas with this wide open space that is warm and relaxing. I end up sitting on the floor quite a bit instead of on the sofa. I wander around in my bare feet all the time too. It was a lot of money and quite messy and disruptive to have the work done, but I love it.'

Bedroom Flooring

The debate goes on over what flooring is best in a bedroom. Some people swear by carpet and others hardwood or laminate. As the bedroom is meant to be your private sanctuary and the floor is one of its largest surfaces, the choice of covering is important. You don't need to worry about maintenance in the same way as the bathroom or kitchen – with the exception of children's rooms – so you can opt for comfort and relative silence instead. Warmth is another crucial factor, so you can be enticed out from under your duvet on a cold morning.

A popular choice is carpet, which is cosy and warm. Try to buy the best carpeting you can afford – cheap nylon versions won't wear well and can be disappointing; carpet tiles cost a bit more than wall-to-wall carpeting, but they might last longer and be worth the extra cost. The only problem is if you suffer from allergies. Carpets hold dust mites, pet dander and other allergens. This could put off a potential purchaser when you sell.

Solid wood is a good choice and quite timeless. If you are concerned about the floorboards feeling cold, you can put some rugs down, which warms up the room and is a nice touch. The look can be updated, depending on which rugs are down.

Laminate could suit those on a budget. If you choose a decent grade, it can have the same effect as hardwood but for far less money. Laminate is easy to look after and lasts for years. Installation is fairly straightforward too.

Cork is an eco-friendly alternative. It is soft and warm and will keep the noise out, as it is a good insulator. Cork is stain-resistant, hygienic and will not form mould or mildew. Allergy sufferers like cork too.

PHIL'S TOP TIP

Surfaces such as rubber can feel a bit clinical in a bedroom, with the exception possibly of a children's room. Vinyl can look cheap, and while hard stone or tile floors might look good they are not all that cosy in a bedroom.

Flooring for Halls and Staircases

Common areas used by everyone, including halls and stairways, look best if they all conform to the same design scheme. For instance, if wood is your choice, then lay it all through these areas. The same applies to carpets: use the same one right through. This is a style choice, but remember 'flow' and how it is good to lead the eye from one area to another.

Noise can be a real issue. If you have ever been woken by someone thumping up the stairs and along a hallway – and don't you notice creaky floorboards? – you know how important noise insulation can be. It might be a good idea to carpet the staircase or – another stylish option – fit a stair runner, a carpet that goes up the middle of a staircase but doesn't reach either edge. Either option makes the staircase quieter as well as safer, as people are less likely to slip and fall.

Paying extra to have carpet in communal places protected against stains could be money well spent. You can spray on the protective chemicals yourself (a tin starts at about £5), or get it professionally done. If you live in the country, you need to think about wear and tear and the 'mud factor'. Rather than complain about the amount of mud being tracked into the house, it might be more sensible to choose easy-care flooring in communal parts. Flagstones, limestone, wood and good ceramic tiles might be preferable to light carpet if you want to keep your sanity.

In my opinion, the wider floorboards are, the better they look. Engineered board, which works well if you have under-floor heating, can look just as good as solid wood (if chosen properly) and can be cheaper. Expect to pay about £20 to £80 a square metre for wooden flooring. Give some thought to the colour. Although I love the dark woods, such as American black walnut, you can see the scratches more than you would in a lighter oak or beech. As long as you don't mind the wood developing a patina in this way, it shouldn't matter. But lighter woods are probably more practical for families, while darker woods are more appropriate for child-free homes, or homes with older children.

Pay particular attention to thresholds when you go from one room to another. Where solid wood meets carpet or carpet meets carpet, a wooden or metal strip is used to conceal the join. These come in all shapes and sizes, but get a decent-quality strip and put it on properly, joining them under the door where it isn't as noticeable.

> ### PHIL'S TOP TIP
>
> *Ideally, wood runs under skirting boards. Or run it up to the board and place an expansion strip along the edge. If you don't want to see the strips, run the wood floor to the skirting board and attach a strip of beading to cover up the edge. Paint the beading the same colour as the skirting board so it looks neat and tidy.*

Mats

Mats are good things to have. They make people feel welcome when they arrive and give them somewhere to wipe their feet and leave wet gear, including umbrellas and boots. If you think ahead, you can have a recessed space set into the floor just inside the door that can hold some matting. A compromise is to have a mat outside, although it can get wet or even be blown away. I like having two mats, particularly in the country: one inside and one outside.

PHIL'S TRADE SECRET

I have seen a very high-end house builder recess a round space in a living room where he inset a beautiful, plush carpet into a wooden floor. An expensive Italian sofa and chair went on top, making this area look wonderfully relaxed and elegant at the same time. A design feature like this doesn't come cheap, mind, and you need to plan everything well in advance.

Flooring for Disabilities

If someone is unsteady on his feet or has a disability, the correct flooring can be important. Blind people might prefer wood or laminate so they can hear someone coming and won't have to worry about stains if they spill something. Those with dementia often cope best with pattern-free carpet or flooring all on the same level, while the hard of hearing with a hearing dog will want something easy to clean. If someone struggles with walking, non-slip well-laid flooring is a sensible idea, and a wheelchair user will need flooring that is totally flat and hardwearing.

LIGHTING

Until recently, lighting was pretty much ignored when it came to building or doing up a property. Just having a light hanging from the middle of the ceiling was thought to suffice, and the idea of dimming lights to create different effects would have been laughable unless you were a lighting director in a film studio or in a West End theatre.

Today, lighting is a key part of making a house appealing, practical and interesting. Because we might use one area in the house in several ways – a bedroom can double up as a study, for instance, or the place where you eat can also be the place where you entertain and relax – we can make a distinction between these zones with clever lighting.

Essentially there are two sorts of lighting: mood and practical. Mood lighting is gentle and makes the room look interesting, while practical lights are more directional and are there to help you see when involved in an activity.

In kitchens, it is important to have practical pools of light shining on to work surfaces so you can see what you are doing. When installing a kitchen, work out how you will use the room and where these lights should go. There is no point in lighting the floor when you can't see to chop the vegetables. You can have mood lighting in a kitchen as well, to wash light over walls and units.

Centre or Wall Lights

Traditional centre lights hanging from ceilings can be quite practical, producing maximum light for one place. But they are not particularly attractive, especially in a modern house with low ceilings. Yet a splendid chandelier – there are some funky ones now from about £100 – hanging over a dining table or a fine pendant light in a hallway both have their place. The downside of centre lights can be that wherever you are in a room, they are likely to cast a shadow, and they are not ideal for certain activities, such as reading a book.

Wall lights are often more useful and attractive. The light comes from behind you, which is better for reading and other close pursuits. Wall lighting is softer and mellower. Unless you are building a house from scratch or renovating, there is a wiring issue. You need to 'chase' – or feed – cable into the wall and dig a hole about an inch deep all the way up the wall. This can be quite a production.

Up-lighters, Down-lighters and Lamps

These lights do exactly what it says on the tin. Up-lighters point up and down-lighters, often in the ceiling, point down. Variations on a theme include recessed lights that are set into walls and ceilings, and wash lights. These are down-lighters used to wash light over a wall or area.

Alternatively, you can use standard and table lamps. The advantage is you can put them wherever you want, move them about and position them to get the light exactly how you want it. They also look nice, and enable more than one person to use a space and benefit from it. For example, if you want to watch TV and your partner wants to read, a standard or table lamp can cast a small pool of light that is good for reading, while you can carry on watching television without any light spilling on to the screen.

Spotlights

A very good solution, although it is expensive, is to inset ceiling spotlights. This requires a great deal of forward planning, preferably before building the house. Spotlights are harder to fit afterwards, but not impossible.

In the Seventies spotlights were mains powered, but in the Nineties dimmable halogen low-voltage lighting was introduced. This revolution meant lights could be positioned more subtly and accurately, with the added bonus of being dimmable for when you want gentle washes of light.

Low-voltage halogen lights come with a transformer – a tube about the length of a cigarette packet. You can have one transformer per light, or one larger transformer with four lights in one unit. They transform 230 volts into 12 volts in the lights, which means you can get a great deal of extra light coming out of a smaller element.

The downside is the expense: the lights start at about £10 each and each transformer is £10 or £15 on top. Also, the light fittings are more expensive to start with – a good one is in the region of £75. Cheaper versions work, but the light can be quite bright and it can flare.

Low-voltage halogens have some drawbacks. When bulbs go, they can be difficult to change. Unless they have been correctly installed, the transformers can sing a bit, making a funny humming noise. They also can overheat and you will have to change them. This is not a DIY job for everyone, so these lights are potentially high maintenance.

Now, a new generation of halogens that look almost identical – the main difference is the bulbs are slightly bigger – operate from the mains. They are a little cheaper too and don't have transformers (which have been known to go expensively wrong).

PHIL'S TOP TIP

I think low-voltage lights are at their best when you have lots of them, giving washes of light over walls or counters. This can be really effective and change the mood of a room from day to night when you dim them or raise the lighting level. I equate good lighting with good design. If something, whether a suit, fireplace or chair, is well designed you don't notice it. You don't know why you like it, it is just right. This applies to lighting as well. If it is really good, it is just there – but it is perfect.

LED Lighting

An LED (light-emitting diode) is an electronic light source. LED lights have many advantages over traditional light sources, such as having lower energy consumption and being longer lasting and quite robust. LED lighting is good in confined spaces, like cupboards and under shelves. Light and bright, they don't heat up, which is safer, and they are waterproof. This makes them ideal for bathrooms, for example, where you can fit them under shelves above the sink.

Low Light and Night Lights

I love low lighting on staircases. Effectively a permanent night light, these lights are inset at a low level in the walls and shine down so you can see to go up and down the stairs at night. You get a terrific effect from low lighting and a low-level floor wash looks good too. These lights are not too dear –

cheaper versions are from about £20 each, while a higher-end steel light is £80 – but you will have to pay to have them 'chased' or installed into the walls. If you are carrying out renovation work and plan to repaint or wallpaper the walls, this probably won't be too much of a problem.

Other interesting lights that subtly add value to your home are 'arty' night lights. These are special low-level lights that gently highlight certain areas. For instance, you can set a light – waterproof, of course – into the tiles at the bottom of a wall in a shower. The light shines on to the shower tray, which looks terrific.

Hall Lighting

This is the first part of your house people see when they arrive, so it is essential to get the lighting right. You don't want bright light shining in people's eyes when they walk through the door, which could be a bit alarming. A good pendant light could work well here if your ceiling is high enough. You could also have low-level lighting along the walls – this works in corridors as well.

I also suggest that a wall light splashing a soft wash on to the face will do more for someone checking their appearance in a hall mirror than a glaring light that makes you feel like you are trapped in a municipal car park.

PHIL'S TOP TIP

Don't light spaces, light places. It is best to light a place you want lit for a reason. Pools of light from behind a sofa or good bedside lights – they can be cabled into the wall either side of a bed, if you want – can be used specifically for reading, while a wall or stairs can have gentle washes of light. One of the most attractive lights is candlelight, of course, which creates a soft wash of its own. Firelight can add to the ambience of a room as well.

Five-amp Circuits

Putting five-amp circuits into living rooms and bedrooms can add value to a property. The lamps in the room — standard, table and bedside, typically — can then be put on the single circuit and be turned on or off, or dimmed, at one flick of a wall switch.

Mirror Lighting and Automatic Sensors

People sometimes get lighting very wrong. They light themselves from above so they can see their images in front of a mirror when getting dressed, putting on make-up or shaving. Yet it is money well spent on a mirror with the light set into it. This has the benefit of light shining from behind the mirror towards you, so you can see what you are doing.

Automatic lights on a sensor are an interesting notion too. I have seen these come on as soon as you enter a bathroom – a sort of more upmarket night light. I am not sure these are worth putting into a bathroom unless you are happy about them coming on whenever you enter the room. They could suit an older person or someone with disabilities. Some automatic lights are 'zoned' – they might light a particular area for those having to get up at night, taking you along a hallway and into a bathroom, for instance.

I have heard of people putting an automatic sensor light into a child's room. It turns on automatically when the child enters the room and shuts off again when the child leaves. I'm not convinced about this, for two reasons. First, the child will never learn that he should turn lights off, which doesn't really help him become eco-friendly. And what about when you want the room to be in darkness when the child is having a nap or is sleeping at night? If someone comes into the room for whatever reason, the child will wake up when the light clicks on.

> ### Fluorescent Lighting
>
> Fluorescent lighting, normally used in office and public spaces, can be unkind and severe in a domestic setting. A fluorescent strip might be useful in a garden workshop, and I've also seen small fluorescent strips set behind mirrors in dressing rooms. But otherwise I would steer clear of fluorescent lights in a private home.

Outdoor Lighting

Good outdoor lighting can add real value to your home. A must is good lighting around the front door. In the past, most of us put up with a rather harsh big light over the front door, but now exterior lighting is subtler and more fashionable.

An automatic light that turns on when someone approaches – and off again when they depart – will conserve energy and provide security. You will be able to find your keys and open the door easily, and if a burglar comes on to your property the automatic light will deter him. There are a number of automatic sensor lights – they are called lights with PIR sensors – on the market now. A basic black rectangular sensor light costs £13, white globe-style £16 and a lantern light £26. There is even a solar security sensor light for sale at £45, where you don't need to wire any electrics. This light uses natural renewable solar energy.

You can have lights set into the ground, mounted on the wall or, my favourite, mounted on to trees and allowing a wash of light to spill down the trunk. Both up-lighters and down-lighters look quite beautiful, as well as serving the function of lighting up the front of your house to keep you safe and deter intruders.

Think of lighting paths and driveways, particularly in the country if you have no streetlights near your house and a long drive to get to your property. You need to invest in special waterproof lights outside, which start at about £40. Pay attention to cabling that needs to be to exterior standard and resilient. I would get a qualified electrician to wire up outside lights for safety reasons.

Designer Lighting

A lighting designer charges about £65 an hour, and I would recommend getting one round for a couple of hours. A good lighting designer will save you money in the long run. He or she will do a lighting electrical chart to make sure the electrician gets everything right. This certainly adds value, because lighting your house well will improve it hugely. Even small things can be bright ideas, like installing interior wardrobe lights, and an automatic light under the stairs that goes on and off when you open and close the door.

A designer might suggest you install a lighting control dimmer system – two of the best-known brands are Lutron and Crestron, although there are several other lower-priced versions on the market now. A Lutron system, or something similar, costs about £1,000 plus, while you can pick up less-expensive dimmer controls for around half that amount.

PHIL'S TRADE SECRET

I spotted a switched-on idea in the wardrobe of a London flat. The light not only went on automatically when you opened the wardrobe door, but it was set into the rail itself. This looked very clean and sharp, as well as making it easier to see the clothing. Wardrobe rails with integrated lights can be found from about £35.

New Eco-friendly Rules for Lights

The European Commission has ruled to stop the sale of certain environmentally inefficient lamps in four stages leading up to 2016. Retailers are asked to stop selling the lights by certain dates. The first deadline was

September 2009, when all frosted lamps (apart from anything labelled Energy Class A) were banned, along with clear incandescent lamps of 100 watts or above.

Other bans include clear incandescent lamps over 75 watts by September 2010, clear incandescent lamps over 60 watts by September 2011 and all incandescent lamps by September 2012. Tungsten halogen lamps that are typically found in ceiling-recessed down-lights will be phased out by 2016. The European Commission wants us to become more eco-friendly by purchasing energy-efficient lights that use less electricity.

However, complaints about the new energy-efficient lights include the fact that they take ages to warm up when first switched on and there is a problem with putting most of them on to a dimmer switch. When you can put them on a dimmer, the light tends to be greyer, rather than warmer. Also, some of the new fluorescent bulbs are said to emit a harsh white light and lighting designers are unhappy that some lights are bulky and not all that attractive.

The good news is lighting designers are already working closely with light manufacturers to improve the energy efficiency of many types of lights, such as tungsten halogens. They hope to produce an energy-compliant halogen tungsten lamp by 2016, for instance. I imagine there will be further advances in the technology behind energy-efficient lighting, producing light fittings that not only look good but also help us to be greener and cut our energy bills.

Building Regulations on Lighting

There are building control rules you have to adhere to when installing and working with lighting. In bathrooms, for example, you cannot use light fittings on leads, or run a supply from an adjoining room. This means you are forbidden from plugging a light into a socket in a bedroom and then bringing it into the bathroom. This is potentially highly dangerous: you could get a shock from the electricity supply, or even be badly injured or killed.

When putting lights into an area that is moist or wet, such as a bathroom, you need to choose those with a high ingress protection (IP) rating. They are waterproofed and keep moisture out. You will need different lights, some with higher IP ratings, in different areas (or zones) of a bathroom, depending on the amount of water likely to accumulate. Above a bath, for instance, a light fitting with a high IP rating of 68 or greater is necessary, while in the area around the bath, where some water might splash, the IP rating is a bit lower at 44.

Even in zones of the bathroom where there is no specific IP rating that needs to be adhered to – above the sink, for instance – it is still wise to use an enclosed fitting that keeps the water out, and to hire a skilled electrician to make sure your lights meet the current building regulation standards.

Cloakrooms with sinks but no baths or showers do not have to comply with zoning regulations. I would still consult a skilled electrician to make sure you know which lights to install correctly if you go down the DIY route. Better still, employ one to do the job for you. It is not worth taking a risk and harming yourself or others.

PHIL'S CONTACTS BOOK

- Contract Flooring Association, www.cfa.org.uk – trade organisation for carpet and hard-surface flooring contractors, manufacturers, distributors and consultants.
- National Wood Flooring Association, www.woodfloors.org – information on wood floors and tips on refinishing wooden flooring.
- The Lighting Association, www.lightingassociation.com – a website for professionals, but there is information on lighting your home and energy-efficient lighting solutions for the public too.

CHAPTER TEN

Gardens and Outside Space

Gardens are the new home extension, so make this valuable space work

The English have an out-and-out passion for gardens. No matter how much or little space you have, from a tiny city patio to a grander walled country garden, every square inch of coveted green land counts. Gardens are an antidote to the bustling, crazy life most of us lead these days. Being able to sit and enjoy a few minutes' peace breathing in some fresh air in a sunny spot, or even simply just being able to look out at a garden, can regenerate the body and soul. The desire to create little Arcadias in our own back yards is part of the consciousness of those living in the British Isles. Rough and wild or planned and orderly, our gardens, roof terraces and other outdoor nooks are all part of our identity.

The number of people who like to visit great gardens like Sissinghurst in Kent, Barnsdale Gardens in Leicestershire and Castle Howard in Yorkshire always staggers me. Over 3 million belong to the National Trust in order to see gardens that cost £11 million per annum to maintain. This illustrates how the opportunity to possess even a sliver of the great outdoors is crucial.

Recent research shows that Britons spend more than £5 billion per year on their gardens. Bling gardens are going out of favour, according to the latest statistics, which have recorded a drop in the sales of garden furniture and barbecues, while grow-your-own products and low-maintenance items for city gardens are in favour. People are more aware that a garden is a living thing and not just outdoor wallpaper. Less is more – with simpler designs – is the new garden mantra.

Having our own little piece of countryside just outside our door has always been important, and I believe it is becoming even more important as more of Britain is steadily being concreted over. Many people move on simply to upgrade to somewhere with a patio, roof terrace, garden, or to gain a bigger garden than they had before. Therefore, eking out any kind of green patch outside adds significant value to your life – and your home.

Estate agents say that a garden is one of the best value-adders to a property, swelling value by 20 per cent or more. The jury is out, however, on which outdoor features add the most worth. Some agents are fans of gardens big enough to hold a decent piece of lawn, while others favour space to park a car. There is great debate over whether swimming pools or tennis courts add any significant value to property. I think they can add value, but under certain circumstances, which I'll discuss in this chapter.

A balcony and terrace are both thought to add between 5 and 15 per cent to a property's price tag, and communal garden facilities at least 5 per cent.

When questioned for a recent survey, 60 per cent of buyers felt that some form of outside space was important, and 78 per cent that owning some kind of garden at the back of a property raised a home's value by 15 per cent or more. A quarter of those interviewed believed a garden upped the value by over 20 per cent. Some of the most prized features are: a spacious garden, easy maintenance, ready-made entertaining areas and mature shrubbery.

Studies like this are all very well, but in the end a lot comes down to what kind of property you own and where it is. In cities and large towns a balcony, terrace or patio augments your home's value, not to mention how much enjoyment you will get out of using it.

Improving a key asset like a garden or patio makes a lot of sense to me. In cramped urban areas, gardens are cherished. Even a small, hidden alcove or roof terrace where people can escape and enjoy a drink on a hot summer night can be a big selling point. In the country, people almost always expect a property to come with a garden. Don't forget that acquiring a generous outside space is why many people move to a rural area in the first place.

Keep in mind that the front garden is the first thing people see when they arrive at your home. Apparently, men, in particular, are put off by a garden that isn't well looked after. It is probably the thought of spending every weekend battling with out-of-control shrubbery, overgrown lawns and crumbling outbuildings that puts them off.

As a property finder, I know that potential buyers are rarely keen to go back for a second viewing to a place with a neglected garden – unless it goes with a house that is a bit of a ruin and they think they can make money upgrading both. Often, people love the house, but they don't love the garden – so they don't buy the house. Another no-no is concreting over a garden. It is depressing and will alienate most buyers.

Planning a Garden

To plan your garden or outdoor space, think carefully and realistically about what you want to do in it, and write a list in order of priority. Next, measure the area and sketch what would suit you, and, ideally one day, the next owner of the house. Show north, south, east and west on your sketch, because it could make a difference as to where you site seating areas or patches to grow vegetables. Watch when the sun comes round and note down which areas get the most light.

When buying a home, some people choose according to when the outdoor space gets the sun, whether in the morning or in the evening. A young professional couple might prefer a place where they can sit outside in the evenings after work, for instance. My favourite times are weekend mornings when I can enjoy breakfast in the garden, but I also love getting some sun in the evening. Which way your garden faces and where you locate seating areas could influence one segment of the market over another when you are looking for a buyer.

If you have a family, or are aiming to sell to a family, you need a bit of lawn where children can play. My big confession is that I have fake grass in our garden. It looks good, is easy to look after and the kids play happily on it. Our neighbour didn't even know our lawn wasn't the real thing and was surprised when she found out.

Artificial grass will not appeal to purists, naturally. If you are in an area where gardening is immensely popular, you might not be advised to opt for an imitation variety. But if you don't have time to look after a lawn – and it can take a lot of care to keep it green and lush – this could be a good alternative. Besides, it won't be difficult to take out the fake lawn and replace it with freshly laid rolls of turf, from about £2.20 a square metre, when it comes to selling your home.

Beware of installing a pond if your house is targeted at families when you sell. It will put off parents concerned that their children could fall into it and drown. If you insist on having a pond, you should at least fence it off or show someone how this could be carried out easily. Also, be careful of placing anything too precious or fiddly in the garden that might be harmed or destroyed by a lively brood. You will forever be scolding your own children while you live there and a potential buyer might be put off too, concerned he will also end up scolding his own offspring.

Artificial Lawns

Imitation lawns have become more sophisticated these days, with a fibre-filled layer adding depth and bounce so synthetic grass is easy to walk on. Fake lawns are fully porous, super tough, no-fade and should be maintenance-free for 20 years. Also, most come with a five-year guarantee.

As well as a substitute lawn surface, fake grass can be good on a patio, roof terrace or around a pool – it is softer than stone and won't crumble. Children and dogs can play on something that isn't the real McCoy without a proud gardener expressing concern about how they are destroying his lawn.

There are several different heights available and a softer variety with two to four different colours of green to make the pretend grass look more natural. It is fairly straightforward to fit an imitation lawn – there are good step-by-step guides with photographs on the Internet – and prices range from £10.95 to £25.95 a square metre.

Although you won't need to mow your lawn, you might need to brush the replica grass with a stiff broom every once in a while. The sand that is put down as a base with most artificial lawns tends to spread to the top and will need to be dusted off. In addition, you might have to hose it down with disinfectant if a dog leaves faeces.

I have built several flowerbeds around my faux lawn and installed some railway sleepers to form pathways and edging for the beds. Railway sleepers come treated with creosote (from £12.50 each), or untreated (£11.50), and you can buy softwood sleepers from Europe (£12) or hardwood African varieties (£12.50).

PHIL'S TOP TIP

Carefully identify the target market for your home when you plan a garden. There is no point putting family-friendly accoutrements in a garden that is likely to be used by older people or a singleton. If you live in an area that is predominantly populated by single people and young couples, smart decking, easy-to-maintain plants and a good table and set of chairs could be more tempting than a complex planting scheme that needs constant watering. Of course, you can add fun additions, such as a stylish treehouse, which children would adore and these are in vogue for adults now too.

Town Gardens

Gardening is one of our biggest hobbies, with 75 per cent of Britons doing some kind of work cultivating a parcel of land or watching over a plant in a pot on a balcony or terrace. I think that in most instances a good garden is not about size but what you do with the space you have got.

You need a mighty big garden before a child can climb a tree, kick a football or ride a bike. In urban areas not everyone will have the luxury of such vast outdoor spaces, so what should they do? I don't believe townie homeowners should get hung up about magnitude. You can do a lot with a little space. So, forget size for the moment, unless you are lucky enough to own a metropolitan property with a large garden. Creating or sprucing up a well-designed garden that is attractive and inviting is what you should aim for.

If you can afford a garden designer for an initial consultation, usually from about £75 to £150, then do pay for one. Some might even do it for free, so it is worth asking. Considering hiring a designer might sound like an indulgence, but getting some good advice at least from an expert is money well spent.

Levels of advice can vary. You could pay for anything from a basic plan to a more detailed map of which plants grow best where or a full-blown scheme involving planting, seating, mature trees and even a water feature. Garden designers can often get discounts on materials and plants, which might make them more cost-efficient to engage than originally thought. Even better, the plants they provide are generally of a higher quality than lower-priced ones sourced from garden superstores, so they are likely to survive longer.

Do not worry about how much you have to spend, but about what you will spend your budgeted sum on. In a town or city, most of the time we are trying to create another room but one that is out of doors. Increasingly, access through French or sliding glass doors carries the house on into the garden and vice versa. All that talk of 'flow' and balance certainly applies to a garden's connection with the property.

At the top end, the furnishings – furniture and accessories – in the garden are becoming ever more important. I saw one garden recently that had furniture specially made for it, along with shelves holding ornaments. If you decide to emulate this design idea, aim for hardwearing furniture that won't be hammered by the weather, and waterproof shelves, or find some way to shelter them from the rain at least.

Town gardens can be tight on space, so use optical tricks to make the area you have appear more generous than it is. One way to visually expand your garden is to have a round section of lawn in the centre, which will make it look wider. I have seen one garden that even opted for two circles: one in the centre with grass and a second one at the bottom of the garden that was laid to stone for a seating area. This was more interesting than a rectangular garden with no definition to it.

Even if you only have a minute patch outside your townhouse or flat, do try to make it look as inviting as possible. No one will be seduced by a muddy, tired-looking bit of ground more accustomed to broken bottles and weeds than pots with pretty flowers and clematis climbing up a trellis. A diminutive outdoor space has great added value for a flat or maisonette. A miniature balcony also can be a big plus if you can squeeze a small table, a couple of chairs and a few pots with plants on to it. After all, it is somewhere to sit out in the open, which is immensely valuable in towns and cities.

Mirrors give the illusion that a garden is bigger. Set at the back of a garden on a wall with trailing plants along the edges to soften it, a mirror can make your garden appear deeper. Another trick is a mirrored gate – a mirror with what looks like a wrought-iron gate in front of it. This costs around £265 and will make your garden feel lighter and larger.

The debate goes on about whether to use wooden decking, slate, stone or even bricks for seating areas and pathways in your garden. Decking was hugely popular a few years back. Then there was a swing back to natural stone and slate when people started to get fed up with decking. I think a lot depends on where you live – what are your neighbours doing? – and your budget. Stone and granite can cost more and labour costs can be higher with workmen having to lug round all those heavy stones. Yet stone can have a timeless quality about it, while decking might suit contemporary homes better.

English gardens can look depressing on grey, rainy days. I always favour something that is light in colour and tone. For instance, a dark grey, brick paved area could look a bit bleak in the winter. Also, if you have too large a swathe of wooden decking it can look somewhat austere unless you break it up visually with pots of colourful plants.

Decking and Paving

If you are into DIY, you can pick up reasonably priced timber decking to install yourself from about £250 to £500. There are simple kits available with all the fittings required to build your deck. Getting someone to supply and lay decking for you would cost in the region of £1,000 to £5,000. The higher end of the scale would get you one of the better hardwoods that have been well treated against the elements.

There is 'composite' decking on the market made up of polymer resins and reclaimed wood fibres. This artificial wood look-alike won't split, rot or warp and is lower maintenance because you won't have to oil or seal anything. This could save you roughly £50 to £300 a year, depending on whether you would seal the wood yourself or hire someone to do the job. Composites generally are about a third less to buy than quality hardwood.

Stylish designs could have a combination of stones and wooden decking. Using a variety of materials results in a less monotone look and breaks your garden up into different areas. I particularly liked one west London house that had dark hardwood floors in the living room that opened on to a garden with dark grey slate on the lower level and white limestone on the top level. Separating the top seating area from the rest of the garden by the use of the lighter stone made it appear like another room.

Some stone and slate can be slippery when wet, as can decking, so be careful what you choose and always keep it free of moss and lichen. Slate costs about £28 a square metre, limestone £17, granite £32, Travertine £25 and sandstone £16. A cheaper alternative is a portable wooden walkway, from £15, that comes in straight or curved sections. One advantage is it can be moved around to various sections of the garden.

Plants

Just like an interior designer can lift a room with rugs, soft furnishings and good lighting, you can inject a lot of colour and personality into your garden with the right plants. Ideally, you want a variety of seasonal plants so there is some colour in the garden all year round. Some plants, such as a crab apple tree, straddle more than one season, offering good colour value. The crab apple produces spring blossom, followed by decorative fruit in the autumn.

Easy tricks include planting a climber, such as the evergreen *Solanum Jasminoides Album* (a climbing potato!) or *Hydrangea Petiolaris* (great for north-facing walls), to cover a nasty-looking wall, and bulbs, which are remarkably cheap and dead easy to plant, to offer a burst of colour in the spring. Fast-spreading climbers include clematis, Virginia creeper and honeysuckle, which smells wonderful. A climbing rose will hide a concrete wall or other unsightly spot as well.

If you want to grow plants in a hurry, three suggestions are the self-seeding (which means you will get more every year) Welsh poppy that rapidly colonises beds and the area under trees, quick-growing golden and black bamboo, and the potentilla shrub with pretty yellow flowers.

Other quick and easy-on-the-pocket fixes are window boxes and hanging baskets with a selection of bright annuals and trailing plants. You can even pick up a selection of well-priced plants for window boxes and baskets that have been specially packaged together, saving you the bother of choosing each plant individually. 'Container gardens' – typically, small patios or terraces that only have room for plants in containers – can be as stylish and varied as a larger garden. Combine flowers with vegetables in the same pot, or in pots standing side by side.

PHIL'S TOP TIP

Get to know which plants grow well in the climate and soil in your area by taking a walk in the park. Some parks label the plants and you can copy down the names of those you like. Or talk to the staff, who will probably be more than happy to give you some guidance. Local garden shops are a good port of call too.

Top 10 trees for small gardens

1. Japanese maple
2. Mountain ash
3. Canary bird
4. Cockspur thorn
5. Golden hornet
6. Bay tree
7. Crab apple
8. Flowering cherry
9. Holly
10. Miniature fir tree

PHIL'S TOP TIP

It is worth keeping an eye out for container-garden road shows, when a gardening expert gives a class on what you can grow in containers and tubs on small patios or terraces. Usually these sessions are free, with tea and biscuits served afterwards. I noted some that were held recently by a top-end house builder keen to attract retirees downsizing from their family homes to an over-50s development.

You can glean ideas from public squares and shopping centres too, where planting is normally restricted to pots and other containers. The sorts of pots and containers used nowadays have broadened considerably – I have seen old wine boxes recycled as window boxes, for example.

Roof Terraces

Roof terraces are an ingenious way to snatch space from an unused area for not a lot of cash. They make sense and bring many advantages, including providing an instant garden for the owner of the property and an extra layer of insulation for the home below. Conservationists are keen on roof terraces, declaring that greenery and plants help keep the air clean and counter climate change. A roof terrace can simply be a place for you to sit and enjoy a drink, or it can be transformed into an imaginative mini-sky-allotment, with a beehive so you can collect your own honey or a home observatory for looking at the stars.

Make sure you have permission to develop a roof terrace above your flat or at the top of your house before you do any work. In a flat, you first need to check that you actually own the space. Even if you do find that you own a flat roof where you can put a terrace, you might still have to get consent from the freeholder.

Illegally developing a roof terrace could result in big problems when you come to sell, so it is worth carefully checking your lease. Ask a solicitor for advice if ownership is not clear. Or contact the Land Registry – the Government department that registers all land titles – at www.landregistry. gov.uk. For a £4 fee, you can download a title plan or register of a property.

A flat-owner has to get planning permission for a roof terrace, while the owner of a house might not have to seek consent under new permitted development rules. You shouldn't have too many problems getting the okay from planners unless the area proposed for your terrace overlooks the neighbour, the alterations will affect the external appearance of the building, or the area is unstable and not deemed a 'proper' roof space suitable for a terrace. There is more on what you are allowed to do in Chapter Fourteen.

Building regulations will need to be followed to make sure you reinforce and toughen up the roof so it can support the weight of the new roof terrace, along with the people, plants and furniture that will go on it. Pipes, gutters and channels will all need to be checked to ensure they are getting rid of rainwater that has gathered. Another key compliance is passing the safety rules about the sort of stairs you have to access the roof and fire exits.

PHIL'S TOP TIP

Local authorities are enthusiastic about encouraging us to become more eco-friendly. There can be nothing more eco-minded than introducing plants and greenery to a roof terrace. When making an application for permission, if it is required, do emphasise the greenery you will be adding and how it will benefit your area. For instance, you can outline which plants you hope to plant and how they might attract butterflies and bees and keep the air clean.

Plants for a Roof Terrace

You need to hunt for hardy, wind-resistant varieties. Up on top of the world there is a tendency for the wind to sweep through, so there is no point having wispy grasses or a fragile clematis. Good suggestions include small-leaved evergreen bamboos and tough plants from New Zealand, such as *Brachyglottis* 'Sunshine' and *Corokia x virgata*, agapanthus, lavender and heuchera, mallow (or lavatera), clover and small patio roses.

Tie plants that look like they are being blown away to railings and fencing (use ties or string of the same colour so they are disguised). Plants in plain terracotta pots need to be watered more often than those in glazed or synthetic pots, and just because it has rained do not assume you do not have to water containers and pots. Putting mulch in tubs and pots can be a good way to help retain water.

BIG HOUSE, TINY GARDEN

The house is spacious with well-proportioned rooms and the location is ideal. But there is a drawback, one typical of a large number of Victorian properties in the UK – the garden is the size of a postage stamp.

Sculptor Jacques Fougere has come up with creative ways to get round the dilemma of a Lilliputian-scale garden at his semi-detached house in Birmingham. He bought it a decade ago for just over £270,000 with his 43-year-old art historian wife Joelle and children Emilie and David, aged 16 and 18.

He has turned the place 'inside out', opening the garden up by installing a floor-to-ceiling glass wall at the end of the kitchen, light stone flooring running from the house outdoors and massive 'architectural' tropical plants in oversized pots both inside and out.

'The house was in a bit of a state when we bought it,' says Jacques, 45. 'But it was on at an affordable price and the rooms were really big for an urban terrace, so we went for it.' His only regret was the tiny garden (about 25- by 20-feet/7.6- by 6.1-metres), not what you would hope for when you buy a large family home of nearly 3,500 square feet (325 square metres).

'I really wanted to get the feeling of more outside space and to bring that feeling of being in the open air inside.'

At least the infrastructure of the house is sound, which saved the Fougeres from having to do major works other than sorting out some of the wiring and re-plumbing. The family moved out for eight months and rented nearby, paying about £150,000 to reconfigure the house, which now has a reception room and a sky-lit family room leading on to the new open-plan kitchen/dining room on the ground floor.

A double reception room covers the first storey with a bathroom off the half landing, while two generous-sized bedrooms and a bathroom are on the second floor. Two more bedrooms and a shower room fashioned from an earlier loft conversion sit at the top.

Trying to manoeuvre the glass wall into the kitchen, which now slides open on to the garden, took a great deal of effort. Jacques remembers having to hire a crane that blocked up the road while it lifted the glass over the top of the house. 'The crane suckered on to the glass and it was quite crazy watching these huge panes come down. It was a very exciting morning.'

The glass wall wasn't cheap (just over £12,000, with the crane hire another £1,000), but as the focus for the whole garden-meets-house design, it is money well spent. Admitting extra light into what was a dark and depressing space, it also blends the exterior with the interior in a subtle way. Another clever way to extend the impression of having a good deal of outdoor space is the creation of a grass roof on top of the kitchen extension that is covered in sedum, a slow-growing flowering alpine plant.

'It looks better than the black tarmac that was there before,' points out Jacques, 'and we get lovely pink and white flowers poking up through the green. You can see the roof from downstairs and it is wonderfully calming. With grass on the roof and stone in the garden, this really is an upside-down house.'

The only problem is the birds that keep turning up to peck at the sedum, annoying Jacques, who has become fond of his eco-friendly roof. He admits he shoos the birdlife away with a water gun, as well as protecting the sedum with netting. Despite this obstacle, he believes everyone should have a grass roof if they can. 'It is surprisingly inexpensive (around £1,000), environmentally friendly, easy to maintain and makes an urban house feel calmer.'

The Fougeres love their tropical-look garden too. Having the gargantuan ferns, bananas, yuccas and palms in huge pots running along both sides of the garden and into the house makes the titchy garden look bigger. A trick of the eye, your vision is drawn upwards and out to the sides of the garden, making the garden appear at least twice as large as it is.

'We do have to wrap up the plants when it becomes colder, but even that can look beautiful. We swathe the plants in white material to keep out the chilly air and then run tiny strings of white lights round the pots. It looks quite misty and eerie, which we love,' adds Jacques.

The other big plus, of course, is the massive glass sliding door that separates the open-plan kitchen/dining room from the garden. Because of the airy contemporary design and transparency of the glass, the garden appears to be part of this larger room and vice-versa.

'This is a great way to open up both your house and garden,' says Jacques. 'And even when it is cold outside, you feel like you could be in California with the glass wall.'

The house is valued at nearly £600,000 today and a local agent believes the refurbishment and inside—outside garden would certainly help the house sell. 'It is hard to definitely say how much the new garden design adds to the house's worth, but I reckon it is in the region of £30,000.'

PHIL'S TRADE SECRET

A unified level of flooring in a living room that extends out into a garden makes the garden appear as a seamless extension of the indoor space. If you keep the same material or at least use similar colours as you make the transition from the inside to outside, the effect is like having one big room. This can be particularly enticing in the summer when you slide open a big glass door and enjoy indoor–outdoor living.

Country Gardens

Most wannabe purchasers hunting for a farmhouse in the country would expect a decent-sized garden to come with the property. Most would want a generous lawn, flowerbeds, shrubbery, trees and a vegetable patch. At the very least, a rural home should offer a bit more space than a town garden to justify moving out of town into the countryside. And in these times, when people are keen to grow their own produce for health reasons or to save a bit of cash, having access to their very own vegetable patch is moving higher up the wish list.

Even those with green fingers might baulk at a massive country garden that is complicated to tend. Ease of maintenance is good, so consider putting in an irrigation system if starting from scratch. Or at least carry out the research to supply information on how it could be done and what it would cost. Raised beds are another good idea – they are easy to access and the garden tends to run less wild if you have them edged with wood or barley-corns (Victorian stone tiles).

Is your garden level? Some gardens spread over one or more tiers, which can look attractive but might put people off when it comes to mowing, edging and climbing up and down. I think people like level gardens, largely for ease of maintenance, particularly if they are laid to lawn.

Just like houses, spend money on the structure of the garden if you can. Buying lots of expensive plants might add less value than working out where a good big feature tree can go, along with a patio and pathways.

Lighting should be part of this design too, from the simple access lights used at night to get around and for security, through to more detailed designer lighting. Lighting walkways can be fun and sensible and up-lighters on trees can look tremendous, washing light over their trunks. I would recommend using a good electrician that knows about safety stand-ards for exterior lighting, keeping water out of specially sealed lights. (See Chapter Nine for more on lighting.)

Pools

Taking the plunge and installing a swimming pool might appeal to the next Olympic champion, but will it add value to your home? The debate over whether a pool will enhance your home and garden or detract from it is not a new one, but getting it right is crucial.

In a poll conducted with 60 country estate agents and house finders, 35 per cent believed a pool, particularly one in bad repair or in the wrong loca-tion in relation to the house, adds no value whatsoever; while an equal number (35 per cent) thought a pool made from good materials and in a good position could help sell a property and boost the price.

In the indoor versus outdoor debate, 60 per cent of those questioned favoured an indoor pool over one out of doors, as long as it doesn't emit the scent of chlorine and fits in with the house design. A further 10 per cent think you might be better off doing nothing, allowing the next owner to construct his own pool. This certainly could save money, as both building a pool and running it – heating, chemicals and cleaning – can be pricey. Outdoor pools can range from £20,000–30,000 up to £100,000 for a massive pool complex, while the finest indoor pool with his and hers changing rooms and trendy barbecue area could cost up to £2 million. Expect a well-designed, high-end outdoor pool to be as much as £100,000, with average running costs at £600 to £1,000 a year (estimate £10 a day for outdoor and £15 a day for indoor pools).

If done well, you will probably get your money back, but I'm not convinced a pool adds a huge amount of value. It should be connected to or near the house – no one wants to venture far at six o'clock in the morning in the cold. You generally do not need planning permission for a pool, unless your property is listed. A covered pool falls within the same restrictions as outbuildings, and a pool cannot take up more than half the area of the garden.

With safety for children and pets a big issue, automatic covers and folding or sliding doors that can be locked when not in use should reassure future buyers.

An outdoor pool should be positioned at the back of the house, but not too far afield so it is easy to access, perhaps in a walled area or surrounded by plants. Modern infinity pools with fabulous views are equally appealing, but do not come cheap. A new high-end trend is to regard a pool as another entertaining space – an area where people can socialise, swim and pamper themselves in the sauna or steam room.

Most important is to determine how a pool will suit its users. Some want to swim lengths and have space to do tumble turns, while children like to jump in and even dive.

If you want to install a pool, make it look as good as you can afford so it becomes a feature of the property. Getting an architect in at the early stages to drive the design could make all the difference. Look at the ergonomics. Try to avoid the natural line of entry into the house from the pool running through the front door.

Agents know that if children accompany their parents on a viewing of a house with a pool, they will try to talk their parents into buying it. So, without going over the top, a few well-placed tasteful pool toys could be a good idea to get them on side.

PHIL'S TOP TIPS

- Keep a pool away from trees, or you will spend your life cleaning it.
- A pool must be proportionate with the value of the house – do not overcapitalise.
- The newest trend is for 'party pool spaces' in blood-red and black colours, as opposed to traditional blues.

Tennis Courts

If asked to choose whether a pool or tennis court adds more value, most estate agents would opt for a tennis court. With so many safety issues linked to pools it can be difficult to sell a house with a pool to some people, while a tennis court might be less controversial.

I think you should put in whichever you prefer and will use, while thinking of ways to make a sporting fixture attractive to the next owner of your home. A tennis court shouldn't be right next to a house, otherwise the noise could be off-putting. Equally, just like a pool, a tennis court should not be in direct vision as not everyone will find it aesthetically pleasing. You need a fair bit of land to make a tennis court fit in with the house – anything less than an acre and a half means the court will take over the garden.

A tennis court costs about £15,000 to £30,000 to build, depending on location, earthworks, type of surface, fencing and lighting. Maintenance costs can mount up with pressure cleaning, binder coating to prolong the court's life, colour coating, lining and resurfacing, which need to take place about every 10 years. Grass is okay if you can look after it, but many people opt for an all-weather porous surface that drains easily.

You should talk to your local planning authority because rules on fence heights, change of land use (you cannot put a tennis court on agricultural land, for instance), surfaces, drainage and lighting vary widely depending on the council.

PHIL'S TRADE SECRET

I have friends who picked up a nice house for a good price. The problem was about 80 per cent of the garden was covered by a tennis court. My friends got the house for a steal, saving over £100,000 off the half-million price tag because of this flaw. Do they play tennis? Well, no, but they covered over the court and replaced it with a garden. This is a good example of someone adding value by removing a perceived blemish, like an unwanted tennis court.

Ponds and Water Features

There are a huge number of water features that can be added to any sort of outside space from a tiny deck right through to the grounds of an imposing country mansion.

Ponds and water features add interest, give an aura of calm, and attract frogs, toads and other water life, which is fun for children and great for the environment. The sound of running water from ponds and water features can also diminish traffic noise. Just as with pools, there are safety concerns with ponds, and water features with lights need to be installed by a professional who knows what he is doing. Or, if you are keen on DIY, you need to be careful – if in doubt, get some help.

Ponds and water features can cost as little as £16 for a small 60-centimetre preformed pond, while a smart deck pond costs £120, water flowing into a wooden barrel is £75 and a typical wall fountain from around £120 to £270.

You can spend many thousands on a state-of-the-art cascade flowing into a Japanese-style pond that will operate using similar technology to a swimming pool. Once you are into this upper-scale league, it is recommended you get a garden designer who will work with a water specialist to create your water feature as part of an overall plan.

As long as your water feature is easy maintenance and as safe as you can make it, it should add value to your home. A number of town and city gardens are having water features installed now. To keep your neighbours on side, remember to turn the water feature off at night so they aren't driven mad by the noise. Even better, hook it up to an automatic timer so you don't have to remember to switch it off.

Sheds, Summerhouses and Other Outbuildings

Sheds and summerhouses used to be somewhere to hang your tools, put out your seedlings or sit with a cuppa. Although some remain fairly humble edifices, others are now becoming glamorous hideaways with all the mod cons.

Research shows that the average man spends three and a half years of his life in his shed. In days gone by, he was probably escaping from his missus and the kiddies while fixing equipment or having a sneaky puff on his pipe. These days, however, shed cred is being embraced by many. A large selection of garden sheds, summerhouses and log cabins is available now and being used as places to relax, entertain, store items, enjoy hobbies and work from home. These are now groovy spaces with televisions, fridges, heating and smart window boxes.

A simple store shed costs about £135 and a tongue and groove apex shed £180, while a bike shed – a good idea to add value as more people are cycling now – costs £175. A reasonable summerhouse starts at just over £300 and an Alpine-style home office with electricity and a power supply is about £3,000.

Outbuildings can add value, as long as they are not desperately rickety and cold. If you can't afford to buy a summerhouse or home office or build one yourself, try to make the best of what you already have. A good clean, reinforcing floors, painting the planks a pretty colour (blue and white can look charming) and growing some roses on a trellis near the door of an old shed or garden building all turn a dreary space into something more inviting.

If you are more serious about using a garden room as a work or entertaining space, you might want to employ a builder to weatherproof the building and install heating, power and electricity.

Another positive notion for a house with small or a limited number of bedrooms is to put a bedroom and maybe even a bathroom into an outbuilding. This could be ideal for houseguests, a nanny, a granny or a teenager. The cost is estimated at about £7,000 to £30,000, depending on the grandeur of your plans and how much of the work you do yourself.

PHIL'S CONTACTS BOOK

- The Association of Professional Landscapers, www.landscaper.org.uk – find a professional garden landscaper in your area.
- The Leisure and Outdoor Furniture Association, www.lofa.com – trade association representing over 80 per cent of the UK's garden furniture manufacturers and suppliers.
- Royal Horticultural Society, www.rhs.org.uk.

CHAPTER ELEVEN

Getting Emotional

Ignore the rational side of your brain and stir
up feelings for your home

You can add value to a home in a practical sense, but emotions also play a huge part, both in how you enjoy living in the property now and in how you reel in prospective buyers when it's time to sell. You would think that I, as a pretty logical English bloke, would steer away from the emotional side of things, but in my experience of showing thousands of people around homes I know that feelings almost always kick in and are often powerful.

The secret is to add passion without being gimmicky. These days, most people see through over-the-top attempts to grab someone's heart as they walk into a property. If you don't feel passionate about your home, then it is unlikely anyone else will. Manufacturing emotion might work in some instances, but you are better advised to tap into what you really care about in your home, and allow that to seep through to a visitor or prospective buyer.

The way to get emotional about a house is to inject the right sort of vibe into its rooms. Creating an ambience that says comfort, serenity and friend-liness is your aim. There is nothing worse than a house – note I didn't say 'home', as the word 'home' conveys something special – that is cold, dreary and just doesn't feel right.

However, if you are not totally in love with your home, then I think it best to step aside and let an estate agent show people around. Let him talk up the positives about your property and point out its key features. If you are not that emotional about it, walk away and let the agent do his job.

What Makes a House a Home

Turning a house into a home isn't as difficult or abstract as it might sound. There are simple ways to tap into the emotions of people coming to your house for the first time. For instance, a friend of mine who is a talented designer and specialises in hand-painting walls once stayed for over a year in a fine period house in the south of England for free. The catch? She was expected to totally redecorate the house for no money so the owner could sell it at a higher price.

She admitted to me that the house was in dreadful condition and felt the owner would be better off spending some money sorting out the damp and replacing rotting window sills. Yet the newly decorated house created such a brilliant atmosphere that its flaws went unnoticed and it sold quickly for more than the asking price.

My advice would always be to do the opposite and spend money on the infrastructure if you can. I would put my cash into coming up with a layout that makes the best use of the space, long-lasting wooden flooring and well-conceived lighting, for example. I think that in most cases it can be a waste of money forking out for twirls and twiddles while the roof is caving in and mould conceals the walls.

Yet sometimes there isn't the time or money to totally revamp a house, so I suggest that you sort out the worst of the cracks and mend what you can at the level you can afford. After your quick renovation, a lick of paint and a few well-chosen pieces of furniture might be your best bet under the circumstances.

As most of us are staying longer in our homes, I think injecting some of your own personality into your residence is a fine idea. It lifts it out of the ordinary, and as long as it isn't too off-putting to potential purchasers, it can remain memorable for the right reasons. With nearly everything else off-white ('landlord beige,' the lettings agents call it), at least your home will stand out if there a few interesting features that mean something to you.

Neutral needn't mean dull and bland either – just don't be too conspicuous and alarming with your taste, so the property appeals to as many people as possible.

However wedded people are to taking a reasoned approach to buying property, tactile fabrics, a carefully selected colour scheme and the odd splash of fun can move even the most dispassionate. Despite arriving armed with a checklist, a buyer will let his heart rule his head at some point at least during his search for a property. I recall escorting one young pregnant woman with a toddler in tow round several houses. Everywhere we went the child screamed the place down. The reason she had engaged my services as a house finder in the first place was because house-hunting with the child was so traumatic. Eventually, we went into a house that exuded an aura of calm and the child didn't scream. The woman was so happy she bought the house.

This might be a rather extreme example of how emotions can influence a purchase, but the buyer was convinced this peaceful-feeling property was the right one for her and her family. We often have a sixth sense about what feels good, a sense that is quite separate from the common sense we normally employ.

Put Yourself in a Buyer's Place

Take a young couple looking to climb up the property ladder, for instance. Newly married, with one of them starting a new job and the other expecting a pay rise and maybe even a baby one day, it is potentially a very exciting time. They want to move to a bigger house in a better area and imagine themselves living a better life.

When a couple like this comes to take a look around your home, do not forget there is a lot going on in the background. There are hopes and expectations and a pledge to make things go well from this point forward. Sometimes people think moving to a new place will wipe the slate clean and they can reinvent themselves in their fresh place of residence. As a seller, you can tap into this. If the couple spot a baby's room with a cot, they can imagine living in the property themselves. The trick is to get someone to believe they can live in your home happily ever after.

When selling, carefully think about the target market for your home. What type of person is likely to buy it? At what stage will he or she be in life? Try to emphasise the features that are most likely to appeal to them. For instance, a great play area for children if you are selling a family home makes sense. Adding one special touch, like a state-of-the-art treehouse or fun playhouse, could help clinch the deal. I have seen prospective buyers won over by the smallest things, like a snug with a comfy velvet sofa and good music system that one downsizing couple fell for. They could already envision themselves sitting there and listening to Bach and Beethoven, they told me.

Between getting out of a car and walking to your house, a visitor can be put off by an uninviting place. Once inside, these negative emotions can take over so your poor home never stands a chance. Sprucing up the front of the house and the access to it is part of this imagined new life. Make sure the façade and immediate surroundings come up to scratch, rather than dent the perceived fantasy.

It is a good idea to give each area or room a positive focus. If you have just one great feature or item, people will remember that room – and, therefore, your property. It could be anything from an ingenious laundry chute in a utility room and clever storage in the hall cupboard, to a fantastic barbecue in a corner of the garden, a well-ordered study in the attic or a built-in iPod dock on the living-

room wall. Remember that if someone is viewing six or even more properties a day, they tend to get muddled up. You want yours to be the one that stands out with subtle, but carefully conceived, touches.

Bear in mind you are not just selling a house, but a lifestyle. Even if people are unlikely to live the life you are unveiling, they might like to think they could. If there is a beautiful polished piano in the sitting room, someone who spots it might think, 'I could learn to play that piano if I lived here and who knows, maybe I could be a concert pianist.'

A wannabe parent could feel equally aspirational in a brightly lit family room with a little table and chairs set out for young children. 'I could have children one day and I can see them painting pictures or playing happily with toys on the floor here.'

When filming *Location, Location, Location,* I go into a huge number of houses and am aware of how books lined up alluringly on bookshelves convey intelligence and an appreciation of culture. I have found that nearly every house I go into won't be without a Jamie Oliver cookbook or a copy of Harry Potter. Good cookbooks in kitchens say that this family eats real food and therefore is healthy and successful. People like to visualise themselves doing the same.

Keep in mind that most people do not embrace change and are uneasy with transitions. Anything you can do to turn a potentially frightening move into an opportunity will encourage and comfort them. Buying a home is not just about handing over some money and taking the keys. It goes much deeper and conjures up childhood recollections.

Tapping into those memories of happy times in what appears to be a happy place to live will get a visit from a friend or a viewing from a buyer off to a good start. There have been reports that in less-secure times when there is a dip in the economy and people feel anxious, they revisit holiday haunts and look for property. The idea of buying at a seaside resort, for instance, where you built sandcastles and ate ice cream cornets as a child is soothing and takes you back to safer and happier days.

PHIL'S TOP TIP

Try to make it easy for people to conceive of living in your home. Open up what people can do with your house. For instance, rather than just state on the floor plan that a room can be a bedroom/ study, visually display it. Neatly place a bed and bedside table alongside a desk, chair and bookshelves to demonstrate the fact. Show people what is achievable even if you aren't using a room for both functions yourself.

Set the Scene

When transforming a house into a home, use all five senses.

Smell

Aromas can be very evocative, triggering recollections and planting hopes for the future. Do take the rubbish out every day to lose that refuse pong and be careful of pets and their smells. If you have a cat, clean out its litter tray frequently. You might want to banish the tray altogether to a discreet corner or move it outside when people come round.

People love the smell of cooking. Although it sounds corny, it does take them back to their past when someone else prepared delicious food for them, and can also lead them to believe they will entertain and enjoy happy food moments with their loved ones once they unpack the china.

Whatever you do, don't go overboard. Too many scented candles can be funereal and visitors could end up having coughing fits. I'm not enamoured of scented candles. They can smack of desperation. Maybe a wittier idea to get the point across is to buy a fabulous big candle and don't light it. If you insist on having a scented candle, only light it in the evening, which is when you would normally have one burning.

Baking bread every time someone appears can appear a bit gimmicky. Instead, do whatever feels natural, rather than staging what you reckon should happen. A bubbling pot of homemade soup, if this is the sort of household where homemade soup is the norm, is good. As is a sense of olfactory promise: a menu for the week stuck on to the fridge with a magnet, for instance.

Other evocative smells that would naturally be inhaled in a kitchen include home baking, vanilla (a few drops in a low oven can give off a lovely fragrance) and coffee. A good and affordable tip is to rub some essential oil over the top of a radiator with a cloth. It will evaporate slowly into the room, emitting a low-key scent. Avoid cheap plug-in fresheners – they can be sickly sometimes – and anything too pungent.

I believe fresh and simple aromas are best. Nothing can beat freshly laundered towels, polished wood, a small vase of sweet peas or fresh air from an open window. Before you splash round expensive bottled room fragrances, a good natural – and free – airing of a room is preferable.

This might sound obvious, but avoid whipping up overpowering dishes just before someone comes to see your house. The scent of curry or a fry-up can linger and repel visitors. A good extractor fan can help, but enjoying these culinary treats at another time might be the best course of action.

Sight

Getting rid of clutter and giving your house 'a deep clean' (a major spring clean) is the best guidance I can offer. No matter how many times this counsel is offered, however, a number of people still cling to displaying their space-grabbing collection of jugs or presume everyone else will love their dismantled Harley Davidson leaving grease marks on the living-room floor.

It is good for people to see you lead an interesting life, but within reason. If you insist on putting your belongings on show, at least cut down the number; and there is a place for repairing your beloved bike – and it isn't in the main reception room of your house. It is rare to find fellow china-collecting Harley Davidson *aficionados*, so by not clearing up some of the detritus from your hobbies you are cutting down the number of people who will warm to your property. By all means, you can display some fruits of your labour – a shiny and clean bike standing in the corner of a modern living room could provide a great talking point – but anything too messy or discouraging can put people off.

One of my most memorable viewings was when I checked out a house that was owned by a retired milkman in Hertfordshire. He had taken to building replicas of landmark buildings out of matchsticks now that he had more time on his hands. The entire living room – a key space for a family – was filled with a replica of Big Ben. Even worse, the owner had taken a chunk out of the ceiling for the top of Big Ben's tower to poke through as he had miscalculated the height. The sight of this edifice and the damage it had caused to the ceiling was enough to make the young family I was showing the property turn and run.

As dull as it might sound, all most people really want to see is a clean, orderly, bright and friendly home. I would spend money on cleaning the carpets, windows, walls, appliances and sinks and baths. Also, jet spray your terrace, patio, pavements and pathways. If you can afford it, consider getting in professional cleaners, which can make a big difference. Costs vary depending on the state of your home and how big it is, but expect to pay from about £75.

I disagree with some of the experts who tell sellers to strip away all personal effects and turn their home into what is essentially a bland and colourless showroom. It is terrific to see paintings, photographs of weddings, birthdays and family events, as well as the odd knick-knack around the place. Just don't have too many. Less is more and just like when you pack a suitcase, after you put out several things, take one or two items back and store them.

If you are clever, you can display the odd photo that is linked to the house: the family gathered on the lawn enjoying a barbecue or special meal, the children opening their presents at Christmas in the living room next to the tree, or snapshots of friends at a party in the house. This can show how your home opens up when you entertain and how practical and adaptable the spaces can be. It also says this is a place where happy occasions are celebrated with happy people. Depending on what your home is like, a little element of fun can add value. The odd interesting gizmo or bright piece of furniture suggests passion, joy and zeal in how you live – and how others might want to live.

An open-plan kitchen/living room I once saw in a house in Sussex had a table football game, a sofa made from the wood of an old boat the owner found in his garden and a jolly-looking blackboard covering the whole side of a kitchen unit where the family could leave messages for one another. The pièce de resistance, however, was a climbing wall at one end of this large room. 'What a great place and what an interesting family,' instantly came into your head, and I'm sure many people secretly wanted to move in and adopt this quite groovy lifestyle.

Maintaining Your Home

One thing people do not want to see is a home that isn't well maintained. Ongoing upkeep is more crucial than ever, with buyers reluctant to sign up for an untended property that will prove costly to patch up. Properties that have fallen into disrepair might be sellable in boom years, but in cash-strapped times far fewer buyers want to take on a huge project. They prefer something that's been well cared for and isn't going to throw up unpleasant financial surprises. The problem is what starts out as a £50 job can escalate into a £5,000 repair if left unattended. Keeping on top of a property and doing little jobs as they become necessary is the best advice I can offer. It's like looking after your health. Prevention is always better than cure. Regular maintenance of your home is less intrusive and expensive than letting it decay and having to fix it from the bottom up again.

As a trained building surveyor, I like to get my hands dirty checking and repairing my home. In the autumn – a good time to carry out work before winter rains and winds arrive – I clean out gutters, make sure drain holes are clear and airbricks clean. Chimneys get a once-over as well to ensure air is circulating around.

Also, make sure your roof is water-tight, re-fix slipped or missing tiles and remove vegetation growing in masonry. Leaving these items un-repaired will result in frost damage and allow damp to penetrate. It is far cheaper maintaining your house regularly than leaving it for years and having to pay for more serious work.

Good maintenance is important even if you aren't planning to sell. Looking after the place where you live has never been more vital.

PHIL'S TOP TIPS

- Clear plants, leaves and silt from gutters, hopper-heads, flat roofs and drainage channels.
- Check for blocked down-pipes: during heavy rain look to see if water is coming from leaky joints and in dry weather look for stained brickwork.
- Keep gullies and drains at ground level clean and clear of debris, such as leaves, twigs, and even balls and toys.
- Remove potentially damaging vegetation from behind down-pipes by cutting back or removing plants altogether.
- Use a hand mirror to look behind rainwater pipes where splits and cracks in old cast iron and aluminium often occur and are not easily noticed.
- Fit bird or leaf guards to the tops of soil pipes and rainwater outlets to prevent blockage.
- Have gutters re-fixed if they are sloping the wrong way or discharging water on to walls.
- If sections of guttering or pipe work are beyond repair, make sure replacements are made of the same material as the originals. On older listed houses, this is sometimes lead, but more typically, cast iron.
- Regularly paint cast iron to prevent rust and to keep your property looking smart.
- Don't undertake routine maintenance work at high levels unless you are accompanied and have suitable equipment – if in doubt, hire a professional.

Sound

Discordant sounds are likely to put people off when they visit your home. Some will be out of your control, such as a train rumbling past at regular intervals, vibrations from a Tube line below your flat or aeroplanes flying overhead. You can diminish these sounds to a degree with double-glazed windows or by closing heavy drapes or shutters.

Another tip is to play gentle music to mask some of the noise. Be warned, however, that anyone savvy will wonder if you are playing music because there is a problem. As a seasoned house finder, the first thing I do is turn up mood lighting and turn off music in a house that might be hiding difficulties. I want to know about them in order to warn my client. This doesn't necessarily mean someone won't buy your house, but they might want a price reduction.

A better method is to come up with solutions to noise problems. If you are living in a flat and hear constant footsteps above you, you can talk to your upstairs neighbour and the freeholder about trying to diminish the noise. Perhaps they can lay down carpet or insulate in some other way.

If trains thunder by the bottom of your garden, maybe it is better to come clean and admit it. But point out they only run four times a day, have two small carriages and the occasional glide past can be quite charming in its way. Emphasising any positives, while still being honest, is better than pretending the problem doesn't exist. Whatever you do, don't lie. Under new laws, you could be fined if you don't supply accurate information if a buyer asks you a question.

When an agent conducts a viewing, soft music can be played in the background, but don't make this too obvious. It can be embarrassing if people feel you are turning your home into a stage set rather than just letting it remain what it is – your home.

Touch

Touch is an understated sense and one not many people think of when adding romance and passion to a house. Using a variety of textures – a favourite is linen mixed with silk in curtains – can make something appear more interesting and homely than it is. Cushions are obvious candidates –

there is nothing more sensuous than running your hand over a velvet or fluffy cushion as you walk past.

Other touch sensations include a soft carpet – you might even want to encourage people to take off their shoes to feel it, if appropriate – and a velvet or soft leather sofa. Even if you don't actually touch it, you know it will feel nice. A nicely polished piece of wood might invite people to stroke it as well.

Taste

Without anyone actually putting anything in his or her mouth, you can still put across the idea of taste. Setting out a bowl of fresh fruit on the table is a good start and a box of luscious-looking chocolates or a plate of figs and cookies is another way to get the taste buds going. In North America, perky saleswomen often bake chocolate chip cookies in the kitchen and offer them to visitors. It can be quite a treat to eat a freshly basked cookie while looking round a property, but I wouldn't suggest you try this in your home unless it comes naturally to you and is appropriate.

Taste comes into play in the garden too, where grapes, apples and plums hanging tantalisingly off boughs can bring back childhood memories of picking and eating fresh produce. Equally, a kitchen garden growing vegetables, such as tomatoes, beans and courgettes, can make the juices flow.

The other definition of taste comes into play as well. Passions can be aroused for a property if you display a good modicum of taste in decoration and style. It is hard to tell someone how to accrue a sense of élan, but using the 'less is more' maxim and sticking to the best quality you can possibly afford should help your home appear tasteful.

CASE STUDY

THE POWER OF EMOTION OVER REASON

Gina Flynn and her husband Peter, a 60-year-old engineer, ended up buying a thatched cottage when it wasn't even on their wish-list.

'We did our research and came up with a sensible checklist of what we wanted — and what we didn't. One thing that was near the top of the "don't want" list was a thatched cottage. Knowing we would have to maintain and renew the thatch, which can be costly, ruled it out. Also, such a fairytale home might suit some, but we were after a more robust farmhouse or barn conversion,' explains Gina, a 58-year-old dental assistant.

Following a tour around various properties in Suffolk that did fit the bill, Gina was taken to a thatched cottage in a small village just outside Ipswich at the end of the day. The agent knew it wasn't what the couple wanted, but thought it might be interesting to get Gina's reaction anyhow. She was tired and wasn't pleased with the unwanted diversion.

'But I fell totally in love with it the second we came up the path,' Gina confesses. 'There were beautiful old roses growing up the front of the house and the second I came in the door I knew I wanted the cottage.'

Gina, who would describe herself as a rational person, says she can't quite explain what overtook her when she entered the property. Yet breaking it down she thinks it was because a lovely family lived there and everything felt right.

'There was a terrific ambience with a young woman making an apple crumble in a light blue and white tiled kitchen with wooden units. Her little girl was standing on a chair next to her playing with some of the topping and trying to help her mum cook. I remember doing exactly the same when I was a child.'

Other sensations that came to Gina were the smell of leather from the furniture in the living room, the glow of an open fire, birdsong and the sound of running water coming from a small stream in the garden, and the smell of cinnamon from the crumble that had been popped into the Aga.

'I just thought a really nice family lives here and everything feels simple and friendly, but not too overdone. Up until then, we had seen some good houses, but most were quite clinical and cold.'

So seduced was Gina by the cottage, she didn't really think about their earlier concerns with thatch at all and offered the asking price on the spot. 'I'm ashamed to say I went ahead without even consulting Peter, who was sceptical at first. But when he came to look at the cottage I could see it had won him over too.'

Gina and Peter paid £525,000 for the cottage and intended to use it as a weekend getaway. But after a year, they have sold their flat in London and moved into the thatched cottage fulltime.

'It is hard to define, but everything just felt good and I could imagine enjoying life there with Peter. Our children, who are grown-up and aged 30 and 26, love coming here too. It is so serene and relaxing.'

Gina says her family teases her – they call her moment of madness her 'crumble folly'. 'I guess it did come down to seeing that crumble being made by such a nice lady and her sweet little girl, but that was only part of the equation really. The cottage was light and bright, clean and well looked after. I just had a sense that we would settle in okay and not be stuck with tons of work.'

The rational might have been ignored temporarily, but Gina's instincts were right. The Flynns have no plans to leave their cottage in a hurry and intend to retire there permanently.

PHIL'S CONTACTS BOOK

- www.maintainyourbuilding.org.uk for advice, top tips and useful dos and don'ts on maintenance from the Society for the Protection of Ancient Buildings (SPAB).

CHAPTER TWELVE

Ideas from the Professionals

Learn from the big boys

Property developers, architects and designers add value to homes all the time by experimenting with new features, techniques and ideas. It might sound like a bit of a cheek, but borrowing some of their ideas and interpreting them in your own property can be a great way of spreading some added value around.

One clever ruse they like to employ is to put in one or two big features that attract attention and give a home the wow factor. Instead of worrying about getting absolutely everything right – unless they are at the very top of the market where they can afford to splurge on everything – this is a realistic way of making a property top a potential buyer's list without breaking the bank.

House builders realise it may not be cost-effective to make all parts of a house top spec because, like home owners, they want to make as big a profit as possible when it is time to sell. So, learn from the professionals and focus on good ideas in just a few zones in your house. The logic is that if the eye is caught by one really great idea in a room or area, then the rest doesn't matter quite so much. The trick is learning where and when to spend your money.

Spend On the Infrastructure

If you are going to spend money anywhere, spend it on the infrastructure. I know I keep saying this, but I don't think there is any point fiddling about with murals on the walls and swish taps if you haven't made the house solid, safe and structurally sound first. I know this isn't possible in every case – if you are hard-pressed for cash or in a hurry to sell your home, for example – but people aren't stupid and will notice when the basics aren't right. Equally, if you plan spending any time in your flat or house, why not get these fundamentals right so you can enjoy it?

Wearing my surveyor and house-finder hats, I would be far happier recommending my client a house that has a brand-new boiler rather than one with lots of expensive but non-essential gimmicks. You can always add the toys – don't forget they rapidly go out of date and therefore become less desirable – but having to sort out the flooring or plumbing can be expensive and messy for someone to do later.

So, do what the quality house builders do and invest in the basics. If there are problems with any of the following, I'd look at spending money to rectify these issues first:

- the roof
- insulation
- electrics
- plumbing
- flooring
- heating

This way, buyers know you are not hiding anything, and if you're asked about the state of your property, you can produce documentation showing that all the basics are in good order. Although the sexy cappuccino maker and stunning flat-screen plasma television are alluring, it is more important to make sure the house is in a good state first.

How to Make Your House Flow

Getting your house to have some sort of overall theme or feeling, so that when you move from one room to another it doesn't jar, can be an effective way to add value. For instance, you might want to paint all the walls in the house one colour, so 'a journey' through the house, in designer parlance, will feel right. This doesn't necessarily mean boring. Often, the effect is far from dull. And you can always add little touches of colour or the odd roll of wallpaper to make a space stand out.

It is a good idea generally to give a house a style. Whether you opt for minimalist and contemporary or go for a faux-Victorian feel, stick to it throughout. Jumping around the ages and fashions from room to room can appear messy and jumbled, and will confuse buyers when they are thinking how they will live in the property.

Top-end house builders usually opt for a neutral but pleasing tone on all of the walls, such as a greyish-white or very pale taupe shade. This has the advantage of making the house look lighter, brighter and bigger, as well as pulling everything together and marrying it up. If you are worried about a lack of colour or pizzazz, you can employ tricks to add a hint of excitement:

- Decorate one wall in a room with stylish wallpaper to break up an overall monotone colour scheme.
- Introduce vibrant cushions on sofas and beds.
- A brightly coloured patterned rug can make a room feel livelier.
- Artworks on neutral-coloured walls give a bit of verve and depth to a space.
- A corner with family photos introduces warmth.
- Fun touches, such as wallpaper with a books motif in a study, will make you – and a potential buyer – smile.

Add Big Features

Once you've taken care of the basics, or as many as you can get to grips with on your budget and timescale, you may want to have a go at emulating top designers, architects and house builders by installing a few breathtaking features that will make the property more interesting for you – and, ultimately, buyers.

Coming up with 'feature presentations' means focusing on a few really good and different ideas that will make the prospect of living in the house very tempting. These will often be features that a house two doors down the road, or the next-door flat, is unlikely to have, making your property all the more alluring. Although they are luxuries, there must be a good reason for having them –

otherwise, they'll be gimmicks rather than important new additions to your home.

The following are some feature presentations you might want to consider putting in.

Sliding doors

You could invest in a show-stopping sliding-door system that takes up a large part of the back wall of your house and leads people directly out into the garden, patio or terrace. This has several advantages. When pulled back in the summer, the door transforms your garden into another room. But even in the winter this system will work well, letting in more light and allowing you to enjoy the view. So, although this may not come cheap, it will look great and has sound practical applications too.

The other plus is as soon as people enter the house, they will see a view of the garden and it will make a great talking point. Your back wall almost becomes a work of art in its own right, while the ease of sliding the door open will not be lost on guests or wannabe buyers. Some top designers are even able to make whole walls out of glass.

You need to reckon on spending in the region of £5,000 to £10,000, however, so this isn't for the faint-hearted. It can be hugely disruptive as well, as it probably involves propping up the back of your home, installing a steel joist and then fitting the massive glass door. But it could be well worth the effort as this feature will draw everyone to this space and the natural light will permeate the entire level.

Skylights

Another good place to spend money in a home is on skylights. These can add drama to a space as well as simply bringing much-needed light to dim and dreary corners. Where should you put a skylight? Installing one in the ceiling above the kitchen or dining table can make an eating area more appealing. But make sure you have a blind to keep out bright sunlight and heat on a hot summer's day. If it is a place where children naturally lay out their books and do their homework, or you pull out your laptop to do some work away from the office, the skylight can create a friendly 'working' zone.

At night, with the moonlight and stars in the sky twinkling through the glass, it will really come into its own. And even when it is raining, somehow life is a bit less depressing. You can watch the rain patter down on to the skylight and feel in touch with the world outside.

Skylights can be put in all manner of places now. They can make all the difference in a loft conversion – although you need to work closely with the planning office at your local authority to ensure that any change to the exterior view or the roofline of the house is acceptable.

PHIL'S TOP TIP

A large skylight at the top of a house, especially one run along virtually the whole length of the corridor, will bring light flooding in. This can be dramatic, and although it is not a cheap option – expect to spend from about £3,000 – it will attract attention on this top level, even if you've done very little else of interest on this floor. Developers tell me this is a neat trick they use when they have put the bulk of their money into the kitchen, living room, bedrooms and bathrooms. The top storey, historically the servants' quarters, is often ignored and this is one way to add some panache here. Even if you do nothing special to the other rooms on this floor, it won't matter a great deal, because this huge ceiling of glass will captivate visitors. It's the distraction technique – people are so bowled over by the one big feature they don't really mind that everything else in that room or on that floor is pretty ordinary.

I would love to install a huge skylight like this in my house next time I am carrying out any work on the place. It would give me the opportunity to personalise the place a bit, while this feature would appeal to most everyone in general. When the builders come around again, this is a feature I will definitely discuss with them.

Tall doors

A neat trick this one, that I have carried out successfully in my own home. Many developers now replace the doors throughout a property with full-height floor-to-ceiling ones. This makes the house look bigger, the ceilings feel higher and it gives an overall rather grand effect. If you paint the doors to match the walls, you end up with a modern, clean look (remember that 'flow' you are trying to achieve). And if you opt for smart wooden doors, this can add splendour to a period property.

This is fairly easy to do, but of course you have to pay for new doors and have them fitted. If you are going to paint them, they can be made from a cheaper material, as no one will know what is underneath anyhow. Don't stint on door furniture – decent handles are all part of the desired chic look too.

Blinds and shutters

To lift a house out of the ordinary, think about smart coverings for the windows that can be more appealing than your average curtains. Niche house builders often install decent quality Venetian blinds and shutters. Shutters are sturdy and have good security properties too. They are easy to clean – a wipe of a cloth is simpler than taking down curtains and sending them to be dry-cleaned – and manage to be both fashionable and timeless.

You can employ another high-end developer trick and put up good blinds – with blackout material on the back to keep the sunlight out – that are the same tone as the walls. When pulled down, they blend in and make the house look streamlined and large. This also makes a statement about you, the homeowner, as someone stylish enough to tie everything together in your house. Blinds are easy to clean and with blackout material you don't need to worry about the thickness, as you do with curtains.

If you prefer curtains, I would choose materials with natural fibres. Mixing materials can soften harsher fabrics – linen and silk go together well, for instance. This is a good place to introduce vibrant colour to liven up your otherwise neutral scheme, or textural drama with purple velvet or a heavier fabric, which can work well in a country house.

PHIL'S TRADE SECRET

A good idea I have borrowed from an architect that has worked well in my own home is to layer blinds. If you want to soften a window that looks out on to a busy street or an entrance with passers-by, put two blinds up, one in front of the other. The one at the back is in a lighter mesh and semi-transparent material, while the one at the front is solid. You pull down the mesh blind during the day, to soften the look and keep prying eyes from peering into your home, but allowing natural light still to filter in. Then you can bring the solid blind at the front down at night to seal off the window.

This neat 'two blinds' effect needn't cost the earth. In the house where I picked up this idea, the young family was on a budget and their architect says he only spent about £100 to £150 on the two blinds, but the effect was extremely impressive for this amount of cash.

Of course, you can use cheaper or even more expensive fabrics to create a richer look. Using two slightly different tones – two browns or two greys – can look good, particularly if you have the two blinds overlapping at times. For instance, you can pull the light grey semi-transparent blind right down during the day, and have the dark grey solid blind pulled about a third of the way down in front. This overlapping look is very stylish, while solving a practical problem as well.

LEARN FROM THE EXPERTS

Like developers, architects can be good at coming up with solutions to housing problems, so you can take inspiration from them too. I once came across a simple way to get around a planning issue. A young architect helping a family renovate their house in Bristol wanted to install a side window over the main stairs to admit light. But the planners told him this wasn't possible because it would overlook the neighbour's house and be intrusive.

Somewhat discouraged, he went home that evening and wracked his brains for an answer to his problem. While he was sitting on the sofa in the living room, he watched his small son play on the floor with a bag of marbles. That is when inspiration came to him. He went back and submitted a new idea to the planners: a double-glazed window with the gap between the two panes filled totally with marbles.

The planners said yes. After all, the neighbours weren't overlooked, because you couldn't look through the window directly with its marbled interior. Also, light refracted off the marbles, casting fabulous streaks of colour on the walls and stairs, and at a distance, the marbled window looked like expensive stained glass. The other bonus? In cost terms, this was an inexpensive exercise: the window was only a few hundred pounds and the marbles £20 to £30 for several bags.

Period Features Pay

If you are lucky enough to be reconstructing a period flat or house that has some of its original features, you can add value to a home by restoring them. A stained-glass window is a prime example. It might not be a low-cost option, but getting a specialist to remove and restore a piece of stained glass will add to the heritage value of the property and show you care about it. Carrying out research into the particular motif or design of your stained glass can possibly reveal certain information about your home: how old it is and what the design says about the property and area, for instance.

It is hard to quantify what restoring stained glass will cost – a lot depends on the size of the job and the state of the window – but it is well worth the price. If you are short of cash, consider taking it to a college where stained-glass restoration is taught to students. Perhaps you will get a bit of a reduction if students, under the supervision of a tutor, can 'practise' on your window.

Other period features you might be able to bring back to life are: wooden panelling on the walls, vintage wallpaper, stepping around doors, tiered skirting boards, fireplaces (a friend stripped cream paint off a beautiful original marble fireplace in his flat) and paint. If you find a layer of original paint, you can match it these days to one in a range of historic colours.

Cornices, ceiling roses and dado rails are three other popular features you can easily bring back to life. You can replace sections, if some are missing, and find replica lights to hang from ceiling roses (from about £75). Hanging, or picture, rails look great in a period house and are also wonderfully practical when it comes to hanging your artwork.

Be aware that before you begin any work on a listed house, you are likely to need permission from the local authority.

It is hard to quantify how much you have added in value once you repair, restore or replace period features in a house, but I think the benefits of seeing them every day far outweigh any cash returns anyhow. It is terrific pointing out a bread oven or ancient timber beam and ruminating about how old they might be and how earlier inhabitants would have used them.

Period features are bound to lift the saleability of your property, making it more appealing than one up the road that has had everything original torn out. If you carry out the work sympathetically, those who look around your property will notice what you have done and the estate agent can list the period features – with good photographs to back the descriptions – on the sales brochure.

Lighting

Good lighting is something designers and architects have well and truly cracked. Yet many of us are scared to embrace this optical trick to manipulate a room and make spaces really work. You can make an open-plan space light and airy during the day, intimate and cosy in the evening, and can have other settings in between. How about a very full-on setting for when you clean, so you can get right into the corners, for instance? You can't get these effects several times a day by shifting the furniture round and changing the finishes, so clever lighting is a fantastic option.

Top Tips from a Lighting Designer

- Light objects, not people. Create atmosphere with table lamps and portable up-lighters in corners of rooms.
- Use IP-rated lights (ingress protection, which means water-resistant) in bathrooms.
- LED strips (light emitting diodes) that cast a glow look fabulous under a washbasin, shelf or along the tops of kitchen cabinets for more ambient light.
- Dramatic lighting can turn a low-cost table or headboard into something richer-looking with more texture.
- If you are on a budget, simply focus light on some flowers and put four little corner up-lighters in a room for drama that doesn't cost a lot.

Art

Good works of art can contribute hugely to the mood of a property. Top-end house builders hang paintings on the walls of their show apartments and houses as well as display art in communal areas and gardens. Sculptures, small bronzes and specially designed lights also are put on show.

Not everyone has access to real masterpieces, but you can have fake 'old masters' commissioned online (about £1,000 apiece). Old movie film posters (from £20) and a mural featuring a film star (about £150) can liven up a wall too.

It is worth checking out art fairs. Buying something original from a new young artist can add value in the long run, assuming the young artist turns into a Damien Hirst or Tracey Emin. And even if he or she doesn't end up with their work displayed in the Tate one day, you have an original piece of art with a story behind it – where you bought it, what the artist is like and why you like it.

Even humble artworks, such as simple sketches you have collected and drawings by your children, can add warmth and interest to a property. But don't hang anything too raunchy. I recall one bohemian retired couple who insisted on hanging a massive oil painting of them unclothed in a rather odd scene from the Sixties. They gave it pride of place in the living room, but visitors found it pretty disturbing.

If you are hanging very good artwork, you might want to install lighting to show off your pieces. Either ceiling or wall-mounted lights positioned in the right spots will add considerably to the enjoyment of the pictures. The next owner of the house can benefit from this pre-installed lighting.

Dressing Your Home

Heading out for a night on the town means dressing to kill in your favourite frock and stilettos. So when it comes to giving a property its grand showing, developers and designers dress it in its best bib and tucker. Dressing to sell is a major way house builders and agents help shift property quickly, and you can turn your home into the equivalent of a supermodel without breaking the bank. Dressing a home, or house doctoring, is not the same as a complete refurbishment. You just place certain items in an attractive way to make the place inviting, getting buyers interested the second they walk through the door.

Interior designers have been dressing top-end homes for some time, knowing that a sumptuous sofa and bathroom that wouldn't look out of place in the Ritz can have prospective purchasers reaching eagerly for their chequebooks. Designers believe that placing the right furniture and accessories in a home helps buyers envisage being there with their friends.

Little touches can make all the difference, advises one designer. 'Put a decanter of wine on the dining room table, good newspapers and books in the study and products from somewhere like the White Company in bathrooms.' The key, she says, is not to dress a place to your own taste but to the taste of the person who might purchase the property.

TV makeover programmes recommend sticking to neutral colours, but neutral needn't mean boring beige or magnolia. A colour consultant says go for brown and cream shades with tones of pink, blue or yellow underneath. To find the underlying colour, place something white or black next to the main colour. She also points out that 'pale colours create an illusion of space, while warm, darker colours make a room appear smaller'.

Another trick is to move furniture away from walls to make a room look less formal, and to hang mirrors for a bigger, lighter space. Use the 'rule of three', which means arranging paintings, cushions, candles, boxes or knick-knacks in groups of three. Pleasing to the eye, items in clutches of three make an area or room look balanced.

Books and stylish lamps on bedside tables work well. I always want to take a peek at what people read, and whatever reading material you have lined up says a lot about you. A few enticing books off the latest bestseller list mixed with classics and art books can do the trick.

Show generosity with cushions, particularly in bedrooms. I loathe having to deal with cushions in 'real life' – generally I just hurl them to the floor – but somehow, piles of sumptuous-looking cushions look great on show. Other home-stager techniques include a parallel line of candles on a coffee table, two overlapping throws folded at the end of a bed and a hall table with a huge vase of flowers (you see this last trick in big hotels as well).

PHIL'S TRADE SECRET

One designer says she decks out show flats and show houses for house builders by pretending a family already lives in the property. 'I even give them names, ages and occupations. A house I designed recently had a dad who was a photographer I called Paul and I put lots of cameras, photography books and lights in his study. The invented mum called Alice was into making things, so there was an area with cool knitting patterns, colourful skeins of wool and other arts and crafts materials.

'The children were given their own identities too, so one of the children named Kevin had a teenage bolthole with dark walls and a cool globe chair hanging from the ceiling, while his younger sister, Lisa, enjoyed a pink fairy princess bed with pretty white fabric hanging round it.'

You might not want to take things quite this far to create an atmosphere, but giving each room an identity of some sort can help someone else work out what they can do with them.

Another designer, who decorates many of the UK's show flats and dresses private homes for sale, believes different members of the family tend to gravitate to different zones in the house. 'The women almost always flock to the kitchen. Children run out into the garden and men go to practical areas, such as the garage, workshop, outbuildings and study.'

She thinks you can dress your home to a degree, but don't go overboard. 'You can get away with laying a table with all its cutlery, china, white damask napkins and candles in an expensive show flat dining room, for instance, but if you do this in your house it can look a bit too staged – unless you own a huge country palace.'

People can be tempted by quite small ideas as well. One that I have seen women wowed by is having the washing machine and drier up on the same level as the bedrooms. We often carry our laundry down from the bedrooms to ground-floor level to launder and dry our clothes and then cart it all the way back up again.

Another idea that can be seductive to both men and women is to position ironing facilities – as basic as where you store the ironing board, through to a more complicated set-up with big steam iron systems – in the right place. I recently found myself getting out a shirt from the wardrobe that already had been taken downstairs to be laundered and ironed then brought back up again, but it needed touching up. I found myself taking it all the way back down to the basement to iron it. If everything is on the same logical level, it can save time and effort.

PHIL'S TOP TIP

Imagine what someone sees when they first walk into each room and give them something to focus on – a smart bedspread or fresh towel draped over the bath. This needn't cost the earth – you can scour junk shops, skips and even rubbish dumps for low-cost or free items, such as wooden tables you can paint.

Window Dressing

- Make the most of the best features.
- If pushed for cash, borrow good furniture from a friend.
- Hang a mirror in a pokey hallway to make it look bigger.
- If fresh flowers are too expensive, buy an orchid plant that smells nice, but lasts longer.

Tips for a developer-style pad

- Look at the bigger picture. You might be better off spending your hard-earned cash on decent flooring or quality carpets instead of less practical items that can be just as expensive.

- Go for neutral designs that won't put people off, but also try injecting a bit of fun into your home. This will demonstrate that you care and have put thought into making the most of your property.
- Designers of show flats are clever at using space properly. This usually means fewer pieces of furniture to make the room look bigger. Try getting rid of or storing some of your furniture, especially the bigger pieces taking up too much room.
- A bold or intriguing design statement in each room will give visitors somewhere to focus. A vivid sofa, reupholstered chair (from about £60 a chair), repainted cabinet or unusual wallpaper on one wall creates a talking point in each area.
- Introduce a sense of fun that still has a practical vein. For example, providing sensible shelving and storage up high that is accessed by a funky ladder will catch the eye – but it also is useful.
- Developers frequently use sliding doors in en-suites and kitchens in show flats to save on space (a door jutting out into a room looks messy and invades a corner where furniture could go). This is a great idea to nick and transfer to a home, but you need to plan ahead to fit them in.

Show-home Tricks

Show homes and show flats used by developers to help sell new property are full of ways – some a bit devious and some not quite so diabolical – to make a property appear larger, lighter and more luxurious. You might be able to employ some of the following ideas, or variations of them, to make your house more appealing when you sell.

- Leave the lights on to create the impression of more natural light.
- Use glass furniture and mirrors to give a feeling of space.
- Remove internal doors, if possible, to make the house appear larger.

- Fit furniture that is half the normal depth, or children's furniture, to make a room look larger.
- If the heating is turned on a bit higher, people don't linger too long to spot any defects and study anything in detail.
- Lay the dining table with sparkling cutlery and bright dishes to get a party atmosphere in the room.
- A soft fur rug, velvet cushion or textured throw makes a living room seem luxurious.
- Displaying a recipe from a trendy cookbook surrounded by some colourful and exotic vegetables lifts a kitchen from the humdrum to *Masterchef* proportions.
- A smart-looking lead and dog bowl in a utility room or kitchen corner makes it look like you own a pedigree dog.
- A silk negligee placed on a bed with a pair of Marilyn Monroe-style high-heeled slippers next to the bed appears sensuous and inviting.
- Musical instruments make the inhabitants – and, therefore, the house – look cultured.

Budget Dressing

If you are on a tight budget, you can still dress, or arrange, your home to make it more attractive to live in and to buyers. Here are some tips:

- Spend money on the worktop (that's the bit you see) rather than the units in a kitchen.
- Source the majority of materials yourself, to save paying a builder to do it.
- Use colour to create drama and divert the eye from imperfections, such as dents in panelling.
- Re-plate instead of replacing door furniture.
- Re-upholster tired-looking furniture (around £60 a chair) and re-cover cushions (about £20 each).
- Spend money on a few key items and hit the High Street or Internet for the rest.

- Stick to the same footprint for sanitary ware in bathrooms – new pipe work can be costly.

The Second Viewing

When you are selling your house and an interested buyer has come back for a second viewing, you should employ another level of psychology. The second viewing is the time when prospective purchasers are trying to find out what a flat or house 'feels like'. For the more practical purchaser, this could be regarded as an opportunity to ask more questions and get down to the nuts and bolts of how the house operates too.

A seller can supply further evidence of his good lifestyle. If your property is a bachelor pad aimed at young men, the latest DVD or piece of electrical kit will further pull your buyer into this world of great gizmos. Developers employ obvious but neat tricks, like framed photos of exotic vacations, designer carrier bags and a few artfully hung pieces of stylish clothing in wardrobes and bathrooms with luxurious soaps and creams. In fact, I can always determine the level of property simply by looking at the brands of soaps and creams on offer in a show flat bathroom. These ideas might appear a bit cheesy, but they do work. Another effective and simple showstopper is to clear the counters in the kitchen, replacing the tat with a brand-new kettle and toaster.

In addition, I think you should emphasise the fact that this is an organised and well-cared-for property at the second viewing. An MOT-type logbook with receipts and information on your favoured builder and workmen should be produced, and label the stopcock and other valves and taps. Although this might not sound as sexy as dimming lighting and arranging velvet cushions, people also want to know if the boiler has been lagged and regularly serviced.

The second viewing should be about reassuring a guest or buyer that this is a happy home – the feeling of a house does give it value. It is difficult to put your finger on how much value this adds, but the flip side of a house that doesn't feel right certainly takes away value. What you want to achieve is someone to say, 'I know we wanted a fourth bedroom, but it feels so nice here, maybe it doesn't matter.'

PHIL'S CONTACTS BOOK

- *Show House* magazine, www.showhouse.co.uk – although this is the trade bible for house builders in the UK, a consumer can pick up some great ideas on new materials and products builders are putting in new developments.
- Period Property UK, www.periodproperty.co.uk – useful information on period homes, with a directory of craftsmen and other professionals.
- Paint Quality Institute, www.paintquality.co.uk – everything about paint you ever needed to know. A good guide on how to achieve the smooth, professional finish that bespoke builders pull off effortlessly.

CHAPTER THIRTEEN

Gadgets

The cappuccino-maker factor: when gadgets add worth to your home

The choice is yours where you put your money. We all have different tastes and wish lists, but gadgets can add value to your enjoyment of a property and entice buyers when it is time to sell. Yet not all gadgets are guaranteed to net quite as much value as you might think.

Gadgets can be terrific. They look fun and everyone has a bit of a poke or a play with the latest spigot tap that washes seafood and the computerised mirror that lets you look at your back view as well as the front all at the same time. But whether they add value is debatable, particularly if savvy buyers can see through the cosmetic touches. If you are creating an upmarket property, then a number of these toys are taken as read and can pull punters in. But you need to be careful fitting them in your own home, so they are not construed as distractions to divert buyers from other problems or mistakes. Better sort out the damp problem before worrying about choosing an upmarket vegetable steamer system.

There are times when gadgets can add value though. If a stacking car parking system means the new owner can fit in three cars instead of only one in an urban area where parking comes at a premium, then this could make sense. But expect to pay big bucks – we are talking tens of thousands of pounds here – for such an installation, although in some upmarket areas where it costs £100,000 plus to buy a garage or permanent parking space you could be quids in. This is not for everyone, of course, but it does go to show that there are places where spending extra on gadgets can mean you make a good profit in the long run.

Gas Triple-flame Burner

Personally, I love the large triple-flame gas burner – also known as a wok burner, wok hotplate or griddle – you can choose as one of the burners on your hob. It is fantastic if you like stir-frying Chinese or other Asian dishes in a wok, or even in a large frying pan. You can also use this burner to cook meat, fish and vegetables on a griddle pan – a special cast-iron pan that costs from just over £20. The one with ridges, which creates lines on your meat or fish, gives your food a sort of 'indoor barbecue' effect.

Coffeemaker

Boys' toys include a sexy coffeemaker – a big male plus, I'd say, although I'm sure it appeals to women as well. There is a huge range of espresso and cappuccino machines on the market now, including those that take ready-made coffee pods so you don't have to add coffee grounds yourself. Prices vary from around £30 to over a thousand pounds. You can have your cool coffeemaker built into the kitchen. This looks fabulous – but the downside is you won't be able to take it away when you sell. You also need a large enough kitchen to justify losing this space permanently to your coffeemaker.

Wine Fridges and Bars

There are two types of bar you can put into your home – a wet bar (with plumbing and a sink) and a dry bar (with no plumbing or sink). A good dry bar starts at about £1,000 and a wet one costs about double that. Once you install mirrored shelves to reflect the glasses, LED lighting and other goodies, the cost could soar to £5,000.

If you have space for it, I believe a bar can be a jolly addition to a home. Mixing cocktails, punches and having a space where people can hang out will make a party go with a swing. Again, in financial terms it is hard to determine whether a bar will recoup the costs you put into it. It certainly is a good talking point though and could be an extra that shifts your home before the neighbour's.

A wine fridge can be a great asset. Although I'm not really into gadgets, my wine fridge was my 'boy's toy', I have to admit! Even though the fridge probably cost more than it has added to our home's value – mine was about £700 – it is very cool and it was a toy I fancied. There is plenty of choice, based on size, starting at £60 for a small fridge that holds six bottles and rising to £388 for 19 bottles, £724 for 38 bottles and £1,260 for 154 bottles. Sometimes people place small wine fridges in bedrooms, which sounds like a romantic thing to do but they can be noisy. A wine fridge can look very striking in a kitchen and attract a good deal of interest. It also can be practical in a way – wine bottles, cans of beer and soft drinks will no longer be clogging up the kitchen fridge.

Pantry Fridges and Drying Cabinets

Ironically, a number of the latest and coolest gadgets are ideas borrowed from the country, given a 21st-century edge and brought into towns and cities. For instance, we are all familiar with the pantry in a country house with its marble slab to keep food cold and its shelves to store preserves, vegetables, cheese and other food. In fact, a pantry does add value to a country home.

But now manufacturers are providing pantry fridges for those who haven't a pantry in town and would like one. Essentially, it is a small fridge that can be integrated into a kitchen that has pull-out shelves for fruit and vegetables and usually a big space at the bottom for potatoes and onions and also a slot for a few bottles. Just how chic these are is reflected in the price tag, around £700.

Another idea is the drying cabinet – a freestanding unit in white or stainless steel that is designed to dry anything from shoes, Wellington boots, hats, coats and gloves to fine cashmere jumpers. A modern version of the airing cupboard, the cabinet exudes gentle heat on three different settings on a timer that will dry your clothing in a couple of hours. A drying cabinet costs about £800.

Although some people might think these new inventions are a bit of a luxury, which indeed they are, they will certainly be noticed and discussed by anyone who visits your home or is deciding whether to buy it.

Taps

For a relatively reasonable sum, you can add a smart tap to your kitchen. Telescopic taps that pull out from the sink and emit a high pressure jet to clean vegetables or dishes cost about £300 – money well spent, as they do create a talking point. They might not necessarily add any value as such, but your kitchen will be remembered by viewers while others will be forgotten instantly. Another sort of telescopic tap is mounted above a cooker and pulls out so you can easily fill a saucepan to cook pasta, for example. This is a more luxurious touch that is popular in North America. Not quite so well known here, it is quite a nifty device and could be useful for people who find it hard to lift heavy pots.

Water purifiers and softeners

Integrated water purifiers and softeners can be good if you live in an area with particularly hard water. They aren't cheap, starting at around £500, and can take up a lot of room under the sink. Some are high maintenance as well, because you need to add salt at least once a month.

If your water is very hard, these could be a good selling point to protect and prolong the life of a washing machine and dishwasher. Otherwise, I'm not wholly convinced they add all that much value.

Soft-close Hinges

A soft-close hinge is essentially a small toy for those who appreciate the finer details. Soft-close hinges are clever little devices that go on to loo seats and kitchen unit drawers, typically, to stop them slamming noisily when you close them. They cost only a matter of pounds but can make all the difference to a visitor or buyer. Anyone who spots your soft-closing door or loo seat will mention it and look for them forever more in other properties.

Home Entertainment Systems

I think the secret to making gadgets work in a home is for them not to be too overt and 'in your face'. It is okay to be able to pinpoint a gizmo in a room, but you don't want it to dominate. A good way to integrate a large wall-mounted television screen, for instance, is to set it into a redundant chimneybreast. The television remains the focal point of the room, but doesn't stand out in an irritating fashion. Other suggestions are to sit the screen on a low-level unit or house it in a decorative cabinet. This works particularly well in a bedroom, when you reveal the TV only when you want to watch it.

If you are renovating your house or building it from scratch, you are best advised to build in a sound system and run wires and cables into walls for broadband and televisions. This will cut down on messy tangles of cables everywhere. The advantage of running CAT 5 or 6 throughout the house is you can access broadband from your computers quickly. A wireless router is another option – this involves no cables, but is slower than a CAT 5 or 6 link. I call adding such technology to your home, even if you aren't all that fussed yourself, as 'future proofing' as it will be attractive to someone looking to buy your home one day.

If at all possible, run as much cabling into the walls as you can. This means the next owner of the house can just tap into what you have already installed – a huge plus when you sell. By installing a good broadband system, you are demonstrating to a future buyer they will have an instant high-speed link. Installing ethernet sockets in most or all of the rooms is useful too. This means anyone can plug in their computer and have direct access to broadband.

Prices vary, depending on which system you choose, but wireless routers start at just over £30, a good 19-inch television is from £210, while a 46-inch television is about £1,500.

Another fun idea could be putting in a waterproof television in the bathroom (the sort of thing a landlord might entertain to let a property) – a five-inch one starts at £275 – but some lettings agents inform me tenants don't always see the benefit of such a luxury. They claim you are not normally in a bathroom long enough to watch an entire episode of your favourite programme and it can be difficult to see when the room mists up. If you are considering installing a telly in the bathroom, however, it must meet safety standards that cover electrical equipment in wet spaces like bathrooms.

Home cinemas are becoming popular in some quarters, but they don't come cheap. A projector could set you back about £1,200 and a comfortable big cinema seat £1,300. If you are designing a top-end property in an area where this standard of luxury is anticipated, however, it could be a good place to spend your money. My last home had a drop-down screen and projector that cost around £3,500. I knew the target market and sold the house to someone who was quite taken with the system. I played around with it when he came to view and, that was it – he was hooked. A more reasonable option that will almost certainly grab someone's attention is to install a dock for an iPod or other MP3 player that can be used to charge, sync and play music through speakers. I have seen portable docks from only about £50 that sit nicely on a bedside or living-room table. Integrated wall-mounted versions look very sharp too, although these cost several hundred pounds.

The best sound system to install is one that allows you to play different radio stations and music in different zones in the house. It can be annoying if everyone in the house has to listen to the same tracks without being able to control rooms or areas individually. If you are not too fussed about having a sound system yourself, I would still recommend putting in all the wiring anyhow if you are renovating. Then the next owner can lash up a system easily, which is a strong selling point.

In the future, it is likely we will watch television through a broadband link, which might do away with TV screens altogether and usher in a new generation of large computer screens.

Entry Phones and Security Systems

An efficient entry phone system will add value to your home. With an audio or video entry phone you can either hear or see someone before you decide to grant him access to your home – a huge security plus. You can say no to salesmen and identify someone before letting him step over the threshold. The hardware for audio systems – the telephone handsets and operating box – isn't too dear (about £200). Where the money adds up is in labour costs installing all the cabling.

Video entry phones can be quite expensive. A cheap version is about £500, although some of these bargain-basement versions are not all that reliable. A higher-end video entry phone is in the region of £2,000 to £3,000. A black-and-white system is less expensive than a colour one.

Security systems are getting sophisticated these days and are often wired into a TV or computer, so you can see on your TV or computer screen who is at your front door. You could be away in another part of the UK or abroad and still monitor what is going on at your house. This can be marvellous if you want to keep tabs on things at home, but some other extras, such as the ability to run a hot bath when you touch down at your local airport so you can leap into it as soon as you get home, are of exaggerated benefit. It only takes a few minutes to run a bath anyhow, so is this really a bonus?

Good alarm systems give you peace of mind and an alarm box on the front of your house is one of the better burglar deterrents. An alarm system costs roughly £500 to £2,000. A number of insurance companies now insist on an efficient and working alarm system before they will insure your property. Those that don't will sometimes offer you a cheaper policy if you have an alarm system in place. Many companies say your burglar alarm must meet a minimum standard, typically grade two EN50131 for all new alarms, and an approved installer must fit it.

There are wireless alarm systems these days that save you running unsightly cables all round your home. Wireless sensors can detect movement, smoke, fire and water, all integrated into the same system. A wireless system costs about £700, and another £300 to fit.

Doors and Locks

Reinforced doors – with steel running through them – are harder for an intruder to break down. Again, insurers are likely to specify what doors and locks must be used, including external doors with five-lever (at least) mortice deadlocks or double-glazed doors with a three-point locking system. Key-operated window locks might also be required.

If you are not at your property all the time, locked metal gates at the front door or at the top of the drive can be another good security device. Increasingly, smarter versions are being produced so they do not resemble prison bars quite as much as they might have done in the past. Prices vary – automated systems cost far more – but start at around £1,000.

Barbecues

Long gone are the days when a 'barbie' was a simple piece of kit for grilling humble sausages, burgers and cobs of corn over a few hot coals. These days at the higher end of the market we are copying the Americans and Australians and demanding snazzy outdoor kitchens with drinks fridges, teppanyaki hotplates, granite work surfaces and stainless-steel sinks. Guests can perch on bar stools and observe the host whipping up a feast.

A ready-made stainless-steel barbecue with two cupboards either side to store all your equipment and work surfaces on top is £2,295. More substantial outdoor kitchens with overhead canopies to keep the rain out and seating round a counter for eight cost £20,000. Although a modular or fixed gas-fired outdoor kitchen is only for those with plenty of money to spare, I have noted over the years that many upper-scale trends do percolate down to the masses. You can buy the units you want separately and build your own outdoor kitchen in your garden out of bricks, saving significantly on the overall cost (about half, I would estimate).

With more of us staying in our homes for longer and remaining there to holiday on 'staycations', perhaps the concept of outdoor kitchens will grow further. I can see one adding value in terms of the enjoyment you will get while you are in your home. Your outdoor kitchen might make your house more attractive and saleable when you sell – it certainly is a big feature – but I'm not sure if you will add to the overall worth of your home in monetary terms.

Air Conditioning and Comfort Cooling

I am often asked whether it is a good idea to install air conditioning or a comfort cooling system in a home in the UK. As we do not have a tropical climate and it doesn't get outrageously hot here in the summer, it is a personal choice rather than one of necessity, I believe. Some might view air conditioning as a good selling point, especially if you are targeting your house at Americans or other nationalities used to having it. I don't think it would make or break a sale, but it could be one of those extras on the list in a very high-end property.

It is quite a difficult job to retro-fit air conditioning as you need to dig up the house to place ducting and cables inside walls and you might even have to raise ceilings or drop floors to accommodate all the kit. This is best carried out when you are building a new home or refurbishing one. Costs vary and depend on the size of your property and how complicated it will be to install. A small portable fan unit costs anything from £20 and a full-blown A/C unit could run into many thousands of pounds.

Whirlpool Baths

Some people swear by whirlpool baths, that they are relaxing, therapeutic and attractive to buyers. There are basically two ways of installing one. You buy one as it is and simply put it in. Or you can choose the bath you want and then send it off to be customised as a whirlpool bath. It costs about £750 for the former and anything from £1,000 to £3,000 for the latter.

Although they can be great fun and people will notice them when they go round your house, the novelty of owning a whirlpool bath could wear thin. It is hard to quantify if you would get your money back when you sell, so you might want to consider buying one only if you will enjoy it while you are living in your home. I think whirlpool baths are a bit like owning a swimming pool – not everyone regards them as a plus, but those who do will be pleased to see one and it could be one of the reasons why they plump for your property over another.

Cutting-edge Fireplaces

Smart contemporary fireplaces in homes in towns and cities, in particular, can add value to a property. Built-in log gas fires can look very slick and fit into small spaces, lending a room focus and adding some warmth. They cost anything from £500 to about £1,000 and you need a CORGI-registered fitter or a specialist company that employs CORGI-registered personnel to fit it. If you don't want to spend money on one immediately, do think about running a gas pipe to the area where one might go. Then you could add a modern gas fire at a later date, or leave it for the next owner to go ahead with the job.

I think the fireplace surround in the living room can really become a major asset and key focus point if you get it right. Vice versa, if you get it wrong, it can detract from the value of the place as well. I have always gone for as good a surround as I could possibly justify financially.

CASE STUDY

THE GIZMO ROOM

Jason and Rania Burroughs, a 36-year-old legal secretary, wanted a way to jazz up an upstairs reception room in their mews house in central London. Although Rania wasn't convinced at first, Jason talked her round into having an entertainment room with various gadgets.

'She thought it might be a bit tacky having all these toys for boys, but I got a designer friend to give me some guidance on how to make the room fun and as tasteful as possible,' explains Jason, a 37-year-old City accountant.

Jason opted for a wall-mounted iPod docking system to provide music that cost about £450, a table football game at £190 and a replica American-style jukebox with CDs for £600. The décor was relaxing – a black soft leather sofa and matching chair and a couple of matching beanbags so friends could chill out.

'In total, including the toys, furniture and decoration, we spent around £2,500 to £3,000,' says Jason. 'We want to put in a wine fridge as well, but the one we want is pretty expensive at around £1,200, so that might have to wait until later.'

Rania says she was worried about the floor bearing up under the weight of the football game and jukebox, but the builder checked it out and said it didn't need any extra reinforcement. A window had to be removed, however, so the jukebox and table could be hoisted into the small house.

'It is quite fun having a room where we can just relax and all our friends love it. Whether we have added any value to the house is debatable, but if a buyer wanted to purchase any of Jason's gizmos I'm sure we would consider it.'

PHIL'S CONTACTS BOOK

- CORGI (Confederation for the Registration of Gas Installers), www.trustcorgi.com, 0800 915 0485.

CHAPTER FOURTEEN

Planning Permission

How to add value by getting the right permission

The planning system in the UK has been with us since the 19th century and is there to protect the environment of where we live in our towns, cities and in the countryside. Central Government sets out a national planning policy with guidelines, but the main responsibility comes down to the local planning authorities (or councils). Each local authority devises a local development framework that outlines how planning will be managed in an area. The local planning authority decides whether a development – anything from an extension to your house through to the building of a large superstore – should go ahead or not.

If you want to understand a bit more about the planning process and what you can and cannot do, go to the excellent website www.planningportal.gov. uk, a clear guide to planning permission and building regulations approval. You can go round an interactive detached house and terrace for planning information on individual projects, such as adding an extension or a conservatory. There's also a 'green' house you can navigate round to get eco-friendly tips. The guidance given in this chapter is based on what is suggested for homeowners in England. You will need to check for any variants on planning in Scotland and Wales.

As the Government website explains, 'most new buildings or major changes to existing buildings or to the local environment need consent – known as planning permission'. Getting planning permission is separate from building regulations approval. Essentially, planners tell you what you are allowed to do and building regulations inspectors make sure you have carried out the work properly to the correct building code.

If the local authority planners turn down your planning application, you can appeal, but there is no guarantee you will win your case. What could occur is you will be asked to re-submit altered plans and a compromise might be reached.

You need to deal with the local council in your area. Start by looking at the council website to get an idea of local planning guidance. Remember, every council interprets Government legislation in its own way. One planner might be in favour of contemporary designs, while another elsewhere could be less keen.

Planning Permission for Extensions

Under new Government regulations that came into effect in October 2008, it should be easier, in theory, to add an extension on to your house. An extension is considered to be within 'permitted development' – what you can do to your property without having to seek permission. You should not require planning permission to build an extension, subject to the following limits and conditions:

- No more than half the area of the land around the 'original house' (as it was first built or as it stood on 1 July 1948, if built before that date) would be covered by additions or other buildings.
- No extension can be built that is forward of the principal elevation or side elevation fronting a highway.
- No extension to be higher than the highest part of the roof.
- Maximum depth of a single-storey rear extension of 3 metres beyond the rear wall for an attached house and 4 metres beyond the rear wall for a detached house.
- Maximum height of a single-storey extension of 4 metres.
- Maximum depth of a rear extension of more than one storey of 3 metres beyond the rear wall including the ground floor.
- Maximum eaves height of an extension within 2 metres of the boundary of 3 metres.

- Maximum eaves and ridge height of extension no higher than existing house.
- Side extensions to be single storey with maximum height of 4 metres and width no more than half that of original house.
- Two-storey extensions no closer than 7 metres to rear boundary.
- Roof pitch of extensions higher than one storey to match existing house.
- Materials to be similar in appearance to the existing house.
- No verandas, balconies or raised platforms.
- Upper-floor side-facing windows to be obscure-glazed and any opening to be 1.7 metres above the floor.
- On designated land (national parks, the Broads, Areas of Outstanding Natural Beauty, conservation areas and World Heritage Sites), no permitted development for rear extensions of more than one storey.
- On designated land no cladding of exterior.
- On designated land no side extensions.

This list applies only to houses. If you want to add an extension on to a flat or maisonette, you must apply for planning permission.

If your flat is in a listed building, it is likely you will need listed building consent before you start work. You should contact your local planning authority before you start any work.

What is a Listed Building?

A listed building in Britain is a building of interest with exceptional architectural, historical or cultural significance. Nearly 373,000 buildings are listed in England. The older a building is, the more likely it is to be listed, although some newer buildings (they must be over 30 years old) are listed too. A listed building may not be demolished, extended or altered without special permission from the local planning authority. Carrying out any work without consent to a listed building that affects its special historic character is a criminal offence. You could be fined, forced to remove any work already carried out and you could end up with a criminal record.

Attention to detail when making an application

Planning what kind of extension and how you are going to integrate it into the rest of the house is incredibly important. Many experts advise getting the whole family involved so everyone can throw their ideas into the pot. This can be useful, but I'm not wholly convinced decisions 'by committee' achieve the best result. This shouldn't be a quick, gut reaction, and the more you plan up front, the better the extension will look.

A builder working at the top end of the property market has told me he thinks the 'real work' when doing any project is winning planning permission at the start. This is where his ability to 'add value' begins.

He does a great deal of research when seeking permission to extend a house, taking hundreds of photographs of similar schemes in the area and finding out what else has been allowed by the local authority. If the council turns down his plans, he produces his seriously detailed case and documents supporting it. The council doesn't always get on with him and he often has to go to battle appealing against their judgements, but he seems to get mainly what he wants in the end.

Now, I am not suggesting you fall out with your local planning office, and obviously most people do not have the time, money or energy to wage war with officials. But there is a lesson here. Working out in huge detail and doing your research at an early stage could net a better result.

So, don't give up if the local authority's initial answer to your expansion scheme is no. There might be a suitable compromise, leading to a way to give you some, or even most, of what you want. And if you have research and photographic examples to back your case, your argument could be strengthened.

Planning for a Basement

Normally, you don't need planning permission if you are converting an existing basement. You will need to seek permission, however, if you are altering the appearance of the exterior – adding a staircase or light well, for instance – or if you are living in a listed building, a conservation area or an Area of Outstanding Natural Beauty. If you reside in a national park, you will need to get planning permission too.

If you are doing something that affects the 'change of use' of the building under the Town and Country Planning Order of 1987, you need permission from the planners. This could be anything from changing an office into residential space, another kind of dwelling into residential living – say, a barn into a family home – or installing a flat where one did not exist before.

You cannot start work before the local authority signs off on the work you wish to carry out. If you start work without seeking permission first, you might have to pay a fine, the council could take you to court and you could be forced to tear down what you have built. You could even end up with a criminal record.

Check out the planning section of your local authority's website. If someone else is doing something similar below ground, this could strengthen your application. You could even go round and have a look at these projects and talk to the builders on site.

Building regulations need to be followed so the work is carried out in an approved way. This normally means a building inspector checking the work at various stages, or at the end of the job. You will then be issued with a certificate that says the work has been carried out properly. If you don't follow the building regulations code, you could have problems when you sell your house, as you will be expected to present the completion certificate upon exchange of contracts.

Generally, there isn't too much concern from the planners when it comes to a typical underground conversion as long as you meet fire safety regulations. Normally, no one is offended by what you do – after all, they can't see anything from above. Light wells, however, will be visible from outside, so these may need to be checked by planners. In architectural terms, a light well is an open space reaching from a glazed roof down several storeys, typically to the ground floor or basement level.

Light wells reduce the need for electric lighting, can add a central space within the building and provide an internal open space for windows to give an illusion of having a view outside. In terraced, row or tenement housing, it is a phrase for the space between buildings beyond the adjoining front wall to allow natural light – and air circulation – to the lower back rooms of a building. In architectural-speak, this is known as the 'area'.

Light wells peak above ground for most basement conversions, so do not take up much space in a garden and are not particularly obtrusive. They can make a huge difference to the basement, allowing natural light to pour through the glass dome or plate above.

Planning for a Loft Conversion

Planning permission might not be required if you are only carrying out internal works. However, local interpretation can vary, so it might be best to contact your local planning authority for advice.

Permission is required if you extend or alter the roof space.

Make sure to check whether you actually own the roof space that you hope to convert. If you are a leaseholder, you may need to get permission from your landlord, freeholder or management company that looks after the building (and sometimes all three).

Some freeholders might ask for a payment to cover administration costs or to sell you the roof space if you do not own it. This is down to negotiation, and a good solicitor specialising in property law should be able to help.

If you live in a conservation area and your plans involve some demolition, you might need to apply for conservation area consent.

Planning for a Conservatory

The same regulations that apply to extensions also apply to adding on a conservatory.

> ## PHIL'S TOP TIP
>
> *I think you will have a better chance of overcoming any planner's fears if you choose materials that fit in with the building, especially if you live in a country house. Matching the bricks, for instance, and using glass for the roof rather than a synthetic plastic are likely to win a reluctant planner round.*
>
> *Do talk to a local builder who has put up a conservatory in your area or to a specialist company. Both should know what the local planning department favours and what has been passed by the planners recently.*
>
> *Also, it won't hurt to build up a dialogue with the planners. All bureaucrats like to feel they have been consulted along the way. If you engage planners in conversation early, it can only help your relationship with them.*

Planning for a Kitchen and Bathroom

If you are putting a kitchen or bathroom into a room where there wasn't one before, building regulations approval is probably going to be needed to make sure the room has adequate ventilation and drainage. It will also have to meet other requirements, such as structural stability, and electrical and fire safety.

If the use of a room is changed and could result in the load (weight) on the floor structure changing significantly, work to reinforce or strengthen the floor may be necessary. For instance, if a new bathroom suite is installed in a room where the floor is made of timber joists and boards, there is a risk the floor could be overloaded from the bath once it is filled with water and in use. So, work would need to be carried out to strengthen the floor.

A surveyor or structural engineer can look at the floor and work out if the floor does need to be fortified. A good engineer can produce the paperwork the building control inspectors require before you carry out the work.

Ventilation

Each new room needs adequate ventilation (air flow) for general health reasons. Ventilation stops condensation building up that could lead to mould or other fungi growing in the room. Depending on the room, the amount of ventilation will need to be determined.

The general rules for ventilating a room are:

- Purge – achieved by opening a window. The opening should have a typical area of at least one-twentieth of the floor area of the room, unless it is a bathroom, which can be of any openable size.
- Whole building – this is known also as 'trickle ventilation', which means installing a small vent, typically into the top of a window. The vent opens by sliding it over or pulling it down, and air can circulate into the room, to remove moisture. Trickle ventilation is usually needed in a bathroom measuring 4,000 square metres and in any other room of 8,000 square metres.

Both these forms of ventilation are normally required, although alternatives might be acceptable if agreed by the building control department at your local authority.

Mechanical Extractor Fans

Any new kitchen, utility room, bath or shower room or loo without a window that can be opened will need a mechanical extractor fan to reduce condensation and get rid of smells. The required performance of these fans is normally measured in litres per second, as follows:

- Kitchen – 30 litres per second if placed over the hob and 60 if elsewhere.
- Utility room – 30 litres per second.
- Bath or shower room – 15 litres per second with a 15-minute overrun (after the light is switched off) if there is no window that can be opened.
- Loo – 6 litres per second with overrun.

Ground-floor WC

Any home that has been built after 1999 will have a ground-floor WC installed that is designed for visiting wheelchair users. During refurbishments or re-fittings, this WC should not be removed and accessibility should not be restricted, to make sure it is still adequate for wheelchair users.

A building regulations application might be required if any alteration is to take place to an existing ground-floor WC.

Electrical Circuits

Building regulations set out overall criteria and requirements you must follow to ensure electrical safety. There is further practical guidance under approved document P (your building control department can give you more information) to undertake this kind of work. Any electrical work carried out in your home, garden, garden shed and any other storage buildings needs to comply with building regulations.

All electrical work has to follow the wiring regulation safety standards BS 7671 found on the British Standards Institute website (www.bsigroup.co.uk). These rules are there to help cut down the number of deaths, injuries and fires caused by badly installed and faulty electrics.

Building regulations do not restrict who can carry out electrical work. If you want to do the work yourself you need to make sure you know what you need to do before you start. If in any doubt, get a skilled electrician to help.

There are no rules for the safety of electrical appliances, but the building regulations do say that fixed connections of appliances must be safe.

You can check for safety under building regulations in one of two ways:

- Use an electrician registered with a competent person scheme.
- Notify the building control section of your local authority.

You should make a building regulations application if the electrician you are employing is not registered as a competent person under the schemes mentioned below, or if you do the work yourself. Contact the local authority building control department before you start the work and they will explain the procedures to you.

It is also good for you or your builder to talk to the building control department to find out how they wish to inspect your work. This might be carried out in stages during the work and when you finally complete it.

Approved inspector building control

An approved inspector is a body that carries out the same functions as local authority building control. If you use an approved inspector they will explain how the approved inspector system works. If they are satisfied that the work is safe and complies with regulations, you will be given a copy of the final notice at the end of the work.

Competent person scheme

In relation to electrical safety, this means that an electrician registered with an organisation authorised by the Secretary of State is able to certify the work has been carried out safely without you having to notify the building control department.

Once the works are completed, the registered electrician will arrange for you to receive a building regulations compliance certificate within 30 days of the end of the work. The electrician will also notify your local authority about the work and give you a completed electrical installation certificate to prove the work was tested for safety.

PHIL'S TOP TIP

Ask the electrician which scheme he belongs to and for his membership number. Check with the organisation that he is properly registered. Here are the organisations that run competent person schemes for electrical installation work:

- APHC (Association of Plumbing and Heating Contractors), www. aphc.co.uk, 02476 470626
- BSI (British Standards Institution), www.bsigroup.com, 01442 230442
- EC Certification Ltd (ELECSA), www.elecsa.co.uk, 0845 6349043
- NAPIT Certification Ltd, www.napit.org.uk, 0870 444 1492
- NICEIC Certification Services Ltd, www.niceic.com, 0870 013 0382
- CORGI, www.trustcorgi.com, 0870 401 2300
- OFTEC, www.oftec.co.uk, 0845 658 5080

Minor Works

The building regulations department allows certain works (known as non-notifiable or minor work) to be carried out in your home without your having to contact building control or use a registered electrician. These works include:

- Replacing any electrical fittings, such as socket outlets, light fittings or control switches.
- Adding a fused spur, which is a socket that has a fuse and switch connected to an appliance (such as a heater), to an existing circuit (but not in a kitchen, bathroom or outdoors).
- Any repair or maintenance work.
- Installing cabling at extra-low voltage for signalling, cabling or communication purposes (telephone cabling, cabling for fire alarm or burglar alarm systems, or heating control systems).

If you are not sure if the work is notifiable or not, contact your local building control department for guidance.

If a qualified electrician carries out the work, make sure they give you a minor works certificate to show they have tested the work to ensure it is safe. If you do the work yourself I think it could still be a good idea to get a skilled electrician to check it for you.

Permission for Outbuildings

The same rules for extensions that came into effect on 1 October 2008 also apply to outbuildings. These outbuildings could include sheds, greenhouses, summerhouses and garages, as well as ancillary garden buildings, such as swimming pools, ponds, sauna cabins, kennels and enclosures (including tennis courts).

With regard to building control, regulations will not normally apply to putting up a small, detached building in your garden, such as a garden shed or summerhouse, if the floor area of the building is less than 15 square metres. If the area is between 15 and 30 square metres, you don't have to apply for approval providing that the building is either at least one metre from any boundary or it is constructed of substantially non-combustible materials.

In both these cases, building regulations do not apply only if the building does not contain any sleeping accommodation.

PHIL'S TRADE SECRET

If you are struggling to extend a listed house, then converting an outbuilding might be a better solution. Planners worried about what you might do to a listed building might be more sympathetic to the refurbishment of an outbuilding instead. Usually, listings apply to the house and all of the grounds, so check yours first.

Tips for outbuildings

- Always err on the side of caution before you buy a property – you might not get the permission you desire to convert outbuildings.
- Give and take: agree to put something back the way it should be in the house in exchange for the new shed you want to build in the garden.
- Use a local architect or surveyor who knows the planners and your area.
- Building up a good relationship with the decision-makers (the planners) is almost always useful.
- A plan using reclaimed materials that closely match the original outbuildings might have more of a chance of being passed by planners than one that looks radically different.
- Check what has been allowed with your neighbours' outbuildings, which gives you some idea of what you can do.

Planning for a Garage

The same new rules from October 2008 for extensions apply to garages as well, and planning permission is not usually required as long as the work is internal and your plans do not involve enlarging the building.

Beware, however, that sometimes permitted development rights have been removed from some properties when it comes to garage conversions, particularly in conservation areas or on certain housing developments. There has been some controversy about the use of garages, with some councils unhappy that garages are not being used in the way intended – that is, to park cars.

With many people converting external and integral garages into kitchens, playrooms, gyms and storage areas, more cars are filling up the streets, which can be unsightly and a problem if there isn't room for them to park on public roads. Do check with your local authority planning department before converting a garage to find out its policy.

The conversion of a garage, or even part of a garage, into habitable space normally requires approval under building regulations.

Planning on Decking

From 1 October 2008, putting up decking or any other raised platforms in your garden comes under permitted development, which means you do not need to apply for planning permission as long as:

- The decking is no more than 30 centimetres off the ground.
- Together with other extensions and outbuildings, the decking or platforms cover no more than 50 per cent of the garden.

These permitted development allowances apply to houses. If you have a flat, maisonette or other type of building, you might need to apply for planning permission, so check with your council what you can do.

Building regulations will apply to every deck structure that requires planning permission.

Planning on Working from Home

With more of us choosing to work from home these days, I am often asked whether you need planning permission to work in your home. According to planners, the key test is whether you will change the overall character of the home as a result of the business operating there. The guidelines say that if you answer 'yes' to any of these questions, then you probably will need to get permission:

- Will your home no longer be used mainly as a private residence?
- Will your business result in a marked rise in traffic or people calling?
- Will your business involve any activities unusual in a residential area?
- Will your business disturb your neighbours at unreasonable hours or create other forms of nuisance, such as noise or smells?

No matter what business you run from your home, whether it is hairdressing, childminding, teaching music or storing goods connected with the business, the key test is: is it still mainly a home, or has it turned into business premises?

If you are in doubt, you might want to apply for a Certificate of Lawful Use from the council to confirm you have not changed how the building is used ('change of use' is the formal phrase). If there is any dispute, you might have to apply for change of use – but there is no guarantee you will be granted it.

Planning Responsibilities

The law states that with all building work the owner of the property (or land) is ultimately responsible for complying with the relevant planning rules and building regulations. This means that if you do not get the correct planning and building regulations approval, you will be liable for 'remedial action', which could mean having to redo the work you have already carried out, or you might even be told you have to knock it all down. Getting advice in the first place from a planner or someone in the building control service is advisable so that you don't fall into this trap.

If you are carrying out the work yourself, you must make sure you understand what you are allowed to do, and not do, under planning and building control regulations. And if you are employing a builder, the responsibility is usually his – but make sure this is confirmed at the beginning. It might be a good idea to get down in writing what he is proposing, how he is going to carry out the work and what planning consents will be achieved.

PHIL'S TOP TIPS

Sometimes, finding your way round the planning system and dealing with building control regulations can be baffling and frustrating. Here are some tips to help you.

- Do not get into confrontations with planners or building regulation inspectors. Most of them are reasonable and can offer useful suggestions if you enter into a dialogue with them.

- Think of making a trade-off to get most or all of what you want. One example is a building regulations inspector accepting fewer fire doors in exchange for a high-specification fire alarm.
- Overworked and under-resourced planners have to respond to your application within eight weeks by law. Make their job easier by sending in clear information backed up by good pictures. They are more likely to be sympathetic to your proposal if it is presented properly.
- You might want to consider hiring a professional (an architect, surveyor or planning consultant) to prepare your case if you haven't the time, and require expertise.
- Hire a specialist to provide a report on specific problems, such as a 'right to light' expert if you have a wall that potentially could block out your neighbour's light.
- State your needs and the reasons why you want to alter your home. If your teenage children will be spending more time in the family home because they haven't found work and can't afford anywhere else to live, you should state this on your application. A planner might understand then why you want to extend and perhaps be more sympathetic to your circumstances.

How to Submit a Planning Application

You apply to your council for planning permission in writing or online at www.planningportal.gov.uk.

You can submit an application yourself, or get a builder, surveyor, architect or planning consultant to do it for you. Good sources of advice include the local planning office and local estate agents.

The planning department must respond to your application within eight weeks. If you have not received a response within eight weeks or your application has been turned down, you have a right of appeal. Permission might be turned down completely, you might get your permission in full, or you could be asked to re-submit amended plans that could then be approved.

Fees for planning applications

Fees vary depending on what you are applying for and they can be altered from time to time, so it is important to check on what the current fees are before you submit your application.

From October 2009, an application from the owner of a house wanting to build an extension, for instance, costs £150.

You might want to apply for a certificate of lawfulness for £170 if what you are proposing to do is within permitted development. This is a confirmation from the planning department that your proposals are within permitted development and do not need a planning application.

For more guidance on fees, contact your local planning department or go to www.planningportal.gov.uk. You can use the fee calculator on the site to determine what amount you should be paying for your application.

Appealing against a planning decision

If you have not received a reply to your planning application within eight weeks of submitting it or you are unhappy with the response, you can appeal against the decision.

You appeal to the Planning Inspectorate and your appeal will be considered by a planning inspector appointed by the Secretary of State if you are in England, and by the National Assembly if you live in Wales.

You can get the official form online from www.planningportal.gov.uk and you must submit your appeal within six months of receiving the application decision letter from the local authority.

If the matter is complicated and you need expert advice, you could hire an architect or surveyor to help. In certain cases, paying for the services of a planning consultant or property solicitor could be sensible. Costs vary for expert help and could range from a few hundred pounds to thousands of pounds, depending on the complexity of the case and the number of hours worked.

Keep in mind you are responsible for all of your own costs, including expert advice, when mounting an appeal in writing, through a hearing or inquiry. If you win, you could get some or all of your costs back from the local planning authority. However, if you lose, the local planning authority might be able to claim back its costs from you. This is rare, but could happen if you have been thought to have behaved unreasonably and wasted the council's time.

If you need any guidance on planning appeals contact the Customer Service Team on 0117 372 6372 or email enquiries@pins.gsi.gov.uk.

Adding Value Simply by Getting Permission

Getting planning permission for an extension or major improvement – but without bothering to carry out any of the work – can add value to your home. Quite simply, you spot the potential in your home and then get planning permission in place to add, extend or convert before you sell.

Having planning consent in place certainly adds to the saleability of a property. Buyers like the idea that they don't have to spend time or money getting permission, because you have taken the bother to do it for them in advance. Gaining planning permission can be a lengthy and expensive procedure, and if you get turned down, appeals can be costly. Architects' and other specialists' fees keep rising too, so having permission in place can be regarded as a huge bonus.

By getting planning permission in place before you sell your home, you are showing a future buyer what he can do with the property, from adding a parking space to converting the loft. Permission is transferable to the next owner and is valid for three years from when it is granted.

I find that many people want to create something for themselves but do not have the patience or imagination to go ahead. Here, the plans are done and they can tweak them a bit if they want to put their own stamp on the project.

I think having planning consent in place is a great selling point. It makes your property distinctive in a competitive market and, as everyone likes to think there is something they can add to a new property, this helps point them in the right direction.

Getting planning in place is a cheaper option than doing a substantial piece of work on your home. You are only paying a few thousand pounds to add many thousands, providing capital value with less outlay. One thing you have to remember is if the property was extended before you arrived, a planner might say those rights have been used up and you won't get permission. Also, your dreams might not be the same as your potential buyer's. Not everyone fancies a Maharajah temple at the end of the garden.

I helped one young couple with advice on getting planning consent for their three-bedroom cottage in Hampshire, which they wanted to sell. They paid £1,000 in architectural and planning fees for consent to add an extra bedroom and kitchen/diner on to their £290,000 stone cottage in a popular village. Because their cottage had three bedrooms and the 'premium market' required four or more, the permission lifted their house into a new band, which made it more attractive to those hunting for a family home.

I advised them to have the plans highlighting the proposed extension available to show prospective buyers, along with a lump of stone from the quarry and a few sample roof tiles. I reckoned it would cost the new owner about £50,000 to carry out the work, far cheaper than paying £400,000 for a four-bedroom house in the same village.

A straightforward extension to a non-listed four-bedroom house with a new reception room downstairs and master bedroom suite above is about £2,000 for the survey, design work and preparation and submission of the planning application. On top of this is the £150 planning application fee and there might be other fees for supporting work like ecological surveys, which can be an issue if you have bats, newts or badgers. More complicated designs for extensions to listed buildings could increase by up to half the amount (or another £1,000).

PHIL'S TOP TIPS

- Talk to a local planning officer about development opportunities on your land.
- Do not produce extravagant plans that do not appeal to buyers.
- Exploit the eco vogue by asking an environmental consultant how to self-generate energy and get consent for his ideas.

PLANNING PERMISSION FOR A LISTED BUILDING

Edward Norman thought it a good idea to build a detached double garage with a room above in the garden of his 19th-century farmhouse in Sussex. As the building exceeded the height restriction under permitted development and his house is Grade-II listed, Edward had to get planning permission.

'The room at the top could be used as a playroom or maybe even a home cinema room,' suggests Edward, a 47-year-old economist, who regards having planning in place as a way to add value to his property. He paid about £700 for visits from an architect and to have plans drawn up – which potential buyers can examine – and estimates the work would cost about £60,000 to carry out.

The agent currently selling Edward's house, which is on the market at £875,000, believes he has added flexibility to the property, making it attractive to those who could benefit from a large garage and extra room.

The agent says a home office or annexe adds the most value for those keen on space for granny or the nanny, and to situate an office. 'Depending on the council, you might be able to erect a wacky, modern outbuilding, or opt for something more conservative. The questions a local planner will ask are: who will overlook it and what will they see?'

PHIL'S CONTACTS BOOK

- Planning Portal, www.planningportal.gov.uk – free advice on planning from the Government.
- Building Control, www.labc.uk.com – national organisation

representing building control departments in England, Wales and Northern Ireland.

- RIBA (Royal Institute of British Architects), www.architecture.com, 020 7307 3700 – for a list of qualified architects and advice on architecture.
- Law Society, www.lawsociety.org.uk, 020 7242 1222 – information and names of solicitors dealing with property law.
- Planning Inspectorate, www.planning-inspectorate.gov.uk, 0117 372 6372 (England), 029 2082 3866 (Wales).
- Royal Town Planning Institute, www.rtpiconsultants.co.uk, 020 7960 5663 – lists planning consultants in different areas.
- RICS (Royal Institution of Chartered Surveyors), www.rics.org, 0870 333 1600 – for qualified surveyors.

Smart Ways to Add Value

Think laterally and add more worth
to your home

I f you use your imagination, there are a number of ways you can up the
value of your home while you are in situ and when you decide to pack
up and leave. Some initiatives might involve a little bit of time and effort
and some might involve parting with some money, but the end result is
generally worth the investment.

I think the best scenario is coming up with an idea that benefits you while
you are living in your home and that the next owner could find attractive as
well. This way, you can enjoy the alterations you have made while you are
there, and the next owner can be attracted to them too, making your house
easier to sell.

Film Locations

One example is to let your house out occasionally as a film location. You
could pick up several thousand pounds a year letting crews shoot films or
stills for magazines in your home. Besides accruing the extra cash, it could
be quite an interesting exercise having a crew in your home if you like this
kind of thing. And when you go to sell your house, you can put this forward
as a selling point.

A buyer might get a bit of a buzz knowing that your house once starred in a period drama or was used as a gritty location for *The Bill*. He might also be attracted to the notion of carrying on this filmic tradition when he takes over the property. You have already done all the research for him and can pass on details of the location company or companies you are registered with and he can go from there.

A number of TV and film companies tend to prefer property within easy reach of London, so generally anything outside the M25 has to be fairly special for a location company to take on. Having said that, programmes and films are shot in the regions too, so it is worth booking with firms that will advertise your home as well as those in or close to the capital.

Many people believe you need to own a mini-stately home at least to get a film company to take notice of your property. This is not true. Although a grand Georgian house might get about £900 a day for a shoot, humbler homes are required too. A small pretty cottage could be needed, as well as homes further down the property ladder – one ad even specifies, 'shabby elements preferred'. And don't forget, contemporary soaps and dramas, such as *EastEnders* and *Casualty*, need fairly ordinary locations.

There is a certain amount of disruption when a film crew lands on your doorstep, mind. Having turned up with crews and all of our cameras, lights and other equipment, I know just how invasive we can be. I think it is almost best if you can go and stay somewhere else while the crew is in your property, or try to stay out of everyone's way as much as you can.

Although crews are usually quite careful and respect someone else's property, accidents can and do happen, so I would lock away anything that is hugely precious. It is important to check your insurance policy as well, in case you need to let your insurance company know a film crew will be on site. You might need to up your cover too.

Location fees (or facility fees, as film and television companies call them) vary, but a ballpark figure is £750 to £5,000 a day for a 12-hour feature film shoot, £500 to £3,000 for a television drama and £400 to £1,000 for a documentary shoot.

Photo shoots, which generally require fewer people and less equipment so they might not be quite so intrusive, can yield £300 to £1,500 a day. Television commercials will pay about £1,000 to £3,000, and music videos

£500 to £3,000. Shorter shoots sometimes pay a half-day or hourly rate from £75 to £200 an hour.

Preparation and 'reinstatement days' (when they put everything back to normal) are generally paid at between a third and a half of the daily rate. Overtime rates are also paid should the production company overrun and this is set at a pre-agreed hourly rate.

Also, look out for deals where you might not get an actual fee, but your home might get a thorough makeover. Your home might play a role in an instructional DIY DVD shoot, for instance, and have new floors and tiles in lieu of payment. Other bonuses could include being fed the odd three-course meal or snacks from the location catering van on a big shoot and free samples of a product that is being filmed on site.

It is usually free to register your home with a film location agent. Some ask for a fee of around £100 if you want your home to be fast-tracked and appear on the agent's books and website within five days (the norm is 30 days).

Typically, agents take a 15 per cent cut of your fee in exchange for marketing your property, drawing up a contract with the film company and introducing specific conditions, such as no nails in the walls and the props man providing white instead of red wine if an actor needs to drink wine in a scene (spilled red wine can stain a carpet more easily).

Other costs include good photographs of the property. You could photograph your house yourself, but the pictures do need to be of a high standard to attract custom. One agent says she can provide a professional photographer for a £250 fee to take high-calibre pictures of your house.

CASE STUDY

HAVING A FILM CREW ROUND

Sandra Middleton likes to recount the story of when a large film crew camped at her small thatched cottage and also pretty much took over her Dorset village when shooting a television advertisement for cheese five years ago.

'It was amazing. There were about 20 or 30 cars parked

everywhere and there were loads of huge trucks supplying electricity by generator and carrying props and equipment. I would imagine there were around 100 people on set, which is about double the population of the village,' points out Sandra, 63.

Sandra does admit that despite the confusion and obvious disruption the villagers loved the experience. 'We all loved watching them shoot the commercial. Even those who moaned a bit still turned out to see what was going on and dined out on the stories related to the filming along with the rest of us.'

Sandra's idyllic little cottage next to a stream was the main property featured and she received £1,500 a day for five days. 'The money came in very handy. I had a conservatory built with the profits and also had a great holiday in St Kitts.'

Registered with two location agents, Sandra had a photographer friend shoot the pictures of her house, saving her a couple of hundred pounds. She pays the agent that finds work for her house a 15 per cent cut of the fee.

'You do get other perks,' she explains. 'The designer had the woodwork in the cottage repainted a lovely pale French blue and I asked if he could leave it like that when they finished filming. They were happy to do so – it did save them having to repaint at the end – and even left me the leftover tins of paints for retouching in the future. I also received a massive hamper of cheese, which was enough to last me for rather a long time.'

Sandra would advise homeowners to decamp while the crew is on site – 'I stayed with my sister in a nearby town and her reward was going on holiday with me' – and get the rest of the village on side. Luckily, the film company gave a facility fee to the village too, which paid for a summer party and fireworks for bonfire night that year.

Check out the contract and do question anything you don't understand and ask for clauses to be added to cover anything special, adds Sandra. 'I asked that they leave all the plants and trees as they are, because I have some quite rare, mature species in the garden. They also had to agree to replace any plants or items in the house that were damaged during the filming. Luckily, nothing was broken and the whole experience was quite a pleasant one.'

Sandra has a set of photographs and shots of the house and village in the advertisement. 'I can show this to a potential buyer when I decide to sell the cottage and I hope they will think it is interesting.'

It is unlikely anyone would pay more money to own a property that has featured on screen, but as Sandra points out, it should command a certain degree of curiosity and conveys the feeling that the property must be all right if a film company paid to use it.

Parking

Parking can be a big concern in an area where there are very few spaces on the streets and councils charge significant amounts (£200 or more annually) for a resident's parking permit. Some councils are even saying no to parking spaces in some new developments, which is meant to deter people buying cars, but often just pushes more cars out on to the streets.

Creating a parking space in front of your house can add value to your home, especially in these hard-pushed areas where parking spaces are rare or expensive. In London, there have been reports of people paying £100,000 or higher – the price of a house in some parts of the country – just for a good underground parking space. Being able to come up with parking outside your home can be like gold dust to buyers.

Keep in mind, however, that not all councils are happy to give permission for you to pave over your front garden and turn it into a parking space. There can be eco concerns as green space turns to concrete, driving away birds and butterflies, and with fewer places for water to drain some believe this could lead to flooding in the area. Also, you will need to have the pavement lowered outside your house to gain access to your new drive, which cuts down on parking spaces in the street, exacerbating the problem further.

Getting a parking space outside your home can be costly too. You will need to get planning permission and the cost of doing the work is likely to be in the region of £10,000 to £20,000.

I reckon getting a parking space, especially in a cramped town or city, could add several thousand pounds on to the price of your property, if not more. In some quarters, it could add as much as £50,000 plus.

Increasingly, homeowners are regarding urban and even some suburban homes if you are near a popular train station with off-street parking as highly valuable commodities. You can earn hundreds of pounds a month letting out the parking space if you don't need it.

A recent survey shows that rent for driveways and private parking spaces in popular London postcodes could average at least £273 a month. Driveways and off-street parking spots most in demand include those spaces near sports and leisure stadiums, airports, train stations and the congestion charge zone. As well as regular commuters renting spaces, people going to one-off events like concerts at Wembley Stadium also are willing to pay for good parking places.

You need to check your home insurance covers you for any problems and you mustn't ever considering selling on local authority parking permits, which is against the law. A number of websites list rentable private parking spaces for free.

Extend the Lease or Buy the Freehold

You can lift the worth of your home by extending the lease on it or buying the freehold. The cost to extend the lease will be easily recouped when you go to sell your property.

What is freehold and leasehold?

The terms 'freehold' and 'leasehold' refer to different ways property in England and Wales can be owned. Scotland has its own version ('feuhold'). Leasehold exists in Scotland, but it isn't as common as in England and Wales.

If you have a freehold home, this means you own it and the land on which it is built. When you die, it is part of your estate and can be left to your heirs. Your entitlement to do what you wish with your freehold property is only limited by planning and other laws. You are responsible for the property and its repairs.

Leasehold applies mainly to flats (houses are almost always freehold). Under a leasehold agreement, you own your property only for the time stated in the lease (or contract with the freeholder). The freeholder grants you the right to have the property for the length of the lease, and the owner-ship reverts back to the freeholder once the lease expires.

The length of a lease can vary, but its initial term can run for up to 999 years. The longer a lease runs, the higher the value of a property. As the time on the lease ticks down, so too does the worth of the property.

Because having a lease is a sort of tenancy, the leaseholder has to pay an annual ground rent to the freeholder. Normally, this is a nominal sum of no more than a few hundred pounds, but it can be more. A maintenance (or service) charge has to be paid too, to cover items such as managing the building, cleaning communal areas (hallways and staircases), getting the external part of the building redecorated and repaired and for insurance on the communal parts.

It can sometimes be more difficult to get a mortgage from the bank or building society on a leasehold property compared to a freehold property. A lot can depend on how much time is left to run on the lease after the end of the mortgage term.

New rules introduced under the 1993 Leasehold Reform Housing and Urban Development Act and its amendments have given flat owners the opportunity to extend their leases. Lease extensions are granted in 90-year blocks and a tenant must have owned the property for two years before the date of the claim to extend the lease. You do not have to occupy the property, however, and the original lease must have been for a term of over 21 years.

Picking up a home on a short lease and then extending it can be a clever way of adding value. You pay less than the market rate to get a home on a short lease, and then after a few years, you can get the lease extended (a 'buy now, pay later' concept). This can be of huge benefit to first-time buyers or anyone else who might not have a great deal of money when they buy a home, but when they are earning a bit more several years later they can pay to extend the lease.

To give you an idea of how short-lease properties sell at considerable discounts: as a general rule, a property with a 25-year lease could sell for as little as half the freehold value, while a property with 50 years left on the lease might cost about 70 to 75 per cent of the freehold value.

Also, as the lease drops below 80 years, it costs more to extend as the 'marriage value' (the amount that the property will then be deemed to be worth when the lease is extended) rises. As a result, the freeholder may try to get more money from the leaseholder, knowing that the property will be more valuable when the lease is extended. A general formula to work out what you have to pay to extend the lease is estimating half the marriage value plus compensation for any loss in value of other property owned by the freeholder that may occur as a result of extending the lease.

It can be quite complicated working out the cost of extending a lease – this is an area where you really do need expert advice. Costs can be high as you pay the landlord's and your legal fees. Consulting a good property lawyer that specialises in leasehold extensions or a consultant at an estate agency that helps flat owners extend leases would be a wise move.

Leaseholders also have the right in most cases to buy the freehold of their property. This process, known as 'enfranchisement', means leasehold- ers can club together and manage the building themselves. The Leasehold Advisory Service (www.lease-advice.org) can give information and advice. This process isn't always quick and can be costly (say, around £30,000), but I think being able to own the freehold is well worth the angst and expense.

A new system of joint ownership called 'commonhold' was introduced in 2004. Under commonhold, a company known as a commonhold association owns the freehold of the building and is responsible for looking after the communal parts (the main hallway, stairs, roof and shared gardens, for instance).

The owner of each flat is a member of the commonhold association and must agree to its terms and conditions (not unlike those in a lease). You might be able to convert an existing leasehold into a commonhold, but you would need to consult a solicitor to see if this is the right route for you to go down to obtain the freehold.

It is hard to put a figure on costs to extend a lease or buy a freehold, but you will need to employ a property lawyer or consultant that charges by the hour. When extending a lease, a lot can come down to negotiation, so you might end up paying a freeholder anything from £10,000 to several hundred thousand pounds or more, depending on location, the sort of property involved and other factors.

Although this might sound complicated and even curious – and it is both in many ways – I believe that almost certainly you will benefit from getting your hands on the freehold of a property. When it comes time to sell, purchasers are generally keener on a freehold property than one with a leasehold.

CASE STUDY

BUYING A FREEHOLD

Jenny and Robert Stuart from north-west London are buying the freehold for the terrace building where they own the top flat. They will have to pay £8,000 for the freehold. Their neighbours in the other flats are happy to remain as leaseholders, as they can't be bothered getting involved with buying the freehold themselves.

The value added is two-fold. Getting the freehold on the entire building holds a certain value in itself, and the Stuarts are also benefiting because they can grant themselves permission as the new freeholder to extend into the loft of their flat. This will make them about £10,000 in profit once they have the loft conversion work carried out.

Being able to control the building and its communal parts is a strong plus too. When it is time to sell their flat, the couple has a say in how the redecoration and any repairs should be done.

Green Features

Putting eco-friendly features into your home can take you to the forefront of green living, helping save the planet and cutting down on ever-increasing bills. With people staying in their homes longer and more concerned about buy-to-live rather than buy-to-let, installing sensible green devices could certainly add worth to your home.

Few estate agents today think a house will sell at a higher profit just because it has money-saving and, ultimately, world-saving green features, but I think that eco issues are becoming more important to many home-owners. In cash terms alone, who wants to pay over the odds for heating from a gas-guzzling heating system when you can replace it with the eco equivalent and save hundreds of pounds?

Besides, attitudes are changing. Recent research by the Energy Saving Trust shows that a third of those polled said they would be willing to pay more for a home where some of the energy supplied comes from renewable resources, such as wind, solar or hydropower. And almost half of those surveyed (49 per cent) said they would like to know if their home is suitable for renewable energy.

I think a solar panel or wood turbine on your home could add to the resale value in the future as much as solid wooden flooring or a new kitchen. We don't know what the rules and regulations to help save energy will be in a few years' time, but I reckon they will only get tougher.

Already, the Energy Saving Trust, a tax-payer-funded Government quango, is keen to ban 5.5 million homes from being sold until thousands of pounds have been spent on improvements. Energy performance certificates, which are part of the HIP (the Home Information Pack that every property has to have before it goes on to the sales market), rate homes from A to G and the trust wants to make it illegal from 2015 for homes in the two lowest bands to be sold or rented until they are improved.

If you have already tackled some of these eco issues – adding cavity-wall insulation, double-glazing your property and converting a solid-fuel open fire to a glass-fronted one, for example – you could stand a better chance when your property goes on to the sales board than one that is a less pleasant shade of green.

Here are some ideas to make your home an eco-friendlier place for you and the next owner.

Solar roof tiles

Solar panels can generate roughly a third of the hot water required for the typical family home. They don't necessarily have to be on the roof – a sunny patch in the garden will do – but generally are on top of the house.

Fitted like ordinary roof tiles, solar roof tiles usually are small panels made up of silicone rubber absorbent strips that use energy from the sun to heat water in pipes connected to the hot-water cylinder. These absorbent strips are covered by toughened glass slates.

Up to 70 per cent of energy needed to heat an average home's water will be produced by about 6 to 8 square metres of solar panelling, saving about £180 a year in heating bills. Mind, it could take a while to get your money back as the materials cost about £125 a square metre, with installation by a plumber and roofer extra at around £75 a square metre. This translates to about £3,000 to £7,000.

Installing solar panels probably only makes financial sense if you are substantially fixing your roof, replacing it or building a new house and starting from scratch. There are some Government grants available from your local authority (check out www.communities.gov.uk if you need directing to your local authority), but generally these are only a few hundred pounds. Some might go as high as a couple of thousand pounds, but a lot depends on how many grants are allocated each year from your council.

Rainwater harvesting

Essentially, rainwater harvesting is when rainwater is collected and reused for all household needs except for drinking. Because the water is soft it is good to use it to water the garden, flush loos, wash your hair and run washing machines.

At the lower end, it can be simple gathering up rainwater by connecting a container to the down-pipe and channelling it into a butt (usually, a wooden barrel or flatter version that fits up to walls). However, you could suffer from flooding when the run-off is greater than the storage capacity of your butt. One easy and low-cost solution is to buy a diverter for less than £10 that sends water into the drain when the butt is full. Butts range from about £15 to several hundreds of pounds.

Heat exchange systems

Ground-source heat pumps operate with underground pipes laid in a loop, or by digging deep down into a borehole (a narrow shaft drilled in the ground). Often the pumps are linked into under-floor heating and savings of about 40 per cent can be expected off your heating bills.

It can take a while to get your money back, because heat exchange systems are not cheap (estimate about £4,000 per kilowatt required in the home). Individuals installing these systems are mainly looking to the future to benefit the next generation, to be honest, and most heat exchange systems are found on larger housing developments. I think this could change over the next few years as people band together in streets or communities to share the costs of installation.

Biomass boilers

Biomass boilers are boilers that mainly burn wood chips, pellets or logs to generate hot water for a home. This can be much cheaper than using oil or gas and can be particularly sensible if you have a large house to heat. You need to have quite a bit of room to store the chips, logs or pellets in your garden and it costs about £2,000 to £4,000 to put in a biomass boiler. As costs rise for fuels like oil and gas, I think this could be a good eco investment.

Energy monitors

This is a low-cost green idea that can become quite compelling. Basically, an energy monitor, from about £20, keeps track of the amount of energy your household appliances are using. You attach a meter to an electrical socket and then plug the appliance into the meter. Voltage, current and wattage consumed are all displayed on a small screen and the total amount of electricity is racked up in kilowatt-hours.

Knowing how much every appliance uses – some versions even estimate the cost of using each appliance for you – is very handy. It can be quite sobering, too, when you discover that raising the temperature setting on a washing machine from 30 degrees centigrade to 40 degrees can consume another 70 per cent of power.

You can involve the whole family in watching energy monitors tick away. This is a good way to teach children to switch things off they are not using and be aware of how much energy is eaten up leaving a television on standby or a mobile phone charger left dangling from a socket without the phone still plugged into it.

Another version – the smart meter – is attached to your incoming mains cable and the remote monitor identifies excessive electricity usage. They cost from just over £30 to £100.

Smart wiring is a more sophisticated variation where you can save on electricity by installing a system programmed to turn off sockets, lights and heating automatically. Individual set-ups for audio or heating, for instance, start at around £1,000, while a bespoke system integrating heating, lighting and alarms is more expensive at £20,000.

De-scaling conditioner

This is a favourite of mine, because you can install it yourself and it isn't too dear. The most common brand is Scalewizard. Essentially this is an electronic water conditioner unit that removes existing limescale and controls the build-up of any more limescale.

You fit the unit to the rising main pipe and it generates an electric field that gets dissolved calcium in water to gather in tiny crystals. These crystals then pass through appliances, rather than stick on to them as limescale. The electrical socket has to be within 3 metres of the rising main pipe where you attach the unit.

A build-up of limescale on appliances adds about £175 a year to the average household's energy bill, so for very little outlay (about £90 for the unit and £3 a year to run), you will get your money back quickly and cut down on future bills.

Insulate the loft

Insulating the loft could save about £150 a year and cavity-wall insulation about £250 on your heating bills. Installing both costs about £500, but you should get this money back in about two years. Again, there are some grants available (contact the Energy Saving Trust for more information on grants and 'pay as you save' loans, www.energysavingtrust.org.uk, or your local authority).

According to the trust, 33 per cent of heat in an un-insulated house is lost through the walls, so producing improved heating bills to show a prospective buyer could make them appreciate the effort you have made to add insulation. And while you are living in your home, you will appreciate the added warmth in the winter and also a cooler atmosphere during a hot summer.

Bike sheds

As simple as it might sound, secure bike storage can be a great selling point for a home. With more people cycling to stations, work or school these days, having good bicycle storage is becoming as important as having car parking space or being near to good public transport.

Estate agents are telling me that buyers, particularly first-time buyers, want a bike rack or shed to store their cycle, so it isn't soaked in a downpour or stolen. If you live in an urban area or on a commuter route, it is worth thinking about keeping cyclists in your family or buyers who cycle happy.

Figures from Transport for London show a 107 per cent increase in cycle journeys since 2000, with a 9 per cent rise in the last few years. The need for security is heightened with Metropolitan Police statistics revealing that 18,218 cycles were nicked last year, a 1,036 rise on the previous year.

People are looking for bicycle sheds – a ready-made one costs about £400 – or even a simple bike rack. Bike racks are effectively a metal bar bolted to the ground and they cost less than £100. I would advise you to talk to your local bicycle shop about various options for storage and security.

Extra Land

This might sound obvious, but I'm constantly surprised by how many people forget about the value of land next to or near their house. When I first started out in the property world as a surveyor, and even later when I worked as an estate agent and now that I work as a property finder, I could and still can always sniff out the potential of land that could be linked to a property.

If there is a patch of land – big or small – it is always worth doing your research to find out who owns it and see whether you can rent or buy it. With more of us spending longer in our homes these days, you can gain huge pleasure from having an extra chunk of land on your doorstep. You can do anything from keep a pony for your children, have a wide open space to throw a ball for the dog, grow an orchard, establish a kitchen garden, install a tennis court or pool, or just have a view across a green and pleasant field. In fact, there are so many options for how you might use your extra land, including a secret garden with a hideaway shed, studio or office, a children's play area and as a meadow, that having this extra bit of green space will certainly increase the value of your home.

First, you need to determine who owns the land. Start by talking to your neighbours. They might well know the owner and about the history of the land. They can fill you in on why nothing has been built on the land and whether it is likely you can buy or rent it.

Also, you can do a check with Land Registry (www.landregistry.gov.uk) and find out who owns the title to the land. For a £4 fee you can download a copy of the title registered. This shows you what is owned and points out the boundaries.

PHIL'S TRADE SECRET

You might even be entitled to land you didn't know you could have. This is known as 'encroachment', where you go over a border or boundary, sometimes by default. Typically, someone starts to build an extension, placing the external wall right on the boundary with the foundations and guttering extending beyond their property. This could have happened even before you bought the property.

Another form of land acquisition is 'adverse possession', a sort of squatter's rights where someone might notice a bit of unloved wasteland out back. What normally happens is someone just purloins it by moving the fence over a couple of yards. He can become the rightful owner if it can be proven he has been in possession of the land for 12 years without any objections from the real owner.

I've noticed this second form of land attainment is on the up, with less time and money for councils to look after every postage stamp of land. Some might not even realise they own it as it gets lost in the bureaucratic machine. It is worth contacting your local council, or you can get a surveyor or architect to do so on your behalf, as they might be happy to let you have this small piece of land. To find out how to get in touch with your local council with regard to adverse possession or encroachment, go to www.communities.gov.uk.

When buying a property, it makes sense to check that the land you believe comes with your new home actually does. Even top experts don't always get things totally right. A solicitor casting an eye over the boundaries during a property search might miss something – often, the lines have been drawn with a thick felt pen and boundaries aren't always determined in the close detail you might imagine – so literally walking the plot can be quite revealing.

I was a bit puzzled once – this time I was wearing my house-finder hat – by the boundaries of a property I was checking out for a client. I was concerned the boundaries did not follow the title plan, and as it was all fairly complicated with the land going through some woodland, it wasn't surprising there was some confusion. I managed to make my way through the woods and take a good look at how this matched the title plan – but it didn't.

Next, I hired a surveyor to plot the existing fenced boundaries and compare them with the plan. They were very different. It turns out Land Registry had drawn the boundaries in the wrong place, with important bits of the property – like the gates and lawn in front of the house – included incorrectly on the neighbour's patch.

After I got legal advice, I had to get the current and previous two owners to make statutory declarations confirming they had enjoyed unhindered access to the property over the last decade. I also got the current owner to take out a £1,500 insurance policy for the new buyer in case the neighbour tried to make a claim on the land. Although the property had changed hands twice over the last few years, no one had picked up the mistake.

So, look for obvious signs of discrepancy. Fences, hedges and ditch lines are not always clearly defined and you need to determine which is the 'real' boundary. A good lawyer should check title plans carefully before you exchange contracts, but some are more deskbound than others in their approach and might not spot inconsistencies.

When it comes to pricing a piece of land, it can vary hugely from a few thousand pounds to many thousand pounds, depending on where you live and what the land consists of. A lot might come down to negotiation, so research what equivalent land in your area might fetch to give you some idea of a starting point at least.

A good property lawyer can do a search to check the title of the land and see if there are any covenants (enforceable agreements or promises that are part of a deed or contract) stopping you from doing something in particular with the land.

For example, you might not be allowed to use the land for certain purposes or there might be a right-of-way covenant giving someone access to your land. And a local chartered surveyor can check you are not being asked a silly price for the land.

Even if the land is only rented, it could be of value to someone who is pleased to have the extra outdoor space for a period of time. If it is rented, you might want to extend the contract, or at least get some idea from the owner how much longer the new owner could rent it for and what he is likely to charge. Getting something in writing would be reassuring for a future owner as well.

I think it could be well worth buying or renting land that isn't exactly adjacent to your land as well. It might seem odd parting with cash for something that isn't right next door and can't be added to your own garden, but it could still be a good selling point. This is even more important if you have a garden that is on the small side or isn't deemed big enough to go with the size of your property. Over the years, land can be sold off and reasonably large houses can have less than the owner would like. People buying a country house expect a certain amount of land and if yours isn't adequate, having thought ahead to purchase or lease some more could help if someone is wavering over buying your home.

If you don't actually go ahead and buy the land, at least do the research and offer some options to a potential buyer. If this is the main sticking point against clinching that deal for your home, offering a positive, helpful solution could make all the difference.

> ### PHIL'S TOP TIP
>
> *Even if the landowner initially says no to your request to buy the extra piece of land, do keep talking to him. One day he might decide to sell and you want to be uppermost in his mind so he comes to you first.*
>
> *You could even show your willingness to let the village or community use the land on occasions for a summer party or fete. This might make the landowner feel you are community minded and aren't just after the land for yourself. By demonstrating how others can enjoy the land as well as yourself, you might get the backing of your village or street too, which could strengthen your case.*

The History of Your Home

One fun way to add value to your property is to research its past. Almost everyone is keen to know about the history of a home and the nearby area. Taking a bit of time to work out who lived in your house and whether it had any ghosts could be of great interest to the next owner. It is hard to formulate what this addition of property genealogy would mean in cash terms, but I don't think this matters. Having a well-researched document with pictures and a more modern history section – the memories you have acquired about the house and village while living there – could make your home more attractive and interesting than a similar history-less house in the same street.

Here are ten top tips on how to research the history of your home:

1. General history First, look into the general history of your street, and then branch out more broadly into the area. Find out how your patch was developed and determine whether your house was once part of an estate linked to a big mansion or landowner, or part of a brave new housing scheme in the Twenties or Fifties. Go to your local records office or borough archives (many are online now) with local history information. A good general starting point is the site www.british-history.ac.uk.

2. Work backwards Historians advise you to start with the present day and work backwards. Current records and information from the 20th and 21st centuries are likely to be easier to locate and sometimes more accurate than those from the distant past. Many areas, towns and villages have books with local information that might mention your house and street.

3. Old identity House names and numbers and street plans change over the years. Check to see if your house had a name as well as, or instead of, a number. Number one, Acacia Drive might have been known as Kingfisher Cottage, or, if you talk to locals, even Jim Robsons' cottage. It might help you find more information on your house if you check out other names it once had. Different spellings might have been used too, so keep this in mind while you research.

4. Maps These are hugely useful when determining your home's history. See if you can find old maps of your area in junk shops, second-hand shops and local antique shops. Ordnance Survey maps date from about 1860, while tithe maps from the 1830s and 1840s can show you the layout of a street or village at that time. If you live on an estate, the estate owner is likely to have old maps you can look at and possibly copy. Other good sources include Goad fire insurance maps and Second World War bomb damage maps (the Imperial War Museum in south London has a terrific archive). It is worth trying to hunt down old plans for your property – well-established estate agents might hold some on file.

5. Electoral rolls Electoral rolls going back to the late 19th century list the names of residents that were eligible to vote. Remember, non-nationals were not allowed to vote, and women weren't allowed to put an X in a box before 1928.

6. Local directories Trade and local directories, not unlike today's telephone books, list many addresses. Some date back to the early 19th century, but earlier versions are not quite as specific as ones printed in later years.

7. Census records The census reveals a great deal about who lived where, with information about age, birthplace and disabilities. The census has been taken every decade since 1801, with more personal information provided since 1841. In country areas, whole streets or villages might be listed instead of individual houses.

8. Tax records Parish and national tax records can help you research the history of your home. When a new land tax was introduced in 1910 an Inland Revenue Valuation Survey was taken, giving the names of the owner, occupants, how much rent was paid, house layout and number of rooms. Local parish rate books reveal when a house was completed along with information about the owner, other occupants and the value of the property.

9. Old documents Old deeds, leases, wills and other documents related to the property might be found on the National Archives website. If your house is listed, there is a brief description of it on www.imagesofengland.org.uk. Check out your local newspaper and library – both should have good collections. National newspapers hold impressive archives too, although many have put only later years online so far.

10. Junk shops House clearances often take place when someone wants to get rid of old junk, or when someone dies, with unwanted items ending up in junk or second-hand shops. Sometimes, they offer boxes or suitcases of old postcards with photographs, maps, letters and record books that could be useful when you turn amateur historian.

PHIL'S CONTACTS BOOK

- www.british-history.ac.uk.
- The National Archives, www.nationalarchives.gov.uk.
- London Metropolitan Archives, www.cityoflondon.gov.uk.
- The Guildhall Library, www.cityoflondon.gov.uk.

- The Royal Institute of British Architects library, www.architecture.com.
- www.old-maps.co.uk.
- www.ancestry.co.uk.
- www.findmypast.co.uk.
- www.1911census.co.uk.
- Land Registry, www.landregistry.gov.uk.
- Communities and Local Government, www.communities.gov. uk, 020 7944 4400.
- Leasehold Advisory Service, www.lease-advice.org.
- Energy Saving Trust, www.energysavingtrust.org.uk, 0800 512012.
- Information Centre for Alternative Technology, www.cat.org.uk.
- Environment Agency, www.environment-agency.gov.uk.

Resources

General

www.1911census.co.uk

www.ancestry.co.uk

Association of Plumbing and Heating Contractors (APHC)
www.aphc.co.uk

Bat Conservation Trust
www.bats.org.uk
0845 1300 228

www.bbc.co.uk/homes

www.british-history.ac.uk

Building Control
www.labc.uk.com

www.channel4.com/4homes

Communities and Local Government
www.communities.gov.uk
020 7944 4400

CORGI (Confederation for the Registration of Gas Installers)
www.trustcorgi.com
0800 915 0485

Energy Saving Trust
www.energysavingtrust.org.uk
0800 512012

Environment Agency
www.environment-agency.gov.uk

www.estimators-online.com

Federation of Master Builders
www.findabuilder.co.uk
0800 015 2522

www.findmypast.co.uk

The Guildhall Library
www.cityoflondon.gov.uk

Guild of Master Craftsmen
www.guildmc.com
01273 478449

Information Centre for Alternative Technology
www.cat.org.uk

Kitchen Bathroom Bedroom Specialists Association
www.kbsa.org.uk

Land Registry
www.landregistry.gov.uk

Law Society
www.lawsociety.org.uk
020 7242 1222

Leasehold Advisory Service
www.lease-advice.org

www.localserviceguide.com

London Metropolitan Archives
www.cityoflondon.gov.uk

www.maintainyourbuilding.org.uk

The National Archives
www.nationalarchives.gov.uk

National Association of Estate Agents
www.naea.co.uk
01926 417794

www.old-maps.co.uk

Paint Quality Institute
www.paintquality.co.uk

Period Property UK
www.periodproperty.co.uk

Royal Institute of British Architects (RIBA)
www.architecture.com
020 7580 5533

Royal Institution of Chartered Surveyors (RICS)
www.rics.org
0870 333 1600

Show House magazine
www.showhouse.co.uk

The Society for the Protection of Ancient Buildings
www.spab.org.uk
020 7377 1644

DIY

The Building Skills Academy
www.buildingskillsacademy.co.uk
01635 522007

www.diydoctor.org.uk

www.diyfixit.co.uk

www.diynot.com

Jeff Howell
www.ask-jeff.co.uk

www.ultimatehandyman.co.uk

www.videojug.com

Flooring

Contract Flooring Association
www.cfa.org.uk

National Wood Flooring Association
www.woodfloors.org

Gardens

The Association of Professional Landscapers
www.landscaper.org.uk

The Leisure and Outdoor Furniture Association
www.lofa.com

Royal Horticultural Society
www.rhs.org.uk

Lighting

The Lighting Association
www.lightingassociation.com

Planning

Planning Inspectorate
www.planning-inspectorate.gov.uk
0117 372 6372 (England)
029 2082 3866 (Wales)

Planning Portal
www.planningportal.gov.uk

Royal Town Planning Institute
www.rtpiconsultants.co.uk
020 7960 5663

Recycling

www.allyourjunk.com
0800 032 8972

www.enviroyellowpages.com

Freecycle
www.freecycle.org

Index